Mary Russell

is an Irish journalist who divides her time between England and Ireland. She has an MA in Peace Studies from the University of Bradford and writes for newspapers both here and in Ireland as well as contributing to African and Middle East publications. She is well travelled herself, and recently completed a journey in the Caribbean to visit her daughter, one of three children, now living in Antigua. Mary now spends as much time as she can in her thatched cottage in Donegal.

Granuaile at the court of Elizabeth I

MARY RUSSELL

The Blessings of
a Good Thick Skirt

Women Travellers and their World

Flamingo
An Imprint of HarperCollins*Publishers*

Flamingo
An Imprint of HarperCollins*Publishers*
77–85 Fulham Palace Road
Hammersmith, London W6 8JB

Published by Flamingo 1994
9 8 7 6 5 4 3 2 1

First published in Great Britain by
William Collins Son & Co Ltd 1986

Author photograph by *Irish Times*

ISBN 0 00 654748 6

Set in Monophoto Apollo

Printed in Great Britain by
HarperCollinsManufacturing Glasgow

For Freya, Deirdre and Russell
In memory of their father,
Ian Rodger

'It is at these moments you realise the blessings of a good thick skirt . . . save for a good many bruises here was I with the fullness of my skirt tucked under me, sitting on nine ebony spikes some twelve inches long, in comparative comfort, howling lustily to be hauled out.'

Mary Kingsley

Contents

Illustrations

We would like to acknowledge with gratitude permission from the following sources to reproduce illustrations in the text: pp. 49, 76, 123, 134, 137, 164, the Mary Evans Picture Library; *frontispiece*, Bodleian HOPE ADDS, 260; p. 125, Bodleian 740.11.r.40; p. 131, Bodleian 20661.e.29; pp. 209, 222, Bodleian 753.12.r.6

Acknowledgements

The writing of this book has been, in itself, a journey of sorts – full of dark despondent sloughs, apparently unsurmountable obstacles but, happily, numerous bright and rewarding peaks. In the course of its writing I have been fortunate to meet many women who, during their brief rest periods at home, were kind enough to talk to me about their travels. To these I owe a special debt and would like to thank Lin Rutland, Naomi Mitchison, Christina Dodwell, Virginia Fiennes, Sheila Scott, Christian Miller, Bettina Selby and Dorothea Gravina. I would also like to thank Fay Gillis Wells for writing to me, Ella Maillart for her hospitality in Geneva and for talking to me about her meeting with Amelia Earhart, Eve Jackson for taking me up in her microlight and Dervla Murphy for sharing her home-made Triple-X Guinness with me.

I would also like to thank Bill Russell for his guidance on the genetic make-up of the traveller; Monk Gibbon for entertaining me most gallantly from his hospital bed and for talking to me about his early friendship with Ella Maillart; Shirley Ardener who offered help and encouragement; Robert Paine of Memorial University, Newfoundland who provided me with material on Canadian travellers, and Dorothy Middleton whose conversation further enhanced the pleasure I had in reading her own book on women travellers.

In the area of flight, I would like to thank both David Ogilvy of the Shuttleworth Collection who kindly showed me Jean Batten's plane and Ann Bond of the British Women Pilots' Association, and both Whirlybirds Inc. in Washington and Loretta Gregg of the International Womens Pilots' Association (the Ninety Nines) for replying to my queries about early flight.

I am also grateful to Nobby Clarke for sharing so generously his encyclopaedic knowledge of the history of sailing and both Edward Pyatt, former editor of the *Alpine Journal*, and the Pinnacle Club for answering my queries on mountaineering.

In the course of my researches I used many libraries and would like to thank Miss Tasker of New Zealand House, C. F. Jones of the Information Research Unit at Australia House and Muriel McCarthy of Archbishop Marsh's Library, Dublin, together with the staff of the library and map room of the Royal Geographical Society. I would also like to thank the curator and library staff at Woburn Abbey who made it possible for me to read the diaries of Mary, Duchess of Bedford and I must acknowledge an enormous debt to the Bodleian Library in Oxford, especially Rhodes House and the Indian Institute.

I would like to thank Michael Traynor in County Limerick, Ireland who alerted me to the existence of the Newcastle West Historical Society and John Cussen for providing me with the Society's Journal which contained such excellent material on the flier Sophie Pierce (Lady Heath) who came from that part of the world.

Thanks must go to Frances Cairncross, former Women's Editor of the *Guardian*, who commissioned me to write the series of articles on women travellers from which the idea for this book grew, to Anne McDermid for her supportive help throughout the writing of the book, to Katherine Broome for her much-needed comments on the text and to Victor Gollancz Ltd for permission to quote from *Castaway* by Lucy Irvine.

I must also acknowledge the inspiring nerve of my daughter Deirdre who, while this book was being written, embodied the spirit of the women in it by stepping into a sailing boat for the first time and, without further ado, crossing the Atlantic. Further, I would like to thank Ronnie for interrupting me, Tony Roberts of Peanut Computers for turning out during unsociable hours to repair my word-processor with a matchstick and loo paper and Margaret Mullet and Michael McGann for calming my panic when all my notes went missing at Belfast Airport.

Lastly, I must acknowledge my gratitude to the vast number of women travellers now dead who, as prolific writers, have made such an important and entertaining contribution to literature. It has been a joy to travel with them.

Had it not been for the help and support of all these friends I might never have reached journey's end.

CHAPTER 1

———◆◆◆———

'A Most Excellent Reason'

'Then the tall cliff was upon us with a splintering crash. The bow-sprit snapped like kindling. The flare was out. The night was dark. We clung to the mainsheets in a pool of light thrown by the lamps in front of the wheelhouse. She began to roll from side to side, rails under with incredible speed as if she would roll right over. A colossal jolt, the shock travelled from stem to stern. The mainmast sagged, came over, seemed to hang suspended. The boom dropped and we leapt from under. Before our horrified eyes the bows of the vessel buried into the very face of the cliff.'

Husband and wife were thrown into the sea. It was a June night off Portland Bill, but the seas were running fast and cold. They clambered onto their float and watched the flares going up from the cliff. At least they, if not their precious boat, would be saved. Later, miserable and helpless, they watched it break up under the relentless pounding of the waves.

Clinging to the float they saw, with relief, the beam of the life-boat shining through the giant waves. Suddenly it disappeared as the float, caught by a wave, rose and turned over, throwing them into the sea yet again. By the time they had climbed back in again, the lifeboat had passed, missing them in the dark. With the realization that they were not going to be saved came the icy fingers of fear, plucking at their minds.

Again and again they were thrown into the sea, and with their hands rendered numb and clumsy by the cold, the effort of hauling themselves back into the float became increasingly difficult. They were both experienced enough to know how remorseless the sea can be, but by now the battering they were getting had numbed even their minds. Then it happened.

'A monster wave rose above the rest. Fury piled upon fury. Curling foaming crest. Sweeping down upon us. Inescapable. I

11

threw an arm around Frank, leant forward. The little float drove into the wall of water and was lost within it. When it broke free, Frank was dead.'

For her, there was no such release. Instead, flung again from the float, she was hurled through the sea and washed up onto the rocks, a reject of the gods. The float disappeared and with it the body of her husband. She had lost everything.

In the cold dawn, exhausted and alone, she looked up at the high cliff. Like someone who, having attempted suicide, wakes up to find the nightmare of life still continuing, she was filled with the desperate knowledge that at the top she would have to face again all the problems from which she and her husband had fled when they first set out on their tragic journey. The cliff was sixty feet high. Slowly, she began to claw her way up its crumbling face.

With nothing to sustain her but her courage and her will of iron, she pulled together the torn threads of her life and over the next years began life anew. Survival, however, was not enough. She had a further task to perform – the completion of that fatal journey. This second attempt was both an act of homage to her dead partner and, perhaps more important, a personal test of all that had gone before. Although she did something never before achieved by a woman – and with minimal resources – she remains unknown to most people for she was not a publicity-seeker and her memorable journey was made without the razzmatazz of Fleet Street.

Her name was Ann Davison and in 1953 she became the first woman to sail single-handed across the Atlantic. In a tiny sloop not much bigger than a lorry, she sailed the 3310 miles from Plymouth to Antigua, travelling the last sixty-five days in complete solitude.

*   *   *

To those of us for whom a comfortable bed, running water and the probability of living at least until tomorrow is of prime importance, the phenomenon of the traveller appears as incomprehensible as it is intriguing. Here are people who have succumbed to the treacherous seduction of the unknown, who actually choose to put their lives at risk by climbing the sheer and icy face of an avalanche-ridden mountain; who sail alone in frail craft through towering seas; who will eat maggots and river insects if nothing more palatable is on offer and who can live, day and night for months on end, in the shadow, and the promise, of the unknown.

It is easy to dismiss such people as oddities – as indeed they are – to be relegated to the bedlam of flat-earthers, freefall divers or indeed writers. That they exist cannot be denied, but the strange, uncomfortable world they occupy lies well outside our everyday experience and can be dismissed, we tell ourselves, as an irrelevancy. We can shrug our shoulders and return thankfully to the twentieth-century world of microwave food and answerphones, glad that the only risks to our own health are the predictable ones of smoking, eating hydrolyzed animal protein or making a kamikaze dash across a city street.

Yet turning away is not enough. There is a residual, nagging curiosity, an invisible thread that pulls us back to seek an explanation. Travellers consciously choose a life of discomfort and danger and somehow their choice of lifestyle is a challenge to our own. We may even harbour the uneasy thought that in so choosing they have acted with more freedom than the rest of us who remain in bondage to the comforts of materialism.

For Ann Davison and her husband Frank, their fatal attempt to cross the Atlantic was a matter of expediency rather than choice, for the wolf, in bailiff's clothing, was at the door. Though pressed unwillingly into this last desperate step, it was a logical result of the precarious lifestyle they had chosen. Almost from the start, they were dogged by financial problems.

They had met when she was a commercial pilot, flying planes in and out of the small aerodrome which he at that time owned. Later, they tried to set up a hill farm and when this ran into difficulties they devised the plan of sailing across the Atlantic and capitalizing on what would undoubtedly have been a great adventure. Before they had time to plan it, however, they found that the bailiffs were intending to impound their boat and, in desperation, they fled, leaving home and debts behind. It was a gamble that failed to come off, but there was no other option – the die had been cast a long time ago. They were both adventurous people who could never be content with a nine-to-five existence devoid of challenge. In the air, at sea or out on a lonely, inhospitable hillside, they set themselves tasks the achievement of which took them far beyond the goals aimed at, let alone won, by most people.

The reasons why men and women set themselves the challenge of going beyond the limits of everyday endurance are numerous, complex and mysterious. Few can articulate their motives and fewer still feel it necessary so to do. Their actions speak for themselves. It is usually only after the journey has been completed that travellers will allow themselves the luxury of attempting an analysis, constructing a package of reasons which seem rational and can be presented to the questioner as a sort of peace-offering.

Most, however, are in thrall to a driving force within them which pushes them onward – a force which they seem powerless to resist. The force has no name but its function is to explore the potential of the human species to adapt to conditions that are both challenging and dangerous. By so doing, it increases our potential for survival. One could argue that a few individuals – sailors, fliers, travellers or mountaineers – while appearing needlessly to expose themselves to danger and death may, in fact, be unconsciously serving the interests of us all.

There are, of course, many more mundane reasons why travellers and explorers set out into the unknown, pitting their wits against the elements, testing their physical and mental endurance, and exposing themselves to unforeseen perils.

Commercial interests, religion, and personal satisfaction have all been strong motivating forces. So too has been the craving for adventure, the complicated need for approval and acclaim. All these factors contribute towards that complex spirit known as the explorer, and standing apart from these reasons is the insatiable, intellectual need to know the unknown, to grasp the mercurial mystery of life itself.

*   *   *

And where do women fit in to this? It seems a contradiction and denial of their sex that women should risk the very thing which only they can nurture and sustain, namely life itself. Yet despite being hemmed in by society's barriers, their vision obscured by fixed horizons, their growth stunted and their potential to develop forced into the narrow channels leading to marriage and mother-hood, women throughout the centuries have managed to transcend their condition and reach out for the world. The reason is clear. If they are to do more than simply give life – if they are to enrich it as well – then the journey must be made which takes them beyond the physical and mental confines set by society. That women are capable of grasping this aspect of their destiny has been ably demonstrated by those pioneers who, valuing freedom more than conformity, have walked out into the world and taken possession of it.

This book, however, is less concerned with theories than with the reasons offered by women themselves as to why they soar off into the dawn skies, trudge across deserts, sail into uncharted waters or cling perilously to the peaks of snowbound mountains. And these reasons are myriad: to escape from domesticity or the drudgery of a routine job; to recover from a broken love affair; to experience the thrill of danger; to demonstrate that woman's name is definitely not frailty; to bring the Bible to China; to study plant life or unknown peoples; to delve into the past; to expiate a private guilt; to honour a dead partner; to glorify their country; to find something interesting to write about – or simply to have fun.

That some set out with no motive other than to enjoy themselves is clear – and to me this is the best reason of all. Our stern society, however, requires reasons for such extraordinary behaviour, reasons which the good-humoured traveller is usually prepared to give. 'I know in my heart of hearts that it is a most excellent reason to do things merely because one likes the doing of them. However, I would advise all those who wish to see unwrinkled brows at passport offices to start out ready labelled as entomologists, anthropologists or whatever other ology they think suitable and propitious.' If a scholar as emminent as Freya Stark advises travellers to don a cloak of respectability then we can safely assume that many of the 'reasons' offered are nothing more than protective clothing.

Whatever the reality may be, we would be unwise to ignore the reasons which women travellers themselves offer, for they provide us with a real insight into their minds, backgrounds and attitudes. Nor can we ignore the likelihood that of all the reasons offered, there may be no single one which predominates over all others. Like any spirited individual, each traveller is a conundrum, a tapestry of experiences whose pattern is so complex as to defy the simple definition.

Naomi Mitchison is an energetic and forthright traveller now in her eighties. She has witnessed, over the years, an enormous change in the fortunes of women and has herself been instrumental in that change. Born at the turn of the century into an academic family in Oxford, she grew up during the pre-war years when there was neither the time nor the opportunity for the sort of excitement a spirited young girl such as she might have enjoyed. Instead, marriage at sixteen followed by a large family left her with a yearning for something more than the daily domestic and social round, and with an aplomb that some career-minded mothers today might envy, she left her family – the youngest was only two – in the care of a team of servants and set sail from the Thames for Leningrad, bearing greetings to Russian writers. Later, in America during the 1930s, she travelled to the southern cotton fields, lending support to striking farmers. 'Pitch it strong, sister,' they told her. Domesticity could hold little attraction from then on and travelling became not merely an escape, but an essential part of her life.

While a dislike of domestic routine may have prompted some women to travel abroad, others, though not many, left to forget a lost love. In 1810 Hester Stanhope, grieving over the death at Corunna of the man she loved – Sir John Moore – left England on a journey which she hoped would help her forget. She was never to return. Gertrude Bell, forbidden by a possessive father to marry the man she loved, sought solace by immersing herself in study and set out to embark on a lifetime of travel throughout the ageless deserts of Arabia. More recently, Christina Dodwell, explorer and fearless whitewater canoeist, set off on her first trek through Africa as a result of a broken love affair; her heart however, like so many others', mended quickly – if it had ever really been shattered in the first place – and indeed the travellers' road is not as littered with the fractured dreams of the heart as the romantic among us might wish to think. Many women have found that the thwarted love which provided the original impulse to set out is swiftly superseded by the real romance of travel.

Travel, of course, can provide not only an escape from love but also its promise. The young and beautiful Lady Jane Digby found herself at the centre of a scandal that was to end in a notorious divorce. Fleeing from England in 1823, she wandered from country to country and from lover to lover, searching for a happiness which she found, unexpectedly, in the tent of a Bedouin chief. Another spirited woman of later times, Margaret Fountaine, fell victim to a similar weakness for Arab men and took her Lebanese guide as her companion in life – a move that was looked at askance by Victorian society, particularly as she chose to flaunt her sin by bringing her lover back to London.

It is not difficult to see how she and her predecessors found the aristocratic Arabs – courteous and sandalwood-sweet – more pleasing than the well-meaning, dull men whom they were intended to marry and serve.

If sheiks were the answer to some travellers' prayers, there were others who had no time for such frivolities and whose reasons for travelling were altogether more serious – they had work to do. As far back as 1669, Maria Merian, a serious and high-minded German matron, made a perilous sea journey to Surinam in order to make a study of insect life there. Two hundred years later, Marianne North journeyed to Java, Ceylon and India to study plant life and the collection of her paintings at Kew Gardens is a unique example of what could be achieved by a woman of determination, who, though without any formal education, was blessed with an abiding curiosity which found its fulfilment in travel.

By the turn of this century, education was more accessible to women and a driving force of intellectual enquiry was released which took women like Freya Stark and Gertrude Bell across the Arabian desert to study past times and the history of its peoples. It is rare nowadays to find women travellers similarly committed to a lifetime of study. Instead, mortgaged to the twin despots of Time and Jet Travel, researchers and PhD candidates take themselves off on carefully funded field trips, limited in scope and structured round the so-called objectivity of academic study; those of us who like to indulge in second-hand travel must be thankful that there are still some travellers left with the time to stop and stare and write about what they have seen.

Perhaps the most poignant reason for certain women embarking on their travels has been the need to finish the task begun by their partners. The widow of a lost explorer feels a special kind of grief, for she has both to endure the loss of a beloved partner and to live with the knowledge of something uncompleted. For some, the healing has come through retracing the journey to its end and finding in its completion a place to rest the ghosts.

Jane Franklin was a nineteenth-century reformer, committed to working for improved conditions for women prisoners in Van Diemens Land, where she lived for a time after marrying its Governor, John Franklin. A distinguished traveller and mountaineer – she was the first woman both to climb Mount Wellington's 4000-foot peak and to travel overland from Melbourne to Sydney – she became anxious for the safety of her husband when he failed to return from a major expedition to the Arctic begun in 1845. For many years she organized search vessels to look for him, the last of which found evidence that he had discovered the Northwest Passage before succumbing to the icy grasp of an arctic death. While the seven-year-long search for her husband was going on, Jane Franklin herself travelled widely in Japan, India and Hawaii and later, while in her eighties, she sent out a final expedition to the spot where her husband had died. It was her last farewell.

Five years before Jane Franklin died, a small girl was born in Canada who was to make travelling history there, though not in the way she might have wished. Mina Hubbard was thirty-five when her husband perished of starvation before he could complete the journey he had started across the uncharted wastes of the Labrador peninsula. She was a slight young woman with a fragile beauty, whose unsuspected inner strength uncoiled as her plan took shape: she herself would retrace the journey her husband had failed to complete. Two years after his death, she did just that, becoming the first white traveller to follow the hazardous route from North West River to Ungava Bay. She was spurred on not only by the memory of her husband's bravery but also by a determination to vindicate the way in which he died. She was convinced that had his travelling companion, Dillon Wallace, acted more wisely, her husband would have survived.

Mina's journey, however, was more than a memorial to a lost explorer – it was also a race in which stamina and honour were at stake, for on that same day, 25 June 1905, Dillon Wallace too set out to retrace the fateful journey, perhaps seeking to lay the ghost of the previous one. There was no communication between their two camps; Mina's feelings towards Wallace were too bitter to allow that. Two months later she achieved the goal her husband had failed to reach, six weeks ahead of the hated Wallace.

Other women equally unwavering in their iron-willed determination to reach their destination, though for very different reasons, were the Victorian missionaries who felt themselves called upon to bring the word of God to the unwary and who were ready to risk imprisonment and death in order to do it. Their initial testing ground, curiously enough, was usually England, for if commitment to religion and a willingness to undergo hardship were essential requirements of the lady missionary, so too was a mental tenacity in the face of parental opposition. No Victorian father wanted to see his daughter renounce a comfortable home – evidence of his own success – in favour of an impecunious life devoted to bringing religion to distant and inscrutable heathens.

Such a father was John Taylor, prosperous director of a fleet of sailing ships. When Annie, his beloved but independent-minded daughter, announced, at the age of thirteen, that she intended to be a missionary, it was the beginning of many years of conflict between the two. To prepare herself for missionary work, she put her cards firmly on the table by enrolling in a London medical school. John Taylor retaliated by stopping her allowance. It was at this point that the courage and determination which later got her across the hostile Tibetan border began to show itself. Authority, especially paternal authority, was at its most repressive in Victorian times and for a young woman to defy her father was similar to flying in the face of God. Yet for Annie there was no alternative and, selling her jewellery, she left home. It was this last, desperate move that finally broke her father's will. In September 1884, Annie Taylor sailed for Shanghai to take up a post with the Chinese Inland Mission. Her father offered her the return fare, certain that she would soon be back, but he was wrong. She was to be gone for the next twenty years.

When the voyage is an inner one, however, twenty years is not enough – it must last a lifetime. The road towards self-knowledge has been travelled by many but it is a route that women in particular seem drawn to. This is understandable, for when the identity of a group has been overlaid by the over-riding demands of society, it is inevitable that some individuals within that group will reach out for an alternative, spiritual home in which to find their true identity.

Alexandra David-Neel was such an individual. Opera singer, journalist and oriental scholar, she travelled to Darjeeling where she met the exiled Dalai Lama and began to study Tibetan Buddhism. While there, she managed to make two unofficial visits across the border into Tibet, spending some time in a lamaserie before returning to Sikkim to spend the winter of 1914/15 living as a hermit in a cave, her food pushed through the curtain that covered the entrance. The local Sikkimese lamas were so impressed with her steadfastness that they invested her with the title of *lamina* and gave her the lama's red robe to wear.

Annoyed by the audacious toing and froing of this determined Frenchwoman, the British authorities ordered her out of the area. It was this move – red rag to a bull – that finally concentrated her resolve: she would go to Lhasa.

'What right have they,' she asked, 'to erect barriers around a country which is not even lawfully theirs?'

She made her way across to Peking and finally, in 1923, set out on the magnificent journey which was to end with her secret entry into the Forbidden City – the first European woman to reach it. Lhasa was journey's end.

'What an unforgettable vision! I was at last in the calm solitudes of which I had dreamed since my infancy. I felt as if I had come home after a tiring, cheerless pilgrimage.'

Such personal pilgrimages of the soul sometimes ran full circle when the traveller learned to accommodate the life which she had previously found irreconcilable. Ella Maillart, who made a memorable solo journey across Turkestan in the 1930s, found herself bewildered by a warring Europe that seemed bent on destroying itself. She left her native Switzerland and spent the war years in southern India in order to understand why 'cousins killed cousins'. '. . . to understand my innermost soul, I had to live in the immensity of Asia [which] . . . is so vast that man, aware of his own littleness, has given first place to the divine life, bestowing on it alone the glory of true reality.'

Not every traveller, of course, can justify her lifestyle in such a high-minded way. For some, there is simply the unashamed joy of staring at strange places, the pleasure of discovering what lies over the next hill and – most delightful of all – there is the fun and freedom of being alone, unhampered by family or phone, ready for whatever adventure may be on offer. Such are the women, the loners, to whom travelling offers a means of giving rein to that contrary element of human nature which rises belligerently when roads appear impassable, when disinterested border officials shrug their shoulders and well-meaning friends advise against the whole impossible undertaking. Such travellers are adventurers, the intractable die-hards who have caused teachers to shake their heads and would-be employers to despair. They are society's square pegs: the guardians of our right to deviate, should we ever feel brave enough to do so. Compelled always to move on, they travel for the joy of it and often – fortunately for us – can find no way of earning a living other than by writing about their experiences. They have no rational excuse, and can offer no justification for their apparently frivolous way of life.

Distinguished and cheerful, their predecessor is Isabella Bird Bishop, that most exuberant of Victorian travellers who so enjoyed her first solo journey – a six months' ride through the Rockies at the age of forty – that she became an incurable traveller unable to stay put for long. A sickly child, she suffered from a spinal complaint which miraculously disappeared whenever she went abroad but flared up again on her return home. She had originally been sent abroad by the family doctor who thought – rightly enough – that the sea breeze and the whiff of strange places would be beneficial. Dr John Bishop, whom she finally agreed to marry after a long and persistent courtship, commented that her amazing resilience was due to the fact that she had 'the appetite of a tiger and the digestion of an ostrich'. Isabella died in Edinburgh at the age of seventy-three, her bags packed and ready for a trip to China.

She was followed by others equally intrepid. The daughter of a doctor who was himself a bit of an adventurer, Mary Kingsley worked as his unpaid literary assistant (he refused to spend money on her education) until the death of both parents left her free to travel. She had been warned to avoid the rays of the sun and to get an early introduction to the local Wesleyan missionaries as, her

21

death being the most likely outcome of her ill-advised journey, they were the only people on the West Coast of Africa, her destination, who would be able to give her a decent burial, with hearse and black funeral feathers. Despite the morbid advice, she went. 'My mind,' she wrote, 'was set on going and I had to go.'

With a practical rather than a romantic attitude to travel, she set off in 1893 on the first of her two famous journeys to the West Coast, the precursor of many anthropologists who found the tribes of Africa rich in tradition and culture. Armed with a waterproof sack packed tight with books, blankets, boots, mustard leaves, quinine, and a hotwater bottle, she marched up the gangway of the steamer, eager to dispense with prejudices which she regarded as both cumbersome and irrelevant. The other passengers, all male except for the stewardess, viewed this unexpected apparition with alarm, fearing that she was somehow connected with the World's Women's Temperance Association.

Mary Kingsley was thirty when she finally got the chance to break loose from the stultifying drudgery of housekeeping for others. Dervla Murphy was another dutiful, unmarried daughter who devoted herself to caring for an invalid mother until, released by her death, she too set out, at the age of thirty, to cycle all the way to India, for biking and foreign travel had fascinated her since childhood. If asked, however to give a more detailed explanation, she is uncharacteristically at a loss for words. Sitting in her old, stone house in rural Ireland, drinking home-made beer and smoking a cigar, she laughs in amazement when asked if she has a reason for travelling. 'None whatsoever,' she says with the complacent look of a cat who has just swallowed the family goldfish, 'I just go to enjoy myself – I'm completely irresponsible, absolutely no commitment to anything.' Did she never feel she had to justify her journey, pretend she was off to learn about new places?

'Not a bit of it,' she replies, firmly tapping her cigar on a saucer. For such women, there is no way of combatting the compulsion to travel. Like Mary Kingsley, she had to go.

*   *   *

There is nothing new about women travelling the highways of the world and from the early centuries, the Christian Church has offered a useful umbrella to women who had the will and the money to travel the pilgrim route to Rome and Jerusalem.

In 383, Egeria, a Roman citizen from Gaul, travelled to Jerusalem to visit the Holy Land. Luckily for posterity, she was an insatiable pilgrim, recording in detail everything she saw. Writing home to her religious sisters, whom she addressed as 'Lovely Ladies, light of my heart', she unearthed for them as much information as she could, for 'you know how inquisitive I am'.

Later, with England converted to Christianity, the daughters of the great Anglo-Saxon noblemen were sent abroad to France to be educated in the Christian and classical mode. It was an opportunity they seized on eagerly, for their new learning offered them an alternative to marriage – a life of religious scholarship. And if the more ambitious women were to achieve any status in their religious communities they would certainly have to spend some time abroad in one of the major monastic centres of learning. This new development in women's education marked the beginning of a trend which continued through the centuries, giving women of means and status both the opportunity and the incentive to travel.

By the seventeenth century, the pilgrimage had given way to the Grand Tour and it was not unusual for women to travel between the major cities of Europe, sometimes without their husbands but always with a startling entourage of servants and baggage. Products of a sober, post-revolutionary England which offered an enlightened education to its more privileged daughters, women such as Lady Mary Wortley Montagu and Eliza Craven toured Europe, Russia and Turkey, studying the architecture, admiring the paintings, dining with the local nobility and wondering at the strangeness of places like Moscow and Istanbul. They were avid collectors of information and assiduous at recording everything they saw.

By the middle of the nineteenth century, the energy and drive that characterized the great days of the British Empire were beginning to show themselves among travellers. Lady missionaries were storming the citadels of China and Africa and the young Victorian miss – middle-class and energetic – was starting to travel on her own, savouring the freedom of climbing in the Alps or walking in Italy while the older, more intrepid maiden lady was pressing onwards to India, Japan, Hawaii and America. By the turn of the century, the New Woman – confident, educated and financially independent – was further liberated by the arrival of the bicycle and the aeroplane. Fanny Workman's bike took her to North Africa and India and another American, Harriet Quimby, took England by surprise by becoming, in 1912, the first woman to fly across the English Channel. Women such as Gertrude Bell and Freya Stark who found satisfaction in combining travel with serious scholarship became professional travellers, bringing with them an aura of respectability that some equally serious travellers have since sought to cast off.

In the 1950s and 1960s, women travellers and explorers were again soaring towards their dreams, breaking new records in the sky, on land and by sea. Jerrie Mock became the first woman to fly solo round the world, and Sheila Scott, having failed her driving test three times, became the first British woman pilot to solo the earth. Ann Davison, as we have seen, became the first woman to sail solo across the Atlantic and in the 1950s the first British all-women expedition set out for the Himalayas. The small but steady stream of women travellers and explorers continues, hell-bent on getting up and away into the skies, over mountains, down rivers or across deserts, travelling on foot, by bike, in a canoe or on their wits alone.

Robyn Davidson needed all her wits about her when she went to spend a year in the incomparable town of Alice Springs learning how to handle camels before setting out with a dog and two camels (one of which was pregnant) on an astonishing trek across 1700 miles of Australian scrubland. Her stay in Alice Springs was a baptism by alcoholism and sexism, and at times was nothing less than sheer misery, but the experience provided her with the protective armour she needed in order to make the journey.

A university girl, she had been accused of being a bourgeois individualist – an insult too terrible to contemplate. 'For one who associated herself for years with the Left, it was the political equivalent of having VD.' Soon however, the pressing need to organize her trek pushed any such self-centred concerns to the back of her mind. She learned how to scout in the desert, how to saddle a camel and, when one of them became ill, how to inject it with massive doses of antibiotics. More important for her own survival, she learned how to supplement her diet with witchetty grubs. She wasn't altogether sure what she was doing in the middle of this vast nowhere. Perhaps she was expiating a collective guilt? The misery caused by her mother's death had affected her whole family and at times she felt that 'all the stupid, meaningless pain our family had suffered might somehow be symbolically absolved, laid to rest through this gesture of mine'.

Robyn Davidson was twenty-seven when she made her solitary and memorable journey across Australia. She has blond hair and a determined smile and though there is a gentleness in her eyes there is also the self-knowledge she gained during her own remarkable pilgrimage. 'You are as powerful,' she wrote when she reached the Indian Ocean and the end of her journey, 'and as strong as you allow yourself to be.'

Lucy Irvine was strong too, but despite that she nearly succumbed to poisoning on three occasions while spending a year as a castaway on the island of Tuin, which lies between the north coast of Australia and Papua New Guinea. She was a 24-year-old tax clerk when she saw a newspaper notice advertising for a wife to live on a desert island for a year. Gerald Kingsland, who had placed the ad, liked what he saw – her 'bubbling, bucaneering spirit . . . her delicate wrists . . . unwavering eyes – and long, shapely legs'.

On her twenty-fifth birthday they made love. A month later, for his fifty-first birthday, she took him to the Royal Festival Hall and the following month they married. It was a marriage merely of convenience. The Australian immigration authorities would feel happier, they said, about allowing a couple to live together on a deserted island if they were married.

'I'm not in love with you,' Lucy told him, 'but I feel very closely attached to you and who knows what the year will bring?'

How could they have guessed what it would be like? They'd brought only the minimum of food with them – two hundred tea bags, a packet of spaghetti, two kilos of dried beans, a bottle of cooking oil and a few other bits and pieces. It would be enough to keep going until they could grow some things of their own. They drank the milk from the large green coconuts that hung overhead and caught and cooked their own shark. It was an idyll that wasn't to last. Three times Lucy became violently ill from eating wild berries. They ran dangerously short of water and Gerald's extra years began to tell on him. He developed a gangrenous ulcer and they both lost weight. Their affection for each other degenerated into a strained uneasiness and it wasn't until their year was ending that they managed to recapture their earlier feelings. At the end of the year, however, she left both the island and Gerald just as she had always planned to do, marriage or not.

' "I know you've got to go," he said. "Christ, you're only twenty-six, you've got your whole life ahead of you." . . . And with that he pulled me closer and our faces bumped together in a brief kiss.' The year was over.

There have been other women propelled by the same curious combination of determination and vulnerability – a blind woman sets out to climb Kala Patthar, 500 feet above Everest base camp, a grandmother cycles solo across America and Eve Jackson, a young Englishwoman, plans to fly solo in 1986 from England to Australia in a frail microlight aircraft. The list lengthens each year, but spread across the world as they are, spanning the years from youth to old age, these women appear linked by nothing more than their sex and the common experience of travelling. Surprisingly, the link that initially might appear to be a vital one – that of feminism – is rarely to be found.

It may be thought that because a woman attempts to achieve something in what has hitherto been considered a male area she is doing so with the primary intention of making a statement about women. It is abundantly clear, however, that in the case of most women travellers, this is not so. It is true, certainly, that some of them have consciously and deliberately laid their motivations and success on the altar of their womanhood. Others, in the course of travelling, have taken on the mantle of their sisters, as their physical journey has evolved into one also of the soul. But to describe all women travellers as feminists would be to take away from them that very quality which makes each one unique – their individuality.

Put them in a room together, and there is no guarantee that harmony will prevail. In the 1880s, when Marianne North and Constance Gordon Cumming accepted an invitation to meet Isabella

Bird Bishop, their lion-hunting London hostess was overjoyed. 'Three globe-trotteresses,' she trilled, unwisely. The two were not especially amused. Isabella was decked out in gold-embroidered slippers, a silver and gold petticoat from Japan and was sporting a favour presented to her by the King of the Sandwich Islands. 'We withdrew,' said Miss North, somewhat loftily, 'leaving Miss Bird unruffled and equal to the occasion.'

Miss Gordon Cumming, in fact, was not unlike the unruffled Isabella. Born into a wealthy Scottish family – her home was at Gordonstoun – she got her first glimpse of the outside world at the age of thirty-one when she received an invitation from her sister to visit her in India. Visit! She was amazed at the idea and almost turned it down since no one, she felt, went to India unless they had to. Yet on arrival, she was immediately captivated by its mystery and sense of history and especially by the similarities between Hindu and Celtic customs. After a two-year stay, she returned to England and wrote an ecstatic two-volume account of what she saw. A few years later, she received an invitation from the Bishop of Colombo to visit him in Ceylon and her reputation as a traveller began to grow. As soon as she got back home to England, people started asking her where next, to which she replied: 'Fiji, because that was the most absolutely improbable idea that could suggest itself.' But improbable or not, she went, and then on to Japan, Tahiti and San Francisco. Mistress of the throwaway line, her books – she wrote one about each journey – are littered with tantalizing phrases such as 'our acquaintance with camels had hitherto been limited to the Arabian dromedary . . .' An inquisitive, studious lady, she observed misery and poverty with compassion but from a distance and, in common with many travellers, she was not always around when her publishers needed her. In a foreword to one of her books, there is an apology for some inadequacy or other, explained by the telling phrase: 'In the absence of the author, who sailed unexpectedly for Fiji . . .' The proofs, on this occasion, were read by none other than the unruffled Miss Bird.

It is perhaps surprising that the paths of the travelling sisterhood did not cross more often, though had Fanny Workman met up with her contemporary, Gertrude Bell, the political sparks might well have turned into a conflagration. At the very time that Fanny was conducting a series of major climbing expeditions in the Karakorams, resolutely advertising the cause of women's suffrage, Gertrude was helping to found, in England, the Anti-Suffrage League.

Both these women were products of their respective worlds, moulded and influenced by the whims, attitudes, needs and prejudices of those around them. Certain women have set out on their journeys happy not only to take the attitudes of society with them but also to impose them on those they have encountered along the way, whom they perceived to be in some way in need of improvement. Others have found such values false and insufficient, and have felt compelled to go in search of qualities which they feel are lacking in the world they leave behind.

Whatever their needs and motivations have been, travelling has over the centuries offered to women a means both of discovering and expressing their own individuality, for the change in their needs has been one only of degree. Women, said a seventeenth-century writer, should stay at home and attend to their duties, which he kindly characterized as 'subjection, helpfulness and gracefulness'. The tedium of such advice was unbearable. 'The truth is,' commented Margaret Lucas, flamboyant and eccentric Restoration writer, 'we live like Bats or Owls, Labour like Beasts, and Dye like Worms.'

Three hundred years later, Sabina Shalom found herself fat, middle-aged and menopausal – and with a bee in her Miami Beach bonnet about hitch-hiking to Australia: 'The idea obsessed me simply because it was right off the map. It became an excuse, not a reason, for getting away . . . I longed to be free of duties and obligations. Free of thinking, worrying, protecting, mothering. Free of feeling everyone's burdens and making them mine.'

The distant horizon beckons even more urgently now, as the blandness of the mid-twentieth century threatens to render us anonymous, our identity emerging as symbols on a computer printout or fashioned as fodder for the consumer society, for the marketing and media world. Within this murderous matrix, women are tamed and packaged, their new 'liberated' image as steeplejacks, truck-drivers or soldiers glamourized, glitzy and unreal – suitable copy for the propaganda machine anxious to demonstrate society's stifling generosity towards them. For those with the will to escape, a journey outwards into the unseen may be the only hope of finding what lies within. Better the reality of the unknown than the artificiality of the known.

CHAPTER 2

◆•◆

Pilgrims to Freedom

'Nothing could hold her back, whether it was the
labour of travelling the whole world . . . the perils of
sea and rivers . . . the dread crags and fearsome
mountains . . .'
Valerius on Egeria.

Travellers, like the rest of us, need to communicate with someone
even if, by writing a journal, it is at one remove. In 1884 a remarkable book was discovered which tells of a journey made by a
woman who travelled to Jerusalem around the year AD 383.

Its author, Egeria, was a devout Roman citizen of noble birth,
who journeyed from Gaul to the Holy Land and recorded everything
she saw, thus leaving us with both a fascinating traveller's tale and
the only complete account we still have of the fourth century
liturgy. So timeless are some of these liturgical ceremonies that her
description, written sixteen hundred years ago, captures that odd
mixture of gloom and glitter, superstition and ritual that haunts the
dark interiors of present-day Jerusalem: 'All you can see is gold
and jewels and silk; the hangings are entirely silk with gold stripes,
the curtains the same and everything they use for services at the
festival is made of gold and jewels. You simply cannot imagine the
number and the sheer weight of the candles and the tapers and the
lamps . . .'

Travelling through fourth-century Palestine was not without
its dangers. Wild animals roamed the purple hills and the inhospitable locals, weary of seeing endless bands of well-to-do foreigners
pass through their lands, were liable to attack without warning. It
was a formidable undertaking for anyone, let alone a woman on her
own, but as long as travellers stuck to the straight and narrow
Roman roads, they were relatively safe.

By the time Egeria set out on her journey, the pilgrim way was well established. Monasteries dotted the route and quite a few hospices had been set up for the use of Christian travellers, many of whom, of course, were women. In fact, the hospices themselves were often run by women, among them Paula, a Roman matron whose business acumen and managerial skills led her to establish a chain of hospices. Her contemporary, the scholar Jerome, was amazed that a mere woman should be so successful: 'With a zeal and courage unbelievable in a woman she forgot her sex and physical weakness and settled in the heat of Bethlehem for good in the company of many virgins and her daughter' – whom we must charitably assume was one too.

These journeys were far from being temporary religious fads, indulged in by rich women with time on their hands. Egeria and Paula were followed by wave after wave of women who put down lasting roots in Jerusalem and refused to return home. A guide book written nearly four hundred years after Egeria's arrival comments on the presence, just outside the East Gate of the Holy City, of a hundred women living in an enclosed convent, receiving gifts of food which were pushed through a hole in the wall.

By the eighth century, the pilgrim route had become something of a tourist trek with many of the delays, frustrations and unexpected expenses that one might encounter today. Sea-captains refused to allow their passengers to leave ship until they had paid the airport tax of the day, known euphemistically as a 'disembarcation fee' Travellers passing through non-Christian areas were subjected to poll taxes which varied according to their apparent wealth, and one traveller commenting on the bureaucracy of the day, no less autocratic then than now, noted in disgust that 'anyone who is found by night or day without a paper or a stamp issued by one of the kings or princes of that country is sent to prison . . . until he can prove he is not a spy'.

None of these inconveniences, however, deterred women from the journey, and indeed so numerous were they on the road to Rome that they presented a special problem to the church authorities whose attempts to restrain this restless tide were at first paternalistic and benign but were soon revealed in their true, repressive colours. 'It would be well and favourable,' wrote Boniface to the Archbishop of Canterbury, '. . . if your synod would forbid matrons and veiled women to make these frequent journeys back and forth to Rome.' To have wives and mothers straying so far from home was an obvious threat to the institution of marriage. Not only that: despite their respectable status, such matrons, it seems, were in danger of falling by the wayside as so many of their sisters had done previously. 'For,' the anxious cleric continued, 'there are few towns [along the way] in which there is not a courtesan or a harlot of English stock.' He might have taken a more charitable view of his fallen sisters, as one of his predecessors did. St Marcianus, in the fifth century, persuaded a number of prostitutes to reform and to demonstrate their new way of life by making the pilgrimage to Jerusalem – a journey which he thoughtfully financed himself.

*　　　*　　　*

Banditry, piracy, prostitution and smuggling – it was all a long way from the vision of a young, wistful, Anglo-Saxon girl, exiled in a German monastery, who had to content herself with being a second-hand traveller.

> I, unworthy child of the Saxon race, the last of those who have come hither from their land who am, in comparison with these my countrymen, not only in years but in virtue also, only a poor little creature . . . Yet I am a woman, tainted with the frailty of my sex, with no pretensions to wisdom or cleverness to support me, but prompted solely by the violence of my own will like a little ignorant child plucking a few flowers here and there from numerous branches rich in foliage and in fruit.

With painful humility the young Huceburg, amanuensis for the first Englishman to travel to Jerusalem, sat down to write what is the earliest English travel book still available to us.

She had been sent from England to the monastery of Heidenheim, in Germany, where her cousin was Abbess. While there, another member of her family, the monk Willibald, now an old man, returned from his travels to dictate his book to the wide-eyed young girl. The guidebook, *The Hodaeporicon*, written about 780, is full of stories that must have amazed her – how the party saw a lion, how they were arrested by the Saracens on suspicion of spying, how Willibald, later Saint Willibald, smuggled balsam through the customs. First he filled a calabash with the balsam, then he took a hollow cane, filled that with petroleum and concealed it in the calabash so that when the officials came to examine the calabash they were distracted by the smell of petroleum and the balsam went undetected.

Huceburg was the product of her religious education, trained to view herself as a woman and therefore less than nothing, but there was nothing humble about Margery Kempe, the mayor's daughter from Bishop's Lynn who, in 1413, set sail for Jerusalem with a party of pilgrims whose collective and determined aim was to lose her as quickly as they could.

By the fifteenth century, women, despite the prohibitive antics of the church, had established themselves as regular and seasoned travellers on the pilgrim run. Their enthusiasm and ebullient response to religious ceremonies could, at times, be somewhat of an embarrassment but their presence was vital to a church which thrived on ignorance and superstition. It is the women, after all, who keep the candles burning and who see, through the hypnotic haze, the strange shadows of moving statues.

Margery Kempe, voluble, energetic, given to hearing voices and seeing visions, was born in 1373 and at the age of forty set out on a five-month journey to Jerusalem. Margery was obsessed with holiness – her own and everyone else's – and constantly harangued her companions to pray when they would rather have been carousing. Although the threat of piracy had lessened since the Venetian Senate had required all galleys to carry bows, arrows and lances for their own protection, it was still a nerve-wracking journey and most of Margery's companions preferred to take their minds off their fears by drinking and playing cards.

When the pilgrim band reached Jaffa, Margery was so excited at the prospect of seeing Jerusalem that she fell off her donkey and two kind Germans had to help her back on, one of them even going so far as to feed her with spices to ward off travel sickness. It was in Jerusalem that the pilgrimage proper began, with a seemingly endless round of visits to churches, to the River Jordan, and to Bethlehem. Here, Margery's sanctity took hold of her in earnest and 'she fell down because she could not stand or kneel and rolled and wrested with her body, spreading her arms and crying with a loud voice as though her heart burst asunder'. Understandably, the rest of the group thought it best to disassociate itself from this excessive and unseemly display of fervour. On the journey home, they frequently managed to give her the slip and she often found herself trudging alone along unknown roads through foreign countries fearing for her good name. Occasionally, she managed to attach herself to another party or, when the worst came to the worst, to hitch a lift on a passing haycart.

Margery Kempe holds an important position in the history of women travellers. Like many before and after her, she took to the whole paraphernalia of travel with the noisy delight of a drake getting her first sight of water. Although a matron of comfortable means, she stoically endured hardship, danger and illness during the two years she was away from home. Despite the unchristian behaviour of her companions, who cut up her clothes, stole her bed sheets and walked too fast for her, she displayed a dogged determination to complete what she had set out to do. Like many women travellers, however, she enjoyed a privileged position in her own society and it was this which enabled her confidently to deal with officials and critics alike.

In one major aspect, however, she differed from most of the women travellers who were to follow her. She was both ill-educated and ill-prepared to benefit intellectually from her experiences. She died in 1438, untouched by the ripples of humanism and radical religious thinking that were beginning to disturb, yet again, the relatively calm pond of English society. She left behind, however, a record of her travels and the final irony in her tale is that this unique book – the earliest autobiographical travel account still in existence to be written in the vernacular – had to be dictated, for this most exuberant and talkative of women travellers could neither read nor write.

Such a state of ignorance would have been unendurable for those women living around the time of the English Civil War whose lives, for a time, depended on their wits, and consisted of a series of hurried and dangerous escapes made under cover, frequently in disguise and usually at dead of night. Their journeys – hazardous and solitary – were ones they would rather not have made.

Anne Harrison was nineteen when she married Sir Richard Fanshawe, in 1644. Brought up to sew and play the virginal, Anne soon found herself thrust into the role of political refugee, both in her own country and abroad, for Sir Richard, who sided with the King in the Civil War, was frequently on the run from the Roundheads. In the course of her happy marriage, she gave birth to six sons and eight daughters and spent much of her time moving her surviving children from country to country, from safe house to safe house, the burden of planning and negotiating the journeys falling on her shoulders alone. When her husband was finally captured in 1651, she had to make a perilous journey through the London streets to see him.

'During this time of his imprisonment, I failed not constantly to go, when the clock struck four in the morning, with a dark lantern in my hand, all alone and on foot from my lodging in Chancery Lane, and then I would go under his window and softly call him ... sometimes I was so wet with rain that it went in at my neck and out at my heels.'

Like other women travellers who came after her, she became adept at talking her way out of difficult situations – not only her own survival but that of both her husband and her family depended on it. When, on Cromwell's death, Sir Richard left for France, she had to forge a document and disguise herself in order to get past the watchful eye of the Roundhead official. It was a testing time and one to which women responded with courage and vigour. The Restoration period which followed seemed for women so dull, superficial and frustrating in comparison that one of its most famous writers – Margaret Lucas – made a special plea that all women should be 'free, happy and famous as men'. It was a brave, vociferous demand, made at a time when, in fact, changes both economic and social were slowly beginning to take place which would allow women a far greater freedom to move out of the domestic milieu to which Margaret Lucas felt herself to be so unwillingly chained. During the latter part of the seventeenth century trade and commerce were expanding, the navy was growing and women found themselves running import and export businesses, dealing in insurance and acting as shipping agents. It was against this increasingly prosperous setting that Celia Fiennes was born in 1662, of a well-to-do family of Dissenters.

At the age of twenty, she set out on a series of journeys round England and Scotland which would take her ten years to complete. She was a prim and serious young woman who undertook her journeys, usually riding sidesaddle, with the aim of improving both her health and her intellect: 'so that my mind,' she wrote severely, 'should not appear totally unoccupied'. More disconcerting in one so young – she hoped that the account she planned to bring back would give people more serious things to think about than cards or dice. If people were to concern themselves with 'observing the pleasant prospects and the different produces and manufactures of each place . . . they would undoubtedly be cured of the endemic sicknesses of laziness and the vapours'. More to the point, she felt, knowledge of their own country might 'cure (in others) the evil itch of over-valuing foreign parts'.

The English countryside into which she forayed was not altogether hospitable and it took a considerable sense of adventure, allied to a strong puritan desire for self-improvement, to set out on such a venture. Roads were rough and badly signposted. On horseback, she had to negotiate water-filled potholes so big that a man could drown in one. Since the ending of the Civil War soldiers had turned to vagrancy, and it was a sign of their prosperity that footpads had recently taken to horseback in order to make their getaway more efficient. Travellers were especially vulnerable on open heaths and in forests, Epping, Hampstead and Hounslow being the well-known danger spots. A sixteen-year-old heiress was attacked no less than eleven times and women took to travelling with a spare purse of money ready to hand over to robbers. Clearly, even a short journey to market was not to be undertaken lightly.

Without children to leaven her solemn attitudes, Celia Fiennes' view of life tended to be staid and devoid of humour, but her insatiable curiosity and sturdy determination more than compensated for this. Her description of a meeting with highwaymen is typical of her style not only of writing but of living: '. . . two fellows all of a sudden from the wood fell into the road and they looked all trussed up with great coats and as it were, bundles about them which I believe were pistols.' They jostled her horse and tried to get between it and those of her servants and when asked the way said they didn't know the area though later it became obvious that they did. The Fiennes party was saved by the presence of men haymaking nearby. 'It was the only time I had reason to suspect I was engaged with some highwaymen,' she remarked, characteristically omitting to say whether or not she had been frightened.

While Celia was exploring her native England, a contemporary of hers had been making a name for herself first as a spy and later as a writer. Aphra Behn was born in 1640 and brought up in Kent. Details of her childhood are uncertain but in her early twenties she sailed with some of her family to live as part of the household of the Governor of Surinam. Life in the tropics seemed strange to the young girl, but she had a generous, open mind, receptive to the wonder of it all and when, with her brother, she encountered some slaves recently uprooted from their African homes she was ready to approach them with friendliness and compassion. In a long, full dress and with a bonnet covering her unconventionally short hair, her appearance must have seemed as strange to them as theirs did to her. 'They touched us, laying their hands on all the features of our faces, feeling our breasts and arms, taking up one petticoat then wondering to see another; admiring our shoes and stockings but more our garters which we gave them and they tied about their legs, being laced with silver lace at the ends.' The arrival, however, of the chieftains of war was another thing altogether, for they seemed a ferocious bunch with their marks and self-mutilations: '. . . so frightful a vision it was to see them . . . some wanted their noses, some their lips . . . others cut through each cheek'. They wore 'girdles of cotton with their knives naked stuck in it . . . a quiver of arrows on their thighs and feathers on their heads'. Nevertheless, she found them both humane and noble.

Returning to England in 1663, Aphra married a merchant called Behn who died within three years, and she was then sent to Antwerp as a spy, with little more to live on than forty pounds and money from the sale of her rings. It seems that she never married again, for she regarded that institution as 'the cheap drug of a church ceremony'. She received little thanks for the political and naval information she sent back from Antwerp, and on her return she devoted herself to earning a living from her writing, becoming the first Englishwoman to do so and drawing copiously on her travels in Surinam which she recounted as the background to her autobiographical novel *Oroonoko*, published a year before her early death at the age of forty-eight.

It is one of life's small ironies that women – their own position in society not unlike that of a colonized country – were themselves able to take a ride on the great wave of colonization that burst outwards into the unclaimed world. The more ambitious and adventurous among them were quick to grasp the opportunity to travel far beyond the tamer shores of Europe to the unknown excitements of distant colonies. While Aphra Behn was working in Holland to undermine any plans the Dutch might have to defeat the English navy, another woman – also in Holland – was starting to build up a career that would eventually take her, also, to Surinam.

It was unusual for women to travel to the colonies on their own and those who did were usually making the journey in order to marry a merchant or planter. A contemporary writer, therefore, found it 'a kind of phenomenon to see a lady actuated by a love of insects so truly heroic as to induce her to traverse the seas for the purpose of painting and describing them'. To go after a husband was understandable but to endure a journey into the tropics merely to paint insects was another thing altogether!

The amazing lady was the entomological artist, Maria Sibylla Merian who, ten years after Aphra Behn's death, received a grant from the Dutch government which allowed her, at the age of fifty-two, to set out for Surinam. At that time, according to a contemporary report, it was the black spot of the Dutch Empire. If the destination proved unsavoury, the means of getting there was a positive death-trap. Sea travel in the seventeenth century was neither pleasant nor healthy. Scurvy abounded, hygiene was virtually non-existent and the only air that filtered down below deck came through hatches which often had to be battened down to keep out the driving rain. Sailing into the tropics, the air became steamy and foul and this, acting upon the decaying food left lying round the galley, meant that sailors and passengers often fell victim to dysentery. Maria, taking her daughter with her as a companion, survived the journey – no mean feat for a woman who would have hitherto led a very sheltered life. Surinam lies just north of the

Equator and the combination of high temperatures and a copious rainfall meant a plentiful vegetation for Maria to sketch. It was the low, unhealthy marshlands, however, that were too much for this middle-aged matron and she had to return to Holland after two years.

The travels of these three women – and of many others that must go unremarked – are a reflection of the new horizons perceived, for the first time, by people interested in the special qualities of the places they visited and especially, in the case of Aphra Behn, in the lives of those they encountered in the course of their journeys. Celia Fiennes noted with obvious disapproval the increasing interest in things foreign and chose instead to confine herself to a thorough study of her own country. The other two travellers accepted the challenge of adventure and, like so many women before them, found it to their taste.

By the eighteenth century, a steady wave of women travellers was regularly leaving England's shores, some to accompany their husbands on diplomatic missions, and some to participate with them in that great cultural institution – the Grand Tour. Lady Mary Wortley Montagu went with her husband to Constantinople in 1716, where she became a keen and amusing observer of life. She was one of the first travellers daring enough to try out a strange, foreign practice: while in Turkey, she studied the habit of vaccination for smallpox, adopted it for her own children, and later introduced the practice to England.

In 1810, Hester Stanhope left England in search of a new and more exciting life than anything she could possibly find at home. There was no way in which an intelligent and independent-minded woman such as she could satisfy her hunger for both knowledge and adventure. She was the daughter of an illustrious family: her grandfather had been Pitt the Elder, first Earl of Chatham, and her uncle was William Pitt for whom she had acted as hostess during his years of office as Prime Minister. After his death in 1806 there was a vacuum to be filled, and she began to think about ways of satisfying the unbounded curiosity which had ruled her since childhood. She recalled her governesses admonishing her for this awkward trait: 'I was tired of all those around me who to all my questions invariably answered, "My dear, that is not proper for you to know – you must not talk about such things until you are older." ' That she was clever was certain; had not her father, himself hungry for knowledge, said that she was the best logician he knew?

The only man she might have married, Sir John Moore, had been killed at Corunna, and having left behind the suffocating standards of English society, she felt free to take as her lover a man much younger than herself – though she refused to marry him. With a settled home in Syria, she found it possible to live a life of freedom that would have been impossible in England. A commentator of the time noted that she was impervious to public opinion: 'Her intentions were pure but only God was the judge of that and she cared not a fig what men thought.'

Perhaps that was just as well, for England could be unforgiving of those who strayed from the preordained path – and never more so than in its treatment of Hester who, having given her services to her country by acting as advisor, secretary and hostess to its Prime Minister, found her meagre pension cut off by Palmerston in an attempt to get her to mend her profligate ways. It was an attempt that failed, for in protest she walled herself up in her Arab mansion at Dar Djoun, near Mount Lebanon. There, in a bed covered in pipe burns – she had taken to the hookah with as much enthusiasm as she had adopted male Arab dress – and in a room heavy with smoke and scattered about with phials, calico and papers, she died a pauper at the age of sixty-three, owing £12,000 invested in an archaeological dig that had failed to reveal anything startling.

Misunderstood and unforgiven, she was one of those early women travellers who pursued their goals of excitement and learning, encountering discomfort and danger to a degree that could only be imagined by those who were so quick to criticize them.

By the middle of the nineteenth century, conditions were slightly easier for the woman who wanted more from life than anything home and marriage might offer. Attitudes had softened, travel conditions had eased and it was no longer necessary for women travellers to cut the umbilical cord in such dramatic fashion. Moreover, it was now seen that in one area at least, the missionary field, women could serve a very useful purpose indeed. The Victorian era was marked by the great surge of enthusiasm with which its women took to the new lands of Africa, America and China, defying convention, daring fate and stepping outside their appointed positions with a cheery disregard for the consequences. They enjoy a special place in the affections of anyone interested in the history of travel, for the journeys they made were not merely physical ones – they were the embodiment of the female spirit that would never again be content to flutter helplessly at the bars of its cage.

*   *   *

The position of women in the Christian Church – and in many other religions – has always been an ambivalent one, their ability to give birth robed in superstition and their power to nurture life feared. Yet their very closeness to the miracle of life has in the past invested them with a mysticism which the Christian Church saw as a strength upon which it might capitalize.

In Victorian times, bemused and bewildered, women found themselves plucked from the blood and sweat of childbirth and placed high upon the pedestal of perfection – the Angel of the Drawing-Room presiding over her own prison. Marriage, however, was not the destiny of every woman, nor was every woman prepared to be held within this domestic cage, and no book about women travellers would be complete without reference to the band of women who in those days set out with courage and conviction to present their foreign god to the unsuspecting peoples of Africa and China.

Women had always played an important role as missionaries, women whose lives had been illuminated by a vision so compelling that they left family, home and country to pursue it. The great mystic, Teresa of Avila, took to the rough roads of sixteenth-century Spain, preaching reform of the Carmelite Order. In the following century, a Frenchwoman, Marie Guyard, abandoned her child in order to become a missioner. In 1617, at the age of seventeen, she had been forced into marriage much against her will, for she had hoped to become a nun. Within three years, she was widowed and left with a small son. This child she put in the care of a sister before sailing to Canada to set up a convent. Attacked on numerous occasions by the Iroquois Indians whom she had come to convert, she nevertheless survived to the age of seventy-three.

The English tradition of the woman preacher travelling the countryside had been established by the Quakers in the seventeenth century. Later, the wave of energy which surged through England during the Industrial Revolution was reflected in the blossoming of Victorian evangelism, its success due in part to the army of women who carried the message with enthusiasm and vigour to the furthermost points of the empire. It was a time when there was work to be done, coal to be mined, lessons to be learned, money to be made and a Queen to be honoured.

For many women, missionary work provided a most satisfying alternative to marriage or stay-at-home spinsterhood. The empire offered men numerous opportunities to travel abroad: they could serve in the army, take a posting as an army chaplain, or make a career for themselves as administrators. They could even make a name for themselves as explorers. No such options were open to women, who had to content themselves, if they were single, with a position as a governess or lady's companion – both lowly states of existence. There were few acceptable occupations open to the single woman in a society which regarded marriage as the only proper state and in which spinsters were regarded as second-class citizens.

Their value in the missionary field lay in the fact that as members of the gentler sex, they presented little threat to the local people; furthermore they had easy access to the local women – a great advantage, since it was commonly held among missionaries that to convert a family, you need only convert the mother. Their most attractive quality, however, was the simple fact that they were unmarried. As such, they could be relied upon to pursue their goals with a single-minded disregard for the hardships encountered along the thorny path to heaven. Staunch and sensible, they were admirably suited to unceasing and unquestioning labour in the name of all they – and the empire – considered decent.

The rationale of religion is, of course, an excellent ingredient to throw into the traveller's brew. It can be used as an elixir, giving fresh and unsuspected strength to a mind and body exhausted by lack of sleep or sustenance. The missionary traveller knows that despite rejection and ridicule, despite the alien climate, the strange customs and only half-understood language, despite the isolation, discomfort and danger, reward will follow, if not by the end of the day, at least at the end of a lifetime. And which of the ungodly among us can be sure of that? In a perverse way, the hardships suffered reinforced both the missionary's zeal and her determination to carry on, her mental state not unlike that of a patriot waging war. 'I am,' said one, 'a soldier of Christ.'

The British Government was quick to see how useful these women could be with their energy, local knowledge and reputation for being fair. Indeed, in the colonies, the link between Church and state was thinly drawn with no distinction at all existing in the minds of some. Born in 1848 in Aberdeen, little Mary Slessor was a millhand by the time she was eleven – the family of seven children needed her earnings. Her mother was a weaver and her alcoholic father a shoemaker. Determined to free herself from the evils of poverty though not from her family commitments, she educated herself as best she could and in the process learned a lot about the famous Doctor Livingstone, another Scot who had become the inspiration of the empire. She too, she decided, would become a missionary. In 1876, at the age of twenty-eight, she sailed from Liverpool on the SS *Ethiopia*, bound for the Niger region of West Africa. Her salary, as a missionary, would be £60 a year. In Calabar, her practical approach to her work and her expertise in dealing with local disputes led to her appointment as British government agent. She saw nothing incongruous in this dual role, simply viewing her job of conducting judicial courts as an extension of her religious duties. Nor did she feel it was unchristian to administer an occasional box on the ear to a local chief when he spoke out of turn.

It was her humanitarian work in saving the lives of twins that evinced uncharacteristic praise from Mary Kingsley and the two formed an immediate if unlikely partnership, for they were both intent on promoting better understanding of tribal customs. Local animists believed that each person was born with a guardian spirit – an invisible companion. When a woman gave birth to twins, however, the Efiks – among whom Mary Slessor was living – believed that the spirit companion had been displaced and its place taken instead by the human child. There could be only one explanation, the Efiks believed. The woman must have secretly mated with the devil. The punishment was horrific. Both children must be killed – for who could be sure which was the devil-child and which the good one? The mother too must be banished, driven out of her home and away from the tribe. The whole thing, as Mary Kingsley noted, was seen 'as a sort of severe adultery'. Mary Slessor devoted herself to saving the lives of both the babies and their mothers, doing so with such tact and understanding that she was soon able to set up a refuge for the unhappy victims.

Hers was a lonely life, far from family and home, living in the bush surrounded by her African helpers. Her red hair was shorn to a boyish crop and the climate took its toll on her health. At the age of thirty-two, another missionary appeared on the scene and the two formed a friendship that looked as if it might end happily in permanent companionship, but circumstances forced them apart and she devoted the rest of her life to her beloved Africans, to whom she was known simply as Ma. Mary Kingsley, despite her dislike of missionaries, afforded her the highest praise: 'The sort of man Miss Slessor represents is rare.'

Mary Kingsley herself, of course, was something of a rare bird, and through her studies of local customs and beliefs she too hoped to make the African better understood. She drew attention, for instance, to the damage she observed being done in girls' schools in Calabar by ill-informed missioners. It was the custom for the girls to wind a long strip of cloth round their waist and to leave a part of this to trail behind them on the ground to be held by their guardian spirit. In the safety of their homes, this train could be caught up and tucked into their skirt but outside in a public place, where danger lurked, the cloth had to trail along the ground. The missionaries briskly forbade this practice, seeing it as yet another example of the lazy, slovenly habits of the Africans. The girls were torn between the two: no respectable girl would go about without the protection of her guardian spirit; if she did, she must be bad. It was a war, Miss Kingsley noted, between native and Presbyterian respectability and it is not difficult to imagine which practice she favoured.

While she found the work done by Slessor admirable, Mary Kingsley would have found it difficult to applaud the zeal with which Annie Taylor, another of her contemporaries, pursued her missionary work in China and Tibet, for Annie's arrogance fed upon her ignorance: 'I was shocked to see men and women near Ta'ri'si,' she wrote, 'prostrating themselves the whole length of the road . . . Poor things, they know no better; no one has ever told them about Jesus.' How different was Alexandra David-Neel's objective and careful observation of the same scene some fifty years later, written with the intention of understanding, not dismissing, the custom:

> Many of the pilgrims [she wrote] went round the mountain, prostrating themselves at each step, that is to say, stretching their arms as they lay on the ground, and marking with their fingers the length they had covered with their bodies. They would get up and stand at the exact place which their fingers had touched, after which they would again prostrate themselves and measure their length once more, and so on, all the way round.

Annie's was the fixed and limited view of the missioner whose commitment prevented her from appreciating the culture and beliefs of those she wanted to save. But it was that very commitment that led her to journey across China and into Tibet, hopeful of finally entering Lhasa. After Africa, China had become the next focus for nineteenth-century missionary activity. British traders made important economic links there, and in 1878 the first woman missionary was sent into the interior. The fact that the economic links had been forged on the sale of opium – in 1839 British ships were bringing in 2000 tons of opium annually – seems not to have bothered the missionary ladies. Their task was to bring God, not change, to the Chinese millions.

Annie Taylor was accompanied on her journey by her faithful servant, Pontso, and the two of them disguised their true identity by dressing as Tibetans; Annie also cut her hair to look like a Buddhist nun. For the length of their 1300-mile trek they had to ward off bandits and robbers, sleep out in the open and seek sanctuary wherever they could. The rivers they had to cross were often flooded and swollen, posing a considerable obstacle. 'The river is quite impassable, so they say, barring our way, but we are waiting until tomorrow to see if it will be lower in the morning. The Lord can do this for me. My eyes are unto him who made a passage in the Red Sea for the children of Israel.'

When the river finally abated, they had to force their way through biting waters which froze to icicles on the spot. Pressing on along the tea road from China, Annie's difficulties continued. One of the three men she had hired to carry her goods and care for the horses turned troublesome and threatened to reveal her identity. This was dangerous, for Tibet feared invasion both from Britain and China and justifiably viewed all foreigners with suspicion. Another of her men died along the way and a third turned back shortly after the journey had begun. Although armed with a pistol, her real trust lay in the Lord.

Undeterred by the icy nights made worse by the altitude, she sold her tent in order to buy another horse. So high up did the route take them that you could plunge your hand unscathed into a saucepan of boiling water and when she put her Christmas pudding on to boil – for certain traditions after all had to be maintained – its centre was still cold after two hours of cooking. Nevertheless, on that Christmas day in 1892, far from the blazing log fire and roast turkey of childhood days in Egremont, she was cheerful and optimistic, doing what she had chosen to do: 'Quite safe here with Jesus,' she wrote happily in her diary. Her seven-month long journey to Lhasa proved fruitless in the end; she was apprehended within twelve miles of her goal, tried by the local elder and arbitrarily expelled from Tibet. What a long way this rocklike and forceful woman had travelled from a Victorian childhood plagued by heart trouble.

Annie Taylor was a simple, solid soul, well suited to the sort of work which the Inland Mission to China required of its members. She plodded her way through some of the most intriguing places in Tibet, totally unaware of their significance, intent only on revealing to the impoverished peasants the golden gates of heaven through which they could walk one day if only they embraced the Bible. The town of Kum Bum is clustered round the famous Buddhist settlement – then the third largest monastery, housing three thousand lamas – and there the stalwart Annie braved the annual Butter Fair, distributing her evangelical leaflets and urging the holiday crowd to forsake their ancient religion and follow the Lord.

What would have happened to Annie had she been forced to

stay at home in England? Perhaps she would have found some satisfaction in evangelical work among the wretches who worked the dark satanic mills of the Midlands. Those places, after all, were every bit as godforsaken as Lanchow or Shanghai, or even Kum Bum. Instead, she chose to set out for the most impenetrable of countries, circled as it is by a fortress of snow-covered peaks. Like scores of travellers before and since, she was drawn towards Lhasa as if mesmerized by its inaccessibility. Her motivation was religion, but it was a drive fuelled by the challenges which her chosen life had laid before her – challenges to which her brave and adventurous spirit rose with stoical determination.

Consumed by the same missionary zeal was the aptly named Evangeline French. With her sister Francesca and friend Mildred Cable, the three, known as 'the trio', spent fifteen years during the 1920s and 1930s evangelizing in China; they crossed the Gobi Desert five times during that period. Wearing Chinese dress and learning the local dialects, the three women brightly and happily revealed the treasures of the Bible to the nomad tribes until forced to leave by the vagaries of the Chinese/Japanese war.

Sublimely indifferent to their supposed weaknesses, Victorian women missionaries breached the wall of prejudice and proved themselves to be as vigorous and as tenacious as any man, giving practical expression to their spiritual message by setting up schools and hospitals, drawing attention to the difficulties under which the indigenous women laboured, and making representations to governments and royalty on behalf of the poor, the sick and the forgotten.

Four years younger than Annie Taylor, Kate Marsden was caught up in the same wave of religious fervour that swept through Victorian England. After only eight months' training as a missionary nurse, she was sent to Bulgaria in 1877, to tend to Russian soldiers injured in the Russian/Turkish war. The sights she saw were terrifying, for she was still only eighteen and until then had been sheltered by a middle-class upbringing. Especially traumatic was her first and unexpected meeting with two men whose bodies had been hideously eaten away by leprosy. It was this meeting, however, that was to give a focus to her religious zeal and a sense of mission to her life.

Back in England, she continued her nursing career, see-sawing between rationality and periods of disabling self-doubt culminating in a mental disorder which eventually engulfed her. When she recovered, she felt ready to begin her life's work, and started off across Russia to set up a hospital for lepers in the outer reaches of Siberia.

Kate Marsden, above all else, had a sense of humour which got her through many terrible experiences. Her description of her journey across Siberia, undertaken in 1891 before the Trans-Siberian railway had been built, would be unbearable even to imagine were it not for the black humour with which she managed to invest it. She and her woman companion travelled by sledge at night, through forests peppered with the gleam of wolves' eyes. The manic speed at which the sledge was driven was usually due to the intoxicated state of the driver and, on one occasion at least, the company was unceremoniously tipped out into the snow. '. . . we hardly knew whether to laugh or cry,' wrote Kate, 'and chose the former alternative and merrily awaited events.'

The journey soon began to resemble a descent into hell. The dark nights of ice and snow gave way to days of suffocating heat. On horseback now, they traversed a region which trembled beneath them, shaken with subterranean fire: 'Blinding clouds of smoke every now and then swept into our eyes and the hot, stifling air almost choked us. We had to go through the fire: there was no escaping it, unless we chose to turn back. After looking on, aghast, for some time, and trying to prevent our terrified horses from bolting, we moved slowly forward, picking our way as best we could in and out of the flames . . .'

Her journey took her another 1000 miles and led to hell itself where lepers crawled out from the forests, dragging themselves painfully towards this foreign woman who had come to help them. Dressed as she was in trousers to the knee, bag slung over her shoulder, riding whip in hand and the whole thing topped off by her London deerstalker, no one could possibly have mistaken her origins. To the leper colony, she must have seemed like some god-sent apparition. She unpacked her medical supplies, distributed gifts among the stricken people and naively offered up a prayer for the health of her Imperial Majesty the Empress of Russia, noting –

Kate Marsden

no doubt with approval – that the poor lepers joined in heartily.
Like the Light Brigade, hers was not to reason why.

It is hard to believe that in her twenties Kate Marsden had
suffered so badly from a lung disease that she had been pensioned
off from her job in a hospital. She had proved that she would stop

at nothing. Bureaucracy, war, the icy wastes of Siberia – all were mere stumbling blocks to be demolished in her personal campaign to bring help to the lepers whose banishment to Siberia was effectively a way of removing such an unwelcome sight from the public eye.

The Victorian women missionaries formed a travelling brigade that was as unique as it was misguided, but whatever the consequences of their ill-advised activities, we cannot but admire the manner in which these delightful ladies dispensed tea, sugar and the Word of Life.

CHAPTER 3

Flights of Fancy

On a spring day in 1928, a small light aircraft taxied along the runway at Cairo Airport and drew to a halt. Out of the cockpit door swung a slim leg clad in a silk stocking followed by the rest of the pilot dressed in white gloves, necklace, an elegant coat fur-trimmed at neck and wrist, and a natty little cloche hat. 28-year-old Sophie Pierce, who came to be better known later as Lady Heath, news-conscious as well as fashion-conscious, posed for the cameramen before climbing down from the wing of her Avro Avian III aircraft having completed part of her historic flight from South Africa to London – the first woman to fly solo from the Cape to Cairo.

The silk stockings had been put on in rather a hurry, for the last lap of the journey had taken less time than she had expected, largely because it had been relatively trouble-free – unlike the unpropitious start. Setting out from South Africa on 17 February, she had fallen victim to a dangerous attack of sunstroke and, landing in a feverish daze in what she later found was a region of Bulawayo, she immediately blacked out.

Africans are nothing if not flexible and are rarely surprised by the strangeness of European behaviour. The local girls who rescued her cared for her and in a few days she was off again. Flying over Nairobi there were more problems, this time with the engine, and although she was forced to jettison her tennis racquet and a few novels to lighten the load she hung on to six dresses, her Bible and a shotgun.

Before flying over Sudan, she set about making arrangements to find a man to escort her northwards. The number of people flying the African sky was on the increase, as was the number falling out of it. An accident, were the pilot lucky enough to escape death, could be costly. Ransoms were often exacted by locals, and European governments, landed with the task of searching for their own nationals, often found themselves picking up a hefty bill. It was for reasons of safety and economy, therefore, allied to the belief that the sky was really no place for a woman, that women were refused permission to fly over the country. Not at all put out by this restriction, Sophie wrote later: '. . . the Sudanese had forbidden women to fly alone owing to recent outbreaks among the natives who killed a District Commissioner last December . . . an entirely sensible regulation.'

Shortly before setting out from South Africa on her flight northwards, she had waved goodbye to a young man and his bride who were spending their honeymoon flying up through Africa. During the late 1920s and early 1930s, England was gripped by flying fever and pilots were setting out like swallows for destinations which grew more and more distant with each year. Lieutenant Bentley had gained fame the previous year by being the first person to fly solo from England to Cape Town and no doubt this was a spur to Sophie's flight.

Catching up with the honeymooners in Uganda, she now sought Bentley's aid. Chivalry took second place when he was persuaded – or perhaps he even volunteered – to escort the Lady Heath as far as Khartoum. Once they were in the air, however, and all the regulations had been strictly observed, the two planes lost sight of each other and Sophie happily flew on alone. From Khartoum to Cairo the journey was relaxed and carefree. Since maps were a bit dodgy in those days, she navigated by following the course of the Nile.

The gallant Bentley, meanwhile, now back in Khartoum, found his services again required, this time to escort a woman pilot who was flying in the opposite direction. No doubt a trifle exhausted by the excitements of his honeymoon as well as having to escort Sophie up through Sudan, he nevertheless took on the task of escorting the indefatigable Lady Mary Bailey who was on her way south to Juba on *her* historic flight – the first solo round trip between England and South Africa to be made by a woman.

It is interesting to observe the similarities and differences between these two pioneering fliers. They were both Anglo-Irish and had married titled men with enough money to keep their wives in planes and fuel. Lady Mary Bailey – herself the daughter of an

Irish peer – married a South African millionaire, and Lady Heath's husband contributed to her fleet of four planes. Apart from their love of flying and their fearlessness, however, the similarities end there.

Lady Mary, the elder by ten years, was the mother of five children – a scatty individual, easy-going in the extreme. Described by those who knew her as a disorganized will o' the wisp, her flight to South Africa was made simply to pay a visit to her husband there – or so she said. Obviously an astute woman, whatever the impression she gave, she may simply have offered this explanation in order to fend off curious journalists, for she was certainly no stranger to ambition. The first woman to gain a certificate for flying blind, she also broke a number of records including an altitude one for light aircraft. As if to promote further her scatter-brained image, she set out for Africa in a Cirrus II Moth not altogether sure of her precise route and without all the necessary maps. Coming in to land at Tabora in order to enquire the way, she miscalculated her speed and the plane did a spectacular somersault. Not at all deterred, she waited while her compliant husband arranged for a pilot to fly up another Moth – at a cost of about £300. The round trip was completed early the next year, 1929, and newspaper photos show her muffled in leather and scarves with a hat jammed unceremoniously on her head, being welcomed back by two daughters at Croydon Aerodrome.

If Lady Mary Bailey presents a picture of a woman living in comfortable harmony with the many aspects of her life, Lady Heath was a different matter altogether. Born and brought up in Limerick, she went to Trinity College, Dublin where she took a science degree before moving to lecture at Aberdeen University. She began flying at twenty-two and, having taken her A Licence in 1925, she got her commercial B Licence the following year which allowed her to carry paying passengers. An energetic exhibitionist, she took up aerobatics and parachuting and on one occasion, when the engine failed, stood on the wing of the aircraft as it came in to crash land.

She was a courageous person who rushed at life full tilt. Her father was something of an eccentric, given to playing practical jokes on the local Irish constabulary. There had been no joke, however, about the murder charge brought against him when his wife was found dead in their home. Sophie, then a small girl, was put in the care of her paternal grandfather.

By the time she made her historic flight up through Africa, she was married for the second time, to a rich industrialist who was able to finance her flying. The year after the flight, however, tragedy struck. Injured in a flying accident in the US, she suffered severe brain damage which, allied to an increasing drink problem, led from one disaster to another. By the time she made her third and final marriage, to an American flier, things were going badly wrong.

She always made a point of dressing stylishly but never succeeded in totally disarming her critics – the press nicknamed her Lady Hell of a Din because of her feminist stand. She was the sort of pioneer with whom society is ill at ease – daring, outspoken and demanding – and the establishment turned with relief to the less threatening Lady Mary Bailey whose heroic image as an intrepid flier was tempered by her motherly dottiness. It was she who was made a Dame of the British Empire while the vociferous and lively Sophie went without official recognition.

In 1939, eleven years after she had delighted the world's press with her glittering and triumphant flight to Cairo, she fell down the steps of a London bus and died of her injuries.

*   *   *

Flight has preoccupied and delighted the human mind for centuries. The Queen of Sheba's lover promised to give her anything she asked for including 'of splendid things and riches . . . a vessel wherein one could traverse the air and winds which Solomon had made by the wisdom that God had given unto him.' In 1020, Oliver, a Benedictine monk, took off from a tower in Malmesbury and was lucky to break only a leg, and in 1507, John Damian broke his 'thee bane' jumping off the tower of Stirling Castle. Where, you might ask, were the women while their menfolk were flinging themselves into oblivion with such misplaced optimism? Sensibly, they stayed at home by the hearth for, though without the benefit of da Vinci's aeronautical knowledge, they nevertheless shared with him the commonsense view that inspiration and genius must be wedded to appropriate technological development before the body can break free and follow the spirit into the blue.

Until the Age of Reason, the longing to fly had been fulfilled only in myths and legends. Hermes, Icarus and Wayland the Smith soared to the skies while below, earth-bound by reality, women were left to languish, taking to the air only as discredited and troublesome witches. When eventually women did take to the skies, it was with a burst of spectacular and daring exhibitionism.

In 1783, the first balloon went up and the following year the first woman made her ascent. By 1810, Napoleon's Chief of Air Service was the noted balloonist Madame Blanchard. Described as combining 'a rugged character and physique with the charity and delicate exterior demanded of femininity of that period', she was dedicated to ballooning, often staying up all night and descending only at dawn. Appointed by Louis XVIII, she planned for him one of the spectacular aerial firework displays for which she was famous. The Parisian crowd watched enraptured as she ignited a surprise rocket which sprayed a bright light across the sky, unexpectedly, however, sending the balloon with its solitary passenger on a rapidly descending course across the rooftops. The Parisian crowd roared its delight as the balloon disappeared from view. Madame Blanchard's battered body was picked up later by passing workmen. While igniting what was to be her final firework, a rush of hydrogen had escaped from the envelope and the soaring flames had set the balloon alight.

Women, if not actually born managers, must quickly learn the skills of management in order to run their homes, and many found they had great aptitude for organizing public aeronautical displays. The public itself was more than happy to enjoy the intriguing sight of a woman elegantly clothed in empire dress and bonnet leaning langorously over a soaring gondola, one hand graciously scattering rose petals upon the awed, upturned faces, the other waving the national flag.

In England an astute mother of seven built up a whole career for herself as a balloonist. The posters, devised by herself, naturally gave her top billing:

Mrs. Graham, the only Female Aeronaut, accompanied by a party of young ladies . . . in the balloon *The Victoria and Albert*, will make an ascent at Vauxhall on Thursday July 11, 1850.

Intrepid and resourceful, Mrs Graham understood well the psychology of theatre. To whip up the anticipatory excitement, she had the preparations for the flight take place in public. Barrels of acid and old iron were set to bubble near the balloon to form the gas that was piped into it. For a heightened effect she used illuminating gas which she bought from the local gas works. Then the balloon, bedecked with ribbons, streamers, plumes and silks and often filled with delightful young girls chaparoned by the matronly Mrs Graham herself, would waft slowly heavenwards. A keen businesswoman, her capacity for self-advertisement was matched only by her ability to stay alive in this dangerous business. She continued performing for forty years, spanning both the rise and the decline of ballooning in Britain.

After going up in a balloon basket the next thing was to jump out of one, and the organizers at Alexandra Palace, the Londoners' playground, soon realized that the sight of an apparently vulnerable female figure with nipped-in waist and small, buttoned boots was more likely to produce a delicious sense of danger than was a burly, male aeronaut. To that end, and certainly to her own delight, Dolly Shepherd, daughter of a detective in the London Metropolitan Police, was chosen to become part of a parachute team.

In 1903, the 17-year-old Dolly was a smart Edwardian miss, with a good steady job as a waitress at the Ally Pally – steady, that is, until offered the chance of joining Bill Cody's parachute team. Undeterred by the circumstances of the offer – the death of another girl parachutist in Dublin – she seized the chance and was soon being billed all over the country. In her breeches, knee-length boots and brass-buttoned jerkin, Dolly was soon the darling of the Edwardian crowd, who turned up to see her hitched to a trapeze bar and carried thousands of feet into the air by a balloon from which she then freed herself to float gracefully back to earth. Paid £2 10s for each ascent – a lot of money when a portion of fish and chips cost a penny halfpenny – her reputation was hard earned for she frequently took her life in her hands. Apart from a few unrehearsed landings on rooftops, she once drifted helplessly two miles above the earth and was only released from her ethereal prison by the unexpected deflation of the balloon. She came closest to death when, making a spectacular dual ascent, her partner's parachute broke. Eight thousand feet up, she had to swing across to her partner, and strap the other girl to her own parachute so that they could make the dangerous descent together. She escaped with her life but badly injured her back on impact.

Dolly was the last of an era for the skies were now being invaded by a noisier sort of aerial creature – the flying machine. In 1903, the same year that young Dolly made her first ascent in a balloon, the Wright brothers made their first wavering flight at Kitty Hawke. From then on, the skies of Europe and America were filled with machines taking off like feverish gnats and before long, women were up there among them, not only flying but also building their own aircraft.

By 1909, the first fatal air accident had happened, Blériot had flown the Channel and Lilian Bland, granddaughter of the Dean of Belfast, had built and flown her own machine, known as the Bland Mayfly. Constructed of steamed ash, piano wire, bicycle pedals and treated calico, the Bland Mayfly sold for £250 – or £350 with an engine. Lilian's first *ad hoc* fuel tank consisted of a whisky bottle and an ear trumpet. 'It was not a good engine,' she noted, 'a beast to start and it got too hot . . . as the engine is English, its sense of humour is not developed sufficiently.' An issue of *Flight Magazine* shows her flying her magnificent machine across a foggy, frosty field.

It would be unusual these days to read of a woman building her own aircraft but the style, in those early days of flight, was strictly trial and error and anyone who had the inclination and the money could have a go. Surprisingly, for one who had worked so hard and achieved so much, it all came to an end in what seemed, for her, an uncharacteristic way. 'As a consequence of the marriage of Miss Bland,' read the notice in *Flight* in 1911, 'we learn that she is disposing of her aeroplane engine, propellers, plant and machines.'

Although Lilian Bland threw it all up for love, there were countless other young women following her who took to the air with equal joy and alacrity. In 1909, Madame la Baronne de Laroche of France was the first woman ever to gain a pilot's licence. Three years later, on the day following the shattering loss of the *Titanic*, a young American journalist, Harriet Quimby, flew solo across the English Channel, taking less than an hour to do so.

In the States, during the recession, many young people – mostly men – found they could earn a living wing-walking and performing other aerial stunts. For a tired and dispirited populace, these dangerous exploits provided some sort of relief, the contemplation of others in danger somehow lessening the boredom and misery of their own dull or inactive lives. For women fliers, the practice served another, useful purpose. Generally thought not to be such good fliers as their male counterparts, anything which offered them a chance to display their skills could not be ignored. For one woman, at least, the strategy paid off. Phoebe Omlie, a talented and daring wing-walker, became the first person in the States to get a transport licence. For the spirited woman who liked excitement and adventure, flying provided an opportunity for both and once she had access to a plane, she could attain a freedom in the skies not available to her on the ground at all.

By the mid-1920s, however, state bureaucracy had begun to assert itself – almost always a bad omen for women. In 1924, the International Commission for Civil Aviation resolved that 'women shall be excluded from any employment in the operative crew of aircraft engaged in public transport'. Another resolution stated categorically that candidates for such posts 'must have use of all four limbs, be free from hernia and must be of the male sex'. Although these restrictions were later removed, the attitudes which prompted them were not. Some twenty years later, Jacqueline Cochrane, the first woman to break the sound barrier, was 'allowed' to deliver a bomber to England, as part of the war effort, provided that the take-off and landing were done by a male pilot.

Well aware of the problems faced by women in the field of aviation, Stella Wolfe, a journalist specializing in flying in the 1920s, made some points about the suitability of women which might now make us smile but which obviously needed stating then. Women, she said, were eminently suited to flying because they were lighter in weight and could endure cold better than men. Nor did they drink or smoke as much as men. Further, she believed that women, when able properly to sublimate their sex instincts, could use their maternal powers as a driving force in other fields. 'Deprived of the right of motherhood and doomed to enforced celibacy by the ravages of war . . . she can put all that marvellous creative power, that tremendous endurance that enables the mother to undergo the agony of childbirth' into flying. It was unfortunate that she should then have cited Lady Bailey as an example of a woman who had raised a large family and still had energy left for other activities. The privileged Lady Bailey only had surplus energy because she could afford to pay other women to look after her family and home. The Wolfe argument is not one that would appeal to the more independent-minded women of today but it was representative of the feminist thinking of the 1920s.

It was not until a few years later, in the early 1930s, that the public got the full benefit of America's bright star: Amelia Earhart, that stalwart flier whose views on women and their place in society were as clear and determined as her own attitude to flying. 'Unfortunately,' she wrote, 'I was born at a time when girls were still girls.'

Amelia Earhart was brought up in the early years of the century, in a large, pleasant clapboard house in Kansas. Her childhood years were happy and carefree although she learned early on that certain activities were considered 'rough' for a girl. Her father, an amiable man whose weakness for drink eventually led to the break-up of his marriage, made a living as a poorly paid lawyer on the railroad. Any extras the family might need were provided by Amelia's maternal grandfather, who was a judge. Life for the small girl was unruffled and unexciting and there was nothing in her formal education nor in the girls' literature of the day to stimulate a spirit of adventure. '. . . who ever heard of a girl – a pleasant one – skipping on an oil tanker, say, finding the crew about to mutiny and saving the captain's life while quelling the mutiny? No, goings on of this sort are left to the masculine characters . . .'

If there was to be any excitement in her own life then clearly she herself would have to generate it. She enrolled as a medical student in New York but threw this up after a year. Unsettled, she moved to live with her parents in Los Angeles, then the centre of America's aircraft industry. Soon, she had found the activity that was to dominate her whole life – flying. She took a job with a telephone company to pay for her flying lessons and with financial help from her mother, the judge's daughter, she bought a secondhand plane. By 1922, at the age of twenty-four, she not only had her pilot's licence but had also set a women's altitude record for 14,000 feet. When her parents' marriage finally broke up she drifted back across the States and took a job working with deprived children. Her life still had no clear direction. What was she, people asked, a social worker or a woman pilot?

'Personally, I am a social worker who flies for sport,' she tried to explain. 'I cannot claim to be a feminist but do rather enjoy seeing women tackling all kinds of new problems, new for them, that is.'

Then, in 1928, everything fell into place. Could she, someone asked, take part in a flight across the Atlantic? She wouldn't have to fly or anything, just simply be a passenger. The backer, a woman, was financing the flight in order to cement the friendship between America and England and wouldn't it be nice, she said, to have a woman on the plane? Amelia was now thirty and had been drifting for too long. She accepted with alacrity. When a great adventure is offered, she said, you don't refuse. But on this first Atlantic crossing Amelia was merely the token female taken along because the woman sponsor thought it a good idea. Not everyone shared that point of view. Commenting on the landing at Burryport in Wales, a *Flight* editorial said: '. . . in these days of sex equality such a feat should not arouse any particular comment. Compared with the solo flights of such lady pilots as Lady Heath and Lady Bailey, the crossing as a passenger does not appear to us to prove anything in particular.' Such a comment, ungainly as it was, had some justification and Amelia herself felt her presence had added little to aviation history: 'All I did was to sit on the floor of the fuselage like a sack of potatoes.'

To add insult to injury, when the sponsorship money was being handed out, the pilot received $20,000, the mechanic received $5000 and she got nothing. Already an accomplished flier, it must have infuriated her to realize she had allowed herself to be used, and the experience spurred her on to reclaim what she felt she had lost. 'Some day,' she said, 'I will redeem my self-respect. I can't live without it.'

She travelled round the country campaigning on behalf of women pilots but in the midst of it all took a surprising step.

Marriage had never appealed to her and in any case, as she remarked to her sister, having babies took up too much time. She had had a suitor, however, for a number of years. George Putnam, the publisher, had been involved in her first transatlantic flight and found himself attracted by the slight, serious young woman with her open, gamine face and gap-toothed smile. He himself was married but on his divorce offered himself to Amelia. She refused over and over again and then, to his surprise, in the middle of her feminist campaign, she agreed to marry him.

There were now a number of people in the States all sharing Amelia's desire to promote women fliers but it was a difficult time of social change and the women, well aware of the dangers of projecting a feminine image that might be damaging to their reputation as serious pilots, carefully chose to dress without any show of female frippery. The press, reflecting the prejudices of the time, saw only the stereotype woman and not the individual, constantly referring to these early fliers as Petticoat Pilots, Ladybirds and Sweethearts of the Air. It was an uphill struggle and perhaps it was this continuing battle that finally led Amelia Earhart to make her momentous decision – she would fly solo across the Atlantic. It was five years since Charles Lindbergh had made his great flight across to Paris and since then, although a number of women pilots had tried the transatlantic flight, none had succeeded.

On 20 May 1932, flying a red Lockheed Vega, she set out from Harbour Grace, Newfoundland, on her long and lonely journey – not altogether sure why she was doing it. 'To have a purpose,' she wrote, 'is sometimes a deadening thing.'

Things went wrong from the start. Within hours of take-off the altimeter failed. If she went too high she risked the wings icing up and if she flew too low she was blinded by sea fog. She flew on, trying to strike a balance between the two. In the dark Atlantic night, her engine was suddenly illuminated by an eerie blue light. Exhaust flames were beginning to lick out of a broken weld in the engine manifold. There was nothing she could do except watch with horror – and fly on, listening to the increasing noise the manifold made as it started to vibrate in a dangerous manner. On and on through the lonely night until, fifteen hours later, she landed in a boggy field in what she hoped was Ireland. It was. You're in Derry, said Mr Gallagher, the farmer whose cows had been so startled by her noisy arrival.

Her earlier London critics remained unimpressed:

> Miss Earhart is reported to have made the flight for no other reason than that she had long thought she could do it . . . Very probably, Miss Earhart would never have rested content until she had proved to her own satisfaction whether or not she was, if we may use the expression, man enough to do it. She has succeeded and we may congratulate her on her success. But her flight has added precisely nothing to the cause of aviation.

An American reporter was more generous in his praise:

> . . . she isn't a bit pretty but if you can be with her without being conscious of something quietly beautiful you are a peculiarly dull fellow and wholly insensitive. There is a charm there and a sense of perfect control over self and that delightful quality infrequently found in the workers of the world – a rare sense of humour.

Calm and undisturbed by the differing responses she seemed to generate, she smiled her way through the razzmatazz of civic welcomes and tickertape hysteria. She had done it, she said, just for the fun of it. Later she offered something more: 'It was a self-justification, a proving to me and to anyone else interested that a woman with adequate experience could do it.'

With Putnam, she was now leading the life of a socialite, fêted wherever she went. Soon, her face was as well known as her name for, although a non-smoker herself, she appeared in cigarette advertisements to help finance her many flying projects. These advertisements produced a spate of criticism as did her uncompromising stand on feminism but, with her usual single-minded commitment, she refused to allow herself to be distracted.

Her solo transatlantic flight had been a vindication of all the women fliers before her who had set out to do the same and perished in the attempt, and she exulted in her achievement: 'There is no telling now,' she wrote, 'where the limitations to feminine activities, if any, will be henceforth.'

Sadly, she encountered her final limits when her plane disappeared mysteriously in 1937 during her attempt to become the first woman to fly round the world.

* * *

In the year that Amelia Earhart agonized over her decision to enter the 'attractive cage' of marriage, a very different young woman set out to make another famous solo flight.

Born in Hull in 1903 – an auspicious year for a flier – Amy Johnson was five years younger than her American counterpart. After taking an Arts degree from Sheffield University she found life in the north of England unexciting and moved to London where she took a job in the silks department of a large store, earning £5 a week. Amy Johnson's life till then had been taken up with the ephemera of the 1920s: jazz, college rags and a love affair that lasted through her twenties. Despite the three hundred love letters – skittish and innocently provocative – which she wrote during that time, the affair ended dismally; by then, however, she had discovered another passion: flying.

As with all fliers, her main concern was raising money to buy her own aircraft. Some fliers saw the commercial opportunities straight away and set about getting their B Licence which allowed them to carry fee-paying passengers. Amy was lucky enough to be helped out by her father, a prosperous fish-merchant. Her secondhand Gypsy Moth cost £1000, of which he paid half. Her aim in life now seemed clear: she would fly to the furthermost point she could which, looking at the map, seemed to be Australia. With only fifty hours' flying experience behind her, she was off.

There's something lonely about the start of a solo flight. The take-off is usually just before dawn so that the flier can get the benefit of a full day's flying. The excitement and strain of the impending flight means the flier has usually had little more than a few hours' sleep and whether or not she can finally take off must depend on weather reports. A negative one means the agony of a snap decision which could easily turn out to be mistaken.

Jason, the plane in which Amy flew, now hangs suspended in nostalgia from the roof of London's Science Museum. Dark green, with wheels that look as if they could just about support a pram, the whole plane looks as fragile as a child's Meccano toy, dwarfed by the large, ungainly Vickers Vimy hanging alongside it, the plane in which Alcock and Brown had first crossed the Atlantic eleven years before.

On that cold May morning in 1930, Amy set out on her solitary flight, a 27-year-old woman the world had not yet heard about. Flying in an open cockpit, she averaged three hours' sleep a day. Thirteen thousand miles and nineteen and a half days later, she arrived in Darwin. Smiling and unsophisticated, ex-shop girl and onetime secretary, she instantly became the darling of the press. 'Don't call me Miss Johnson,' she told the papers, 'just plain Johnnie will do.' When, three years later, she married Jim Mollison, another well-known flier, the papers were delerious with romantic joy. For Amy, however, it was the moment at which things began to turn sour. Instead of a partnership, the marriage became a competition. Husband and wife vied with each other in the air. When Amy established a record, Jim felt he had to beat it. The strain began to show and a record-breaking flight to the US ended when they had to crash land in Connecticut.

A photo of them with President Roosevelt shows Jim Mollison bandaged after the crash with Amy beside him smiling gently but looking tired and strained. In comparison with Amelia, who seemed to have made such a success of her life, Amy appeared to have gone off course.

Jim Mollison had always been a bit of a playboy and Amy slipped easily into his lifestyle, dressing in a sharp and snappy fashion, posing with long cigarette-holder and affecting hair styles that made her look sophisticated and certainly older than she was. Gone was the vulnerable girl and in was the brittle social butterfly. Though often compared to each other, Amy and Amelia were very different and Amelia's continuing interest in women fliers and her work for that cause must have made Amy suspect that fame might have more to offer than smart clothes and a partner whose drinking and philandering were getting out of hand.

The Mollisons tried to save their tattered marriage by flying together rather than trying to break each other's records but eventually, in 1938, they separated and divorced. When war broke out the following year, Amy volunteered for the Women's Auxiliary

Air Service. In 1941, on a mission from Blackpool to Kidlington, her plane mysteriously went down in the Thames Estuary. Her death was one sad thing she shared with Amelia Earhart, whose plane had disappeared without explanation four years earlier.

*   *   *

Earhart and Johnson's names are well-known because of their pioneering flights but there were many other women who also deserve mention. Ruth Nicholls, a flamboyant young American, had hoped to precede Amelia across the Atlantic. After coaxing an industrialist friend to let her borrow his Lockheed Vega, she took off, dressed as usual in an eye-catching purple flying suit – and crashed within minutes.

New Yorker Elinor Smith was a determined altitude flier who climbed all the way to 24,000 feet and then fainted when her oxygen tube broke. Higher, faster, further – for these women and many others, the freedom of the air presented different challenges. Elinor Smith teamed up with Bobbi Trout to set up a new endurance record. They managed to stay in the air for forty-two hours, becoming the first women to refuel in flight.

On the other side of the Atlantic, things moved at a slower pace and women pilots of the early 1930s in England began to use the plane as they might a motor car, to get them from one place to another.

Most splendid of these was Mary, Duchess of Bedford, who in 1926, at the age of sixty-one, took up flying in an attempt to alleviate the troublesome buzzing noises in her ear which had plagued her later years. Blessed with insatiable curiosity and enormous energy, she was one of the first aviators who actually used her plane to see the world. She was a solid monarchist surprised to meet, at a Buckingham Palace tea-party in 1937, some other guests that she wouldn't have met in the normal run of events. 'It was strange to see at Court for the first time,' she wrote, 'those who I presume were Members of the Labour Government.'

England travelled with her wherever she went. While visiting a mosque in Constantinople, her party had been asked not to speak in case their country of origin, not popular at that time, might be discovered. She questioned the value of this: even though silent,

'. . . the English are always so essentially English that I doubt our guide's having been taken in for a moment.' In her long leather flying coat and helmet, and a gracious if ironic smile on her face, she was the epitome of the English lady abroad. Once, on a flying tour of North Africa, she got up an hour too early by mistake but whiled away the time by doing the tapestry which she had brought along with her. On another occasion, having had to make a forced landing in the desert, she and her pilot played their after-dinner 'three customary games of backgammon with the electric torch' and despite the stones (which she fashioned into a pillow) and the proximity of wildlife, she found it all 'great fun and glorious to sleep out in the open desert with all the romance that accompanies that situation. Secretly, I had rather longed for this to happen.'

Flying as a passenger in those days was not a matter of sitting back and enjoying the scenery: there was work to be done. Her job was to work the petrol pump, for fuel always had to be hand-pumped from the reserve tank up into another tank fixed to the wings from where it dropped by gravity into the engine. At a thousand pumps every fifteen minutes, it was not an easy task for a woman of her age but she did what was expected of her; perhaps she even enjoyed the novelty of being told what to do, despite it always being prefaced by a respectful 'Your Grace'.

Her other task when flying in her Moth was to adjust the compass which was fixed on the back of the pilot's seat. The confined space and the absence on the plane of a tail trimmer made balancing difficult and, at times, taking a reading from the airspeed indicator fixed outside on the wing was positively suicidal. The pilot needed to be told the speed from time to time and the only way to communicate above the roar of the noisy little plane was down a speaking tube.

> Occasionally, the compass needs adjusting . . . and I bend down to do it, an action which the Moth always takes advantage of and dips and rises according to its fancy.
>
> 'About 105 m.p.h., please,' is immediately ordered down the speaking tube so a momentary glance at the pet cloud or landscape has to be made to adjust matters . . . the Moth again soars and dips according to its pleasure. The

speaking tube is again seized, '105 m.p.h., please' is
shouted down a little louder. I do not remonstrate because
the compass was installed to please me . . . so I take it
meekly and say nothing but turn my head to see the airspeed indicator on the wing and then out drops my ear-
piece. Once more the speaking tube is seized and even
with only one ear and that probably the deafest I can hear:
'105 – miles – per – hour, PLEASE, your Grace.'

She made many crash landings, mentioning them casually in
her log book, and declared nonchalantly that she preferred looping
the loop to doing spins. Her plane became her car and she flew to
Aintree for the Grand National and to Putney for the Boat Race.
Sometimes, to brighten things up a little, she went further afield.

At the [African] stations, we were told that the natives are
terrified by aeroplanes and have special charms to ward
off the evils . . . I fear these statements are due to an attack
of Press fever. Careful observation of the innumerable
villages we passed over compels me to say that I never saw
the slightest sign of fright amongst the inhabitants and
only the chickens lived up to their reputation.

While the women fliers of Europe and the United States took
possession of the skies, they were regarded with some wistfulness
by others who felt themselves distanced, geographically, from the
excitement.

In 1933, a newspaper tersely reported that Mrs Bonney of
Brisbane and her plane were missing – for the second time. There
were many such reports in those days for the skies were filling with
ambitious pioneers, some more successful than others. Mrs Bonney,
however, was different. For one thing, she would never give up.
The previous year, while making a circular flight of Australia in a
Gypsy Moth, she had to make a number of forced landings because
of engine trouble and she ran into very real danger once, when her
Moth and an accompanying plane were in a mid-air collision which
bent the rudder of the other plane and ripped the fabric off her
own.

In April 1933, she set off for England with a large rubber tube complete with tin water bottle attached to the bottom of her plane in case she came down in the Timor Sea. She did come down, but fortunately for her not in the sea. Just over the coast of what was then Siam she ran into a violent storm and was forced to land on a sandy beach. One wheel caught the water, the plane turned over and Mrs Bonney was thrown out. It took two days before a boat search party found her on the island of Banbaing, being cared for by the local people. She got her plane to Rangoon, then to Calcutta where it was repaired, and as she flew on towards Europe she was again reported missing, after being forced off course by bad weather. Eventually, on 21 June, she landed at Croydon Aerodrome, the first woman to have flown solo from Australia to England.

The following year, Jean Batten decided the sky must be used as a bridge, not seen as a barrier. Born in New Zealand in 1909, six weeks after Blériot's famous flight across the English Channel, she had watched enthralled first as Alcock and Brown crossed the Atlantic and then as Hinkler made his solo flight from England to Australia. These flights showed that it might now be possible to connect the continents by a network of airlinks and by the age of nineteen, Jean Batten had decided that she wanted to play an active part in forging these links. Selling her piano to raise the money for flying lessons, she travelled with her mother to England and gained her A Licence there in 1930. Determined to follow Amy Johnson to Australia she set about getting her B Licence, which would allow her to make some sort of living and raise the cost of a plane.

In the early 1930s, the cost of hiring a plane for solo flying was £1 10s an hour, well beyond her reach, but her mother stepped in with the necessary financial assistance and by 1934 she had acquired a battered Tiger Moth. With five previous owners and an open cockpit it was not the most suitable of planes to make the long journey to Australia but it was the best she could manage for £260 and, in the event, it stood the course well.

'It was bitterly cold sitting in the open cockpit and exposed to the icy blast of the slipstream from the propeller. Despite the fact that I was wearing a leather helmet, goggles, a heavy lined flying suit and fur gloves, I felt the cold dreadfully.'

South of Paris she had to fly at 7000 feet because of low clouds on the mountains, and very soon her hand, gripping the control column, became numb with the cold. In Syria, she encountered the opposite. Glare from the desert blinded her and the desert dust parched her throat. Further along the route, she hit a monsoon and the driving rain was at times so dense it obscured the wing tips, drenching both her and the cockpit. On 23 May 1934, however, fourteen days after take-off, she reached Darwin, cutting Amy Johnson's record by four days.

Folding up the wings of her Moth, she put it on a boat and sailed for her home in New Zealand, unable to fly the last part of the journey by air because the Moth could only carry enough fuel for eight hundred miles at a time.

*　　　　*　　　　*

While Earhart, Batten and Johnson fall into the category of comfortably well-off fliers whose achievements were helped by the moral and financial support they got from their parents – particularly their mothers – there were others who fell on either side of the fence. The Duchess of Bedford and Lady Heath could afford to run not one but a fleet of planes, but there was one pilot of that time who was born into appalling poverty and had to claw her way out of its destructive trap before she could realize her burning ambition to fly.

Jackie Cochrane was born into the squalid life of a Florida sawmill camp around 1912. As a small child she had never worn shoes and her dresses had been made out of old flour sacks. By the age of eight she was self-supporting, earning six cents an hour, working a twelve-hour night shift pushing carts up and down the aisles of a cotton mill, delivering spools to the weavers. By the age of ten, her determination to make a success of her life was still strong and she was in charge of fifteen other children. To people living in this sort of poverty, the law is largely irrelevant and no one cared much whether or not she went to school, something she was astute enough to capitalize on. By fourteen, she was working in a beauty parlour and a few years later had a well-paid job at Saks on Fifth Avenue, commuting between the social world of New York and Miami.

Aiming to become a top cosmetic sales rep, she realized that the only fast way to get around was by plane. From then on, all thoughts of travelling the skies as a sales rep – top or otherwise – were gone. She wanted to race. Blond, lipsticked and determined to get to the top, she set up her own cosmetics firm, married a millionaire and went on to become the first woman to break the sound barrier. It is understandable that Jackie Cochrane's priority should have been the success of Jackie Cochrane, but the most coolly daring of all the women pilots of that time was motivated by something quite different – patriotism.

Daughter of an eye specialist, there was no hint during Hanna Reitsch's happy if extremely disciplined Silesian childhood of the daredevil way in which she would one day serve her country. 'In our family, it was accepted as a principle so obvious as to be unspoken that a girl could only have one task in life, namely, to marry and become a good mother to her children.'

Looking at her bright and eager young face, it is doubtful if such a life would have satisfied her and it soon became apparent that her obvious skills in gliding would lead her to abandon medical school – she had always wanted to be a missionary doctor – and go into aviation. This later led to her appointment as a gliding instructor and here she encountered the same difficulties that women fliers elsewhere had come across.

'Already during my own training . . . I had learnt that men, while treating their own desire to become glider pilots as natural and normal, tend to look on any girl who professes a similar inclination as the victim of a mere foolish whim . . .' The bravery which she brought to her flying was decidedly not the product of a whim but of a deeply-felt commitment both to her religion and to her country – the two seemed closely intertwined.

Until 1926, gliding had been mostly on up-wind but with the discovery of thermal currents came also the realization that gliders could fly higher and for longer periods of time. It was then that their sinister potential as a weapon of war was recognized. In 1929, the year when the voting age for women in England was lowered to twenty-one and Hanna Reitsch was still a schoolgirl, Stella Wolfe wrote with eerie prescience: 'May we . . . watch against the development of winged warfare, using our newly acquired political power to protest . . . to our representatives in Parliament . . . whenever they show signs of wanting to increase air armaments with which to kill innocent babes, born or unborn.'

Not long after, the young Hanna was taken on as a test pilot for the Luftwaffe. She was thrilled. 'I felt that to be entrusted with a patriotic task of such importance and responsibility was a greater honour than that conferred by any title or honour.' Her work included testing brakes for future use in military aircraft; on one occasion the stress on the glider was so great that the control column was torn from her hand. Her small size and balanced attitude to danger made her especially suited to test flights which became more and more dangerous as Germany began to prepare for war. Seeking to devise a way for planes to land on small ships, she had to land the glider on a bed of ropes which would ensnare the machine. When it became apparent that she was in danger of having her head sliced off by the ropes she was offered a motor cycle helmet as protection.

Once war had started, the testing became urgent. The barrage balloons which the British were sending up to intercept enemy planes had to be disabled and Hanna was given the task of test-flying a plane which had wire cutters fixed to its wings. These, it was hoped, would slice through the cables holding the balloons. Instead, on her test flight, the cables shaved off the lower edge of the propeller blade. The onlookers watched, horrified, as the air was filled with metal fragments. The plane, its engine screaming, hurtled out of sight. Hanna, however, survived – to be awarded the Iron Cross. Göring, arriving to present it to her, looked at the minute test pilot and asked: 'But where's the rest of her?'

Hanna pursued her work in the field of aerial warfare, believing that by helping to destroy the enemy she might also be helping to save lives. Ironically, she was something that a number of her enemy countries, both large and small, might have understood well – a patriot. She wanted to protect, she said, 'ploughland and meadowland . . . my home. Was that not worth flying for?' When the war was over, returning to the work she had originally hoped to do, she went to Africa as a flying missionary.

For all the countries involved, the war had, of course, proved a stimulus to aviation design and in the postwar years women pilots were again seeking to establish new records; Sheila Scott was foremost amongst them. Her mother had broken two taboos of the day – she divorced her husband and then compounded her transgression by marrying an actor. Sheila herself was brought up by grandparents and later by a kindly stepmother. Hers was the usual solitary childhood of the broken home, interspersed with exciting days out with her father to the zoo, to the roller coaster and, on her sixth birthday, to Cobham's Circus, when she was taken up for a ride in a plane piloted by Cobham himself. 'The wind blew away my breath as it sang through the rigging,' she remembered.

At school, she ran into trouble, was suspended and then reprieved because her grandmother had been one of its first pupils. Boarding school and her lonely childhood set her apart and gave her a useful degree of independence; she went on to make an unfortunate marriage. Divorced after six years, she did a bit of modelling and acting – and failed her driving test twice. In 1958, at the age of twenty-eight, she had her first flying lesson. It was a difficult time for a woman to enter a male preserve. After proving their usefulness during the war, women had been swiftly relegated once more to the kitchen, the dance floor and the fashion magazine. When Sheila turned up for her lesson she was ignored – a woman wanting to fly and a pretty blonde at that!

'Please don't clasp the stick as though it's your last possession,' said her instructor. 'Try and hold it as you would your boyfriend on a Saturday night.' In times of masculine uncertainty, sexism offered some protection. The lesson – a special offer in a women's magazine – cost £1 and so ignorant was Sheila Scott of flying safety that she wondered 'what could be wrong with this antique airplane that it needed so much checking'. When she took to the idea of flying with unexpected enthusiasm, her instructor groaned: 'Trust a woman to overdo a good thing.'

She learned to fly in a modified Tiger Moth which she hired but soon found it cheaper to buy her own plane on hire purchase – 'just like buying a car, really'. Winning the first race in which she ever competed, she went on to break more than one hundred records. In 1971, she became the first person to overfly the North Pole in a light aircraft, thus fulfilling the hope expressed over forty years previously by flying campaigner, Stella Wolfe: 'The day will yet come when women will fly to the poles both as pilots and passengers.'

72

The skies, more so perhaps than sea or land, present a continuing challenge to the explorer, for great expanses of them are still untracked and uncharted. But while aircraft become every day more vast, designed for speed and, ominously, for destruction, there has been a counter-trend towards a more basic form of flying which recalls the precarious days of Kitty Hawke. In 1986, Eve Jackson plans to fly from England to Australia in a fragile microlite, the first person to attempt a journey of this sort. And why is she doing it? 'Because no one else is.'

Over the years, there have been many women who have found a place for themselves in the skies and now women such as Valentina Tereshkova and Sally Ride have ventured into space. Encased in steel, wired to their base and monitored by the world, or rather our world, in many ways the space riders of today are more earthbound than those free spirits who, less than a hundred years ago, floated up so trustingly into the sky.

Perhaps the young and hopeful Dolly Shepherd should have the last word:

> Then just as abruptly as I had entered the cloud, I emerged from it, into a new world – into another vast hall of silence and space, this one floored with a fleecy white carpet and with the great dome of the purple skies for a roof. There was nothing to suggest that the earth existed at all. There was just a cloud and space   and the balloon and me!

CHAPTER 4

At Sea

The corridors leading to the royal apartments of Elizabeth I hummed with a tension which mounted ominously when the Irish party came into view. Grace O'Malley, known as Granuaile, leader of her people and self-appointed Queen of Connaught, had come to Greenwich Palace to bargain with the most formidable queen England has ever had. Dressed in the robes of a highborn woman, with a long cloak of fine wool round her shoulders worn over a yellow low-cut cress, long hair piled up and clasped with a bodkin, her face burned by the salt of the Atlantic, Grace's style was far removed from the elegance and grandeur of Elizabeth's court. Yet she had a style of her own.

The difference between the two women lay not only in their appearance: while Elizabeth remained within the safety of her palace, sending her emissaries out to meet death on her behalf, Grace O'Malley stood on the prow of her ship, leading her clan against the enemy, fighting with equal ferocity against the English navy or another warring Irish tribe.

Married at sixteen to a chieftain whose leadership role she assumed, she soon earned a reputation as both fearless sea captain and pirate who inspired dread. Commanding a fleet of ships that patrolled the west coast of Ireland, she divided her time between plundering the unwary and acting as pilot to the foreign ships, usually Spanish, whose captains had to choose between facing the dangers of an Atlantic storm or putting in to a far from safe haven in one of the bays commanded by Grace's sea force.

A political pragmatist and born survivor – she lived until she was nearly seventy – she made deals with friend and enemy alike and prospered in so doing for there was plenty of trading, legal and illegal, to be done along the western coast. She was a formidable fighter, both on land and on sea and, when her son once retreated behind her in the heat of battle, she is reputed to have jeered: 'Is it trying to hide behind my backside you are – the place you came from?' So watchful and wary was she that she kept a length of rope tied to her bed which ran through a hole in the castle wall, connected with her boat outside. She was imprisoned on a number of occasions, to the delight of her enemies, one of whom, affronted by her unwomanly ways, described her as 'a woman that hath impudently passed the part of womanhood and been a great spoiler, and chief commander and director of thieves and murderers'.

This wild and wily woman of the seas amazed Elizabeth's deputy by turning up at his residence to offer her services and to put at his disposal three galleys and two hundred fighting men. A famous, feminine sea captain, he called her, with grudging recognition. Even more amazing was the fact that she brought along her husband, who served under her. The English court was horrorstruck by the audacity of this elderly woman who later dared to show her face to the very Queen whose sovereignty she had so often challenged. Others had died for less and indeed Grace, herself charged with treason, had only recently escaped death by hanging. Now here she was, seeking protection against the punitive measures exacted by Elizabeth's own Governor, who had attacked her castles and confiscated her ships.

Fierce and undaunted she might have been, but she was not unwise and her petition to Elizabeth, couched in suitably humble terms, was accepted. Unfamiliar with the English language, she conversed with Elizabeth in Latin, begging to be allowed to resume her activities on the high seas and piously maintaining that she would be acting only against the enemies of the Crown. Whether or not Elizabeth was taken in by this disarming request is not known, but she ordered Grace's sons to support her in her old age and advised Grace herself to behave in a more orderly fashion during her remaining years. Grace O'Malley's exploits may have been unique, but the sort of courage and determination she displayed is to be found in women sailors – especially single-handed ones – throughout the centuries.

To launch oneself into an alien element in a vessel small and frail takes a sort of faith that can truly be called blind. Some women set to sea as companions to their men – they had little choice. The wife of Thorodd, an Icelander killed in a feud in Greenland, was left without protection, and in 981 sailed home to Norway, the first woman known to make a long sea crossing in a small boat.

Latin texts and legend combined to weave the great epic story of the first Atlantic crossing by an Irish monk, Brendan, who in the fifth century sailed in a leather boat through fog and icebergs to reach Newfoundland. Fourteen hundred years later, Tim Severin, crossing by the same route in his twentieth-century leather boat, was able to give substance to the legend. Other legends remain, likely but unproved. The great missionary exodus from Ireland was in full flood at this time and Brendan was thought to be paying a pastoral visit to monks who had gone out ahead of him. These sea-faring missioners were not all male: legend tells us of a woman who made a successful if dangerous journey from Ireland to England, the voyage a hazardous one because she crossed the sea on a leaf! The story goes that Ia, a fifth-century Irish virgin of noble birth, hoped to accompany a party of monks who were sailing on a proselytizing mission to England. When she reached the Irish shore, she found their ship had already gone. Looking down at the water she saw, through her tears, a floating leaf and prodded it with her stick to see if it would sink. Instead, it grew and grew and she knew that it had been sent by God. Stepping into it, she wafted across the water to the southernmost tip of England and, arriving well ahead of the monks, founded a religious settlement at St Ives.

Ships have long been used by men as a means of increasing their wealth and after Brendan came the Vikings, seeking new lands where their expanding population might settle. Not long after came the great seafaring nations of Europe, bankrupting themselves in their efforts to gain control of the growing world. Their ships became mighty engines of destruction, far removed from the boats of leaf and leather that had sailed the seas a thousand years before. The piracy of distant lands was part and parcel of the legalized piracy on the seas as European navies fought for supremacy and a discontented populace at home was drained of every last penny to finance them.

War on the high seas was a miserable and horrifying thing. Whole ships' crews might be massacred and their cargo of slaves thrown overboard. Torture was rife and one captain had his lips sewn up with sail thread because he kept up a barrage of complaint against his captors. It might be hard to imagine a woman finding a place for herself among such people yet some did, proving themselves even more fearsome than their male comrades.

Although life on board a merchant vessel may have been unbearable at times, it was nothing compared to the misery and hardship that existed on a pirate ship. Overcrowding was inevitable, since each ship needed to carry a crew at least three times larger than that of a merchant ship; there were frequently up to 250 men on a ship built to accommodate eighty. Cockroaches, rats and beetles overran the decks and the first thing a raiding party did was to ransack the medicine chest of the captured vessel, for typhoid and typhus were regular fellow travellers.

If life on a pirate ship was so terrible, why did so many choose it as a way of earning a living? It is often said that after prostitution and medicine, piracy is the third oldest profession and indeed, as long as foreign trade prospered, so too did piracy. The rewards were enormous. Merchant ships returning from the West Indies regularly carried silver coins and gold bullion. Best haul of all were the ships carrying the silver coins worth eight *reales* – the legendary pieces of eight – which could be divided up into eight equal pieces when the booty was being shared out. Such a ship, if raided, could yield as much as £2000 to each pirate. It was a colossal sum when one considers that a sailor was unlikely ever to earn more than £500 in his whole lifetime.

Another thing which made this life attractive was the fact that, just as there is sometimes honour among thieves, there was also a modicum of democracy on board a pirate ship. Some captains sought to run their ships in an orderly fashion and devised rules which pirates were required to sign when joining a vessel. The ship's musicians – valued members of the crew who could be relied upon to create a terrifying cacophony when a raid was in progress – were to have Sundays off. Any pirate losing a limb in the course of his duty was to be paid 800 pieces of eight. And, more relevant to our story, no boy or woman was to be allowed on board. 'If any man shall be found seducing any of the latter sex, he shall suffer death.' The necessity for having such rules points to the fact that women were smuggled on board on numerous occasions either to serve the needs of the men or as pirates themselves.

Consider, then, the predicament of the young pirate who found himself amorously but inexplicably drawn to another member of the crew. The feeling seemed to be reciprocated and complications would undoubtedly have followed had not one of them 'suffered the discovery to be made, by carelessly shewing her breasts, which were very white'. The young woman was Mary Read who, before becoming a pirate, had led an equally wild and dangerous life. She herself was illegitimate; her mother 'who was young and airy, met with an accident, which has often happened to women who are young, and do not take a great deal of care: which was, she soon proved, with child again'. This child turned out to be Mary. The arrival of an unwelcome girl resulted in the child being dressed and brought up as a boy.

Having lived through a tomboy childhood, Mary was not going to be satisfied to stay at home and as soon as she could, she ran away to join a regiment of horse in Flanders. There she fell in love with a young Flemish soldier in the same regiment and soon found herself facing the first of many predicaments for, as Daniel Defoe wrote of her, 'Mars and Venus could not be served at the same time'. Venus won the day and the two were married; the young soldier however died shortly after, leaving Mary once again on her own. Reverting to male attire, she joined a Dutch merchant ship which was captured by the notorious pirate Captain Jack Rackham – Calico Jack to his friends – and signed an agreement to sail with him. Life on board a pirate ship was dangerous enough but another predicament presented itself: having fallen in love with one of the sailors, Mary spent some time 'insinuating herself into his liking' while at the same time having to ward off the attentions of another sailor who had fallen in love with her. In desperation, she revealed to the latter her true identity only to discover to her consternation (though no doubt also to her relief) that this pirate too was a woman. Unknown to himself, Calico Jack was carrying two female pirates on board his vessel.

This second woman was, in fact, Jack's common law wife, an Irish woman called Anne Bonny who had run away from her husband to sail the high seas. Her story had started in Cork where

Mary Read and Anne Bonny

she had been conceived, like Mary Read, on the wrong side of the blanket. Her father was a well-known attorney and her mother was the family's serving maid. Taking mother and child with him, the attorney left Ireland and settled in America where Anne had as many suitors as she could have wished for. In the event, her chosen husband turned out to be a ne'er do well rogue who took her off to the Bahamas – the haunt of pirates. There, he turned informer, an act of treachery which horrified Anne, who was a spirited and independent person. She transferred her affections to Calico Jack who energetically wooed her with jewels and gold, even offering to purchase her from the renegade husband. Eventually, the two ran off together to ransack the seas around the Caribbean, during which Anne took time off to put in at Cuba and have a baby before rejoining Jack.

Dressed in trousers and shirts, a brace of pistols stuck in their belts and armed with cutlasses and boarding axes, Anne and Mary were not the sort of couple you might want to tangle with. Though generous in love and loyal to those they chose as their companions, they were both known to be fearless in battle. Anne had thrashed a young man who had unwisely attempted to rape her and Mary, finding her loved one challenged to a duel, secretly challenged his challenger to a duel an hour earlier and killed him, thus saving her lover the embarrassment of possible death. The two were pirates to be reckoned with though, ironically, their day of reckoning was brought about by another woman.

Storming over the side of a merchant ship off the coast of Jamaica one October day in 1720, they were observed by a woman passenger. Later that same month, Jack's ship was captured and the crew brought to court. Unfortunately for Mary and Anne, the Crown produced the one witness who could identify them with certainty. She had had her suspicions about those two pirates, she said, as soon as they appeared over the side of the ship. There was something oddly familiar about them, almost as if she knew them. Then it had become clear: 'By the largeness of their breasts,' Dorothy Thomas told the court, 'I knew them to be women.'

The death penalty was withdrawn when the two women pleaded their pregnant state. Mary languished in gaol for a time and then died. Calico Jack, however, having allowed himself, unnecessarily Anne thought, to be captured, was executed and went to his death laden with her scorn. 'Had he fought like a man,' she said, 'he need not have died like a dog.' Hard words from a hard woman.

*   *   *

The sea, then, was a place of death, running red with the blood of men and women – not a place of peace where sailors could find a unity with nature. That harmony was not to come until people began to sail alone, moving within the watery elements of the sea, recognizing its power and beauty rather than regarding it as little more than as a terrible theatre of war. Perhaps it was in an attempt to regain a communion with the sea that sailors began again to cross the oceans in small craft, tuning their spirits to the mood of the sea and learning to enjoy peace and isolation.

There were many heroic women in the nineteenth century who sailed the seas with their husbands in clipper ships, whalers and steam packets and who no doubt gained considerable navigational skills *en route*, had they ever been allowed to exercise them. One such woman, who put her life in her husband's hands by sailing across the Atlantic with him, was Joanna Crapo.

In 1876, a Danish-born American, Alfred Johnson, celebrated a hundred years of American Independence by setting off to sail single-handed across the Atlantic from Nova Scotia to Liverpool which he reached fifty-three days later, the first person to have made the crossing. The following year, Joanna and Thomas Crapo sailed off on their journey, no doubt benefiting from the following wind of Johnson's publicity. Thomas knew how to capitalize on this and took the opportunity of selling photographs of his 19-foot boat to the great crowd that turned up at Cape Cod to see them off. Autocratic, like many a ship's captain before him, Thomas resolutely refused to share the helm with his wife and risked both their lives by sailing for twenty hours at a time without a break. Fifty days later and after a marathon seventy-two hours at the helm, Thomas took the ship into a Cornish port.

It can only have been madness or love – and the two are not mutually exclusive – which made Joanna undertake the trip. The staple diet was dried meat and ship's biscuits. The kerosene lamp was in constant danger of exploding and the head room below hatch was only two foot six, so that when resting, you had to get up on hands and knees before turning over. We have no way of knowing if Joanna felt frustrated at not being able to play a more active part in the whole adventure. She had plenty of sailing experience, having sailed many times with Thomas when he was first mate on a brig, and it was reported that she had, in fact, gained enough navigational skills to be a Master Mariner.

Women sailors soon learned, however, that if they wanted to gain control of the helm they would have to paddle their own canoe, so to speak. Many more women were to follow Joanna across the Atlantic, in both directions, but it wasn't until the middle of the twentieth century that a woman was to make a successful solo crossing, taking the difficult east to west route.

The search for Atlantis – that elusive paradise beneath the sea – has continued throughout the ages, for it is in the wistful nature of human beings to seek for something better than can be found on this earth. The green, mysterious world beneath the Atlantic is indeed magical, with mountains higher than Everest and gorges deeper than the Grand Canyon. The biggest range of mountains in the world lie here, submerged beneath the ocean. The Atlantic has always presented a challenge to sailors, dividing them, on either side, from their destiny. Like a nebulous afterlife, dimly perceived by the hopeful, it beckons them across its green waters, offering nothing more than survival – or death.

To sail the Atlantic east to west means running against the winds – the great westerlies which blew Brendan's boat back to Ireland. Known as the Great Circle, it's a difficult crossing to make but the most direct and therefore the shortest, taking as little as thirty days in a fast boat. An alternative east–west route is to head south of the Azores, sail along the coast of Portugal and North Africa, then turn westwards out towards the Canaries and make for the West Indies, three thousand miles away. Here, the waters are warmer and the sailor can pick up the friendly north-east trade winds which will take the boat safely into harbour – or so the theory goes.

The reality is quite different. The lone transatlantic sailor faces gales, icy and torrential rain, seas that could overturn a boat, fog, thunder and lightning, and the danger of being run down by larger ships. If she has no radio telephone, she is cut off completely from the outside world. Unless she has self-steering gear – and that frequently doesn't work – she must heave-to when trying to get some sleep. Even with self-steering gear she will rarely get more than five or six hours of sleep at a time, and in bad weather she may have to wake up to do an hourly check. During a bad patch, one woman sailor got four hours' sleep in two days. Food becomes monotonous, as do the workings of the mind. Three thousand miles without sight of land can do strange things to one's thoughts. 'You become convinced,' said one transatlantic sailor, 'that you are, in fact, sailing in ever increasing circles.'

Can a woman make such a long sea journey on her own? The list of women who have done so grows longer every year: after Ann Davison, with whom this book started, came Sharon Sites who in 1965 sailed the 2480 miles solo from California to Honolulu and four years later sailed back again, this time from Yokohama to San Diego. That same year, a German sailor, Ingeborg von Heister, became the second woman to solo across the Atlantic, sailing from

Las Palmas to Barbados in thirty-three days, and the following year she became the first woman to return in the opposite direction. In 1971, Nicolette Milnes Walker sailed non-stop from Wales to Newport, Rhode Island – a distance of 3400 miles. Three years later, Annette Wilde sailed solo across the Tasman Sea and back again in a 33-foot yacht built by herself and a friend. Then, in 1977, nine years after Bernard Moitessier made the first solo non-stop circumnavigation, Naomi James triumphantly sailed round the world – the first woman to do so on her own.

Ann Davison's journey, however, must be singled out not only because it made sailing history but, more importantly, because it represents a journey of spiritual courage. Stripped of everything except her own will and bravery, she set sail in a 23-foot sloop without even a trial run. Hopeless at calculations, she took a course in celestial navigation which, she said, left her more mystified than before, though her on-target landfall after three thousand miles would suggest otherwise. Like the poker player who believes that over a year her winnings and losses will even out, Ann Davison had the happy facility for believing that a similar balance existed in nature. It was the sort of belief that so infuriates the organized and well-ordered mind. Any navigational errors she made, she felt sure, would cancel themselves out. What took her across the Atlantic, in fact, was not the rickety little boat with its ex-army compass and navigational oil lamp that kept going out, but her own superb sailing skills, allied to a determination to carry on. There was, of course, more to it. 'It wasn't courage that sent me scurrying off across the ocean in a 23-foot sloop. It was a little curiosity and a lot of desperation that went into the making of that particular dream.'

The journey was made in a series of hops from Plymouth to Casablanca to Las Palmas before she finally set out on the long transatlantic haul to the West Indies, with a last leg on to New York via Miami, a journey lasting 454 days in all. In Gibralter, she had a five-week stop, repairing the clutch of the *Felicity Ann* – also known as the *Sweet F.A.* The 600-mile journey from Casablanca to the Canaries became more and more worrying as the 12,000-foot peak of Tenerife, normally visible from a distance of ninety miles, refused to reveal itself through the haze. She later discovered this was quite normal: as she had rightly guessed, these things would balance themselves out.

She embarked on her voyage when roughing it was the order of the day. Having lived through the war years and being, in any case, committed to a style of life that was anything but luxurious, she was well suited to the makeshift life of the sailor. When she hit fog, she fixed flashlights on as many bits of the boat as she could; her oil lamp was constantly going out and therefore served little purpose. Without a foghorn of any sort, she resorted to banging her frying pan as a warning to anything within earshot.

With only one pair of hands to work the bilge pump, operate the radio, navigate, cook the food — and eat it, sleep had to be fitted in to the little time left over and having to do without that was one of the worst tortures. The danger of being run down by larger ships was always present and Ann Davison found herself getting up every twenty minutes during the hours of darkness to keep a look-out. She was not, at that time, a woman in her prime, and the physical strain must have been enormous. She was, however, of that generation of women who were stalwart both in spirit and speech, born at a time when women found difficulty in reconciling the male and female sides of their characters. She was, after all, a trailblazer, standing in proud isolation from both her own and the opposite sex and yet still deriving her identity from a world which thought that only men could embark on such adventures. Perhaps understandably, she saw herself as one of the boys. Referring to her late arrival at one port, an event which had caused some alarm, she wrote: 'It's a sad thing when a chap can't be becalmed without having the ponds dragged, so to speak.' In common with many women travellers and adventurers, she underplayed her achievements, realizing that clever women, then as now, presented something of a threat.

She denied she had any particular mechanical skills but thirteen days out of the Canaries and heading for the more benign trade winds, she managed, 'by dickering', to fix up her own self-steering device. Now the main thing she had to cope with was herself and her thoughts — those same ones that had prompted her to set off in the first instance. She had hoped that by sailing the Atlantic alone, by completing the task left unfinished by the death of her husband, she might find the key to living. That key, of course, she already held within herself, although it took the lone sea voyage to reveal that truth. The key, she found, was courage, not the sort of courage needed to conquer physical fear

> but an acceptance without resignation . . . for courage is a fighting quality. It is the ability to make mistakes and profit by them, to fail and start again, to take heartaches, setbacks and disappointments in your stride, to face every day of your life and every humdrum trivial little detail of it and realize you don't amount to much and accept that fact with equanimity and not let it deter your efforts.

Having achieved that equanimity, she was able to sail serenely into English Harbour, Antigua which less than two hundred years earlier had offered safety to another notable sailor – Nelson.

There remains a question of interest even to the unsceptical – how can a woman have the strength to sail a boat single-handed on a long journey? We know, of course, that strength of a different sort – strength of will – plays a large part but it would be naïve not to consider the physical problems facing a woman whose muscle power is simply not equal to that of the average man. (Though the average man, of course, does not sail solo across the Atlantic.) Careful attention to the selection of gear, economic use of energy and a certain cunning have helped many a woman do what has formerly been considered a man's job. ('You lift with your mind,' says Virginia Fiennes with unquestionable simplicity.) Ann Davison had plenty of cunning: although her boat was small it had a large sail area; by cutting this she was able to make it easier to handle.

Since that historic voyage, the development of lighter craft, more sophisticated self-steering gear, and winches especially suited to single-handed sailing, together with changes in sheeting material, have all made sailing easier, and women sailors have wisely turned these innovations to their particular advantage. A self-tailing winch, for instance, has a special construction which allows the solo sailor to handle both sheets and halyards at the same time. Naomi James had eight fitted to her transworld yacht, *Crusader Express*. The most important change, though, has been the growing confidence among women themselves that the ocean is no longer beyond their reach.

For Clare Francis, it was the combination of persistence and skill which got her across the finishing line in the 1976 transatlantic race, the first woman to reach it. Five foot two and slightly built, she weighed seven stone at the time of the race. Her 32-foot boat was a well-equipped racing yacht with self-steering gear that was both powerful and sensitive – exactly right for racing.

The sea, however, had other ideas. During a mid-Atlantic Force 5 gale, she had to get up every hour to check that things were going alright and at 3 a.m., tired and under pressure, she made a misjudgement that damaged the self-steering gear. Her only option was to make for a port in Newfoundland or Nova Scotia, where she would undoubtedly lose another three days getting the gear fixed. This prospect was not at all pleasing but even less so was that of standing at the tiller for the rest of the journey. In the end, she decided to try to mend the gear herself. The first thing she had to do was heave it out of the water. Made of heavy alloy, it was as long as she was tall and weighed three stone more.

> I didn't quite make it first time and, with a gasp, I had to let the gear fall into the water again. By this time, my arms were very tired and I had to take a long rest before attempting the lift again. I hung there over the stern, holding firmly onto that precious metal, and waited for perhaps a half a minute. A large wave came, I heaved, and got the gear halfway on to the rail. But the weight was still on the wrong side and I felt it slipping back. Summoning some strength, I gave it a last pull and managed to slide it over another inch. At last, by swinging my weight on it, the gear pivoted over onto my side of the rail. Then, after a final heave, it fell on top of me. I lay back on the wet deck, exhausted but very relieved.

She spent five hours battering the struts of the gear back into some sort of shape and then discovered she could have done the whole job in ten minutes if she had used a different method! In the end, by arduously developing a system of rope lashings, she put the gear together again and, up to her elbows in water, with the spindle between her teeth, she manoeuvred the gear back into position – and it worked. With the infuriating throwaway modesty so common among such women, she put it all down to luck. Sailing is not unlike poker: the skill comes in capitalizing on the good luck and turning bad luck into an advantage. Clare Francis had luck indeed but it was her sailing skills that brought her through to the finish.

That year, there had been 125 starters of which forty had retired, five had finished after the official finishing time, five had to be rescued from sinking boats and, sadly, two had been lost at sea. Clare Francis finished thirteenth overall, the first woman to cross the line, and having broken the women's record by three days. She also managed to avoid washing herself on all but three of her twenty-nine days at sea!

What do you do after you've raced across the Atlantic single-handed? There are other races to be won, other journeys to be made, but for Clare Francis adventure lay in other directions. Her first crossing had been made as the result of a bet. Finding, in her late twenties, that she was bored with her London office job, she used some money left to her in a will to buy a boat in which she made a solo crossing to the West Indies.

On the surface, her childhood had been conventional – ballet classes, holidays with grandparents in Yorkshire, university. Below the surface, however, lay a child who wished she was something other than she was – untidy, awkward, messy looking. Instead, she settled for a makebelieve world in which she was always tidy and presentable, a credit to her parents. She was possessed by a burning desire to succeed, to win approval, and found it difficult to be happy. She wasn't to know it then, but there were other horizons which would eventually reveal the satisfactions she sought. Having crossed the Atlantic once, she vowed she would never do it again and, eighteen months later, found herself racing across it. Now she has said never again, for a second time, and turned to a successful career as a writer.

Single-handed sailing presents challenges that are especially appealing to the adventurous woman. Programmed by society to make her own needs subservient to those of others, she is supposed to act upon orders, meet demands, attend to directives, interpret innuendoes, accept advice and guidance while maintaining a calm and cheerful exterior. Crewing on a boat has little to recommend it as long as the women members are confined to the galley and take their orders from the male skipper – it's not much different, in fact, from being on dry land. Single-handed sailing, however, gives a woman a unique opportunity to be in sole command of her own destiny, to test her independence and courage, to extend her sailing skills, to pit her physical strength against that of the sea, to push self-reliance to its limits, and to survive.

If Clare Francis had her fantasies so too had another extra-ordinary sailor. 'In my daydreams, I was always a famous dancer or pianist or explorer, amazing people with my skill and daring.' In reality, she was a 16-year-old hairdresser, slotted neatly into that trap that society sets for the unwary female. Brought up on a farm in New Zealand, the daughter of an Irish immigrant, Naomi James had a conventional, middle-class and happy childhood; if all went according to plan, she would now concentrate on making herself look attractive (the constant company of like-minded women would ensure plenty of advice on that subject) and then, when she had reached a certain age, she would be expected to embark upon marriage and motherhood. She had other ideas, however, and when she was twenty-one, Naomi James sailed from her native New Zealand to see the world. Seven years later, in 1977, she was to do more than see the world – she was to make a solo voyage round it, the first woman to do so. She had recently married Rob James, an attractive Englishman she had met on the quays of St Malo. Why should she put her newly discovered happiness at risk by undertaking such a dangerous and awesome journey?

The world was first circumnavigated by Magellan who set sail under a Spanish flag in 1519. There are many ways of circum-navigating the world and no two routes can really be compared, though in order to establish records such comparisons are fre-quently made. Magellan sailed through the straits named after him (between South America and Tierra del Fuego), thereby avoiding the horrors of the stormy seas round Cape Horn. It wasn't until a hundred years later that the Cape Horn route was taken again, by a Dutch sailor, and it was this route that Naomi James chose, too. The loneliest and most dangerous part of the journey is off Cape

Horn itself, and it was here, five and a half months after she'd left England, that Naomi James capsized. Going into the water is something that every sailor fears, but the single-hander fears it most of all. Earlier, when she had lost overboard her companion, a tiny kitten called Boris, she had rigged some ropes to trail over the stern which she could grab if she herself went over. On this occasion, she was saved by the fact that she was below deck.

Chay Blyth, himself a pioneering sailor who recognized a kindred spirit, had loaned her his boat for the historic voyage. The journey was not made, he commented in the preface to her book, in order to demonstrate women's superiority over men but 'was undertaken for that indefinable reason that makes men climb mountains and soar into the sky and fight the elements'. Women, too, he might have added but curiously didn't, are subject to the same inexplicable urges.

Having experienced the loneliness of a solitary Christmas at sea and the horror of capsizing, the joy of returning after 272 days of solo sailing to the safety of England and the warmth of her husband's arms was immeasurable. It was now time, however, to try to define more clearly – and better than Chay Blyth obviously could – her reasons for the journey. She had risked losing her life at the very moment when it had become fulfilling but by so doing, she felt, she had experienced a second and more complete life. In making this journey, she had also managed to make a clear distinction between herself and her husband, whose own reputation as a sailor was well known.

Since the 1950s, there have been a number of distinguished women sailors who have found their lives enriched by the experience of facing their own mortality. To them we owe a debt, for humanity's potential to survive and prosper lies in the courage of individuals such as they.

CHAPTER 5

Reaching the Summit

Like sirens of the snow, mountain peaks send forth their solitary call, luring climbers upwards towards some undefinable fulfilment. Lodged somewhere in the cliffs of ice there is a mountain mysticism, an intangible presence which draws people to it as inevitably as they move towards their own death. For many a climber, the mountain is their destiny.

We have become accustomed to contemporary climbers making ascents with the help of oxygen, two-way radios and even, in one case, a computer. There was a time, however, when mountaineering, primitive though it was, was considered a gentle and altogether suitable pastime for ladies, as long as they were prepared to trudge through the Alpine snow hampered not only by their reputation for being the weaker sex but also by the heavy and cumbersome clothes they had to wear.

It was the local doctor from Chamonix who made the first ascent of the 15,772-foot peak of Mont Blanc, in 1786. It was not until twenty-two years later that the first woman was to reach the summit. Her ascent, however, could hardly be called a climb for she was dragged to the top in a state of near collapse.

Maria Paradis was a young local girl who had quickly seen the financial possibilities open to those at the bottom of the mountain. More and more climbers were arriving, all requiring guides as well as food and drink. (In 1787, a climber made the ascent taking with him his valet and seventeen guides.) Maria, with her food stall already set up at the base of the mountain, decided it would be quite good for business if she were to make the ascent herself. Accordingly, in 1808, aided and abetted by the local guides, she set off with nothing more than a strong constitution and an eye for business. She climbed unaided as high as she could but eventually had to rely on help from her friends. Even so, she found the going tough and eventually pleaded with the guides to abandon the whole mad idea. 'Throw me in a crevasse,' she begged them, 'and go on yourselves.' The guides refused to oblige, for they had been among the first to encourage her in the whole mad escapade. Instead, she was dragged, protesting, to the top, to take her place in history as the first woman to reach the summit.

The first *climbed* ascent by a woman, however, was made by a French mountaineer, Henriette D'Angeville, in 1838. A highly organized climber, she was the first woman fully to plan her own ascent. Shackled as all women were in those days by their clothes, she nevertheless managed to struggle upwards in a long skirt – with a pair of brightly checked trousers underneath. Modesty was not a virtue with which Henriette was overfamiliar, which may explain why one male commentator described her disparagingly as 'a thwarted maiden lady in her forties'. She gained the maximum publicity for the climb, dramatically announcing that she had made her will before setting out. The news of her successful three-day ascent – brought down from the summit by carrier pigeon – was celebrated by a burst of cannon fire.

From the 1850s onwards, the English had begun to flock across France to the Alps. It was a period of considerable economic prosperity, a time which allowed for philosophical reflection and debate. Walking was a popular activity, appealing to the energetic and the aesthetic alike. Stendhal walked to Moscow and back and Wordsworth from Calais to the Alps and back. The vigour of the Victorian period was mirrored by the energetic walking tours undertaken first at home in places like the Lake District and later in the Alps, where the development of the French railway made those mountains accessible. It was not surprising, since their quest was often a spiritual one, that scientists and clergymen tended to dominate these tours, travelling in the same luxurious style to which they were accustomed at home. One party setting out for Mont Blanc included among its provisions sixty bottles of vin ordinaire, six of Bordeaux, three of Cognac, four legs of mutton, and eleven large and thirty-five small fowl.

Henriette D'Angeville's success had been a great triumph for women climbers and when, sixteen years later, the first English-woman arrived at the summit, it paved the way for wives and daughters to accompany their menfolk on their tours. Until then, the sporting activities of women had been mainly confined to riding – not something that every woman enjoyed – and once climbing became an acceptable form of exercise, they flocked to the mountains. This new acceptance was due in part to the fact that mountaineering was at first seen as little more than a slightly strenuous form of the promenade. The ladies certainly dressed as if all they were doing was setting out on a robust walk and perhaps it was important that they did, for anything more flamboyant might have been counter-productive and provoked a negative response. Once started, however, there was no stopping them and by 1869, Ellen Pigeon, a noted climber of the day, was able to write about herself and her sister: 'Now people are accustomed to lady climbers and even solitary ones. We were the first, I think, to go unattended by a male protector and we got on very well.'

After Mont Blanc, there remained the Matterhorn, perhaps the most famous Alpine peak of all, a tower of stone, steep-sided and triangular like a child's drawing. A thousand feet lower than Mont Blanc, it remained unclimbed until Edward Whymper made his successful though tragic and controversial climb in 1865 – a climb which resulted in the loss of four lives.

Six years after Whymper's success, Lucy Walker, modest and unassuming, became the first Englishwoman to climb the Matterhorn. She had begun climbing in the Alps when she was twenty-two, accompanying her father and brother on the lesser climbs until it became evident that she was capable of far more strenuous challenges. Later, she formed a lifelong partnership with an Alpine guide and with him made ninety-eight climbs in all. A photo of Lucy at eighty-one shows her to be a large, rotund woman, hair drawn back tightly to reveal a strong, square jaw, firm eyes looking out through small round spectacles, the whole face composed and serious but with a certain humorous look in her gaze. It is the face of someone with a lifetime of satisfying climbs behind her.

The Alps held a great attraction for those European women who had the money and the spirit to climb them. They set out using little equipment other than ropes, picks and the ubiquitous alpenstock, but there was a certain style to their climbing, a flamboyance that tells us much about their personalities. Lucy frequently drank champagne while on a climb – accompanied by a slice or two of sponge cake – and Henriette D'Angeville, a staunch Royalist and active self-publicist, celebrated her arrival at the summit of Mont Blanc by toasting the Comte de Paris with a bumper of champagne carried to the top for that purpose.

Later, the stirring notes of the 'Marseillaise', banned at the time lest it threaten the Second Empire, were to ring out from the summit. The singer was Meta Brevoort, educated in a Parisian convent and as staunchly republican as Henriette was royalist. Meta was beaten to the Matterhorn summit by Lucy Walker by only a few days and one cannot help but wonder what ancient national enmities propelled these two very dissimilar young women. While Lucy usually climbed in a white print frock, Meta wore breeches which she kept discreetly hidden beneath a voluminous skirt until she was well up the mountain and out of sight of scandalized eyes. Then the skirt would be removed and either handed to the guide to carry or concealed under a rock until their return. Once she forgot to put it on for the descent and had to spend a whole day searching for it.

Restraints of this sort must have been particularly irksome to such energetic women. Henriette D'Angeville had to bivouac one night in a cave without either food or blankets. For her, the imposition of dresses and skirts must have seemed a gross irrelevancy. Her reluctance to wear a skirt while climbing is even more understandable when one remembers that they were usually made out of a heavy material like tweed which dragged in the snow and added to the climber's weight. Some women devised ways of beating convention which were more cunning than successful. One method was to sew into the seam of the dress small rings through which a cord could be passed. 'The ends could then be knotted together,' advised one lady, 'in such a way that the whole dress might be drawn up at a moment's notice to the required height.' These women were obviously not to be defeated! The method wasn't all that good however, for, coming down the slopes, the snow got into the rings filled the hems, and made them even heavier.

Unsuitable clothing was not the only problem they had to contend with. Getting from England to the Alps in the first place was neither easy nor convenient. Trains existed, it is true, but they were expensive and not always comfortable. From the railway station one hired a horse and carriage which, though expensive, was at least more comfortable than being packed into a diligence. The final climb to the hotel might have to be made on foot or possibly on a mule. The Alpine playground was only just beginning to be developed, and climbers frequently had to stay in inns which were short on fresh meat but long on fleas!

Despite all this, it was a time of vigour and excitement. With their champagne and rousing songs, in delicate white frocks or robust knickerbockers, shaded from the glare of sun and snow by umbrellas and boaters, protected by male relatives or striding out independently on their own, these early mountaineers enjoyed a sparkling new freedom that would never be experienced again.

*   *   *

By the 1870s, the ripples engendered by the women's movement were starting to make themselves felt even in the Alps. The mountains, in fact, proved to be a good testing ground for those young women climbers who, in all other respects, had led a cossetted and comfortable life. 'Never until that moment had I put on my own boots and I was none too sure on which foot which boot should go.'

The mystified girl, marooned overnight in an Alpine hut, was 19-year-old Elizabeth Burnaby, recently married to Colonel Fred Burnaby. Born in 1861 and brought up in Ireland, Elizabeth had been swept off her feet and on towards the altar – the first of her three journeys up the aisle – by the dashing colonel who was twenty years her senior and whose reputation could have rivalled that of the legendary Cuchulain. It was said that he could bend a poker with his bare hands, lift dumbells weighing 170 lbs each and walk round the place with a pony under each arm. That aside, what we know he could do, because he did it, was to go absent without leave from his regiment in order to travel in a balloon across to France where a farmer's wife complained that the aerial apparition had caused her hens to have convulsions. To the young Elizabeth, he was a hero, a thing of wonder, and she marvelled that a creature as magnificent as he should choose her for his bride. The colonel, however, was nearing forty and it was time to settle down. A pretty young 18-year-old, taught to respect and honour her husband but with enough spirit to maintain his interest, was just the rejuvenating elixir a man approaching middle age needed. Elizabeth, privately educated and finished off in Switzerland, had been presented at court and had a proper sense of who was who in society. (She utterly despised middle-class people who referred to table napkins as serviettes.) They were married soon after her eighteenth birthday and among the wedding gifts was one from the Prince of Wales.

A year later a son was born and Fred persuaded Elizabeth to recover from this exhausting ordeal by taking a rest in the mountains. Accordingly, she set out for the Alps and during her so-called recuperation period in Chamonix, managed to climb Mont Blanc not once but twice.

By the time Elizabeth Burnaby arrived in the Alps in 1880, women were finding themselves faced with Hobson's Choice. If they conformed to the conventions of the time, they were likely never to travel at all; if on the other hand they appeared too spirited in their approach to climbing they risked the danger of being labelled a New Woman – a terrible thing to happen to a well-brought-up young lady like Elizabeth Burnaby. In any case, Elizabeth had her own personal battles to fight: 'I had to struggle hard for my freedom. My mother faced the music on my behalf when my great-aunt, Lady Bentinck, sent out a frantic SOS – "Stop her climbing mountains, she is scandalizing all London and looks like a Red Indian." '

Elizabeth did all she could to allay the fears of her aunt, dressing sensibly if most unsuitably in a long skirt, a blouse with leg-of-mutton sleeves and a tie. A photograph shows her knee-deep in snow, all dressed up ready for a climb, with alpenstock at the ready, and hat perched at a stern angle on top of her decorously arranged hair. She got miserably wet and cold on her climbs: '. . . our boots were pulp, our stockings wet sponges, our skirts sodden'. At first, the alternative – breeches – was unthinkable but common sense got the better of breeding and she finally devised a strategy: she would wear breeches but only when up on the mountain and out of public sight, and even then they had to be riding breeches, not knickerbockers. Like others before her, she hid her skirt under a boulder only to discover on one occasion that it had been carried away in an avalanche.

The mountains, however, were the making of this strong-minded young woman. She owed them, she said, a supreme debt of gratitude for knocking from her the shackles of convention. They also proved to be her consolation and her refuge when, at the age of twenty-four, she found herself widowed. Her beloved Fred had been killed trying to reach General Gordon at Khartoum. From then on, she settled in France, devoting herself to climbing and cycling in the days when bikes were known as safety machines, which is the last thing they were. Without brakes, her only means of slowing down when coming down a mountain pass was to tie the branch of a tree to her back wheel and trail it along behind.

Since she had first come to Chamonix, as a faintly notorious young 19-year-old, Elizabeth had toned down her behaviour in order, she said, that she might not discredit women's mountaineering. Indefatigable in her efforts to improve her technique, she stretched herself to the limits, at times detaching herself from the rope in order to display to her guides the degree of confidence she felt in her own skills. In between climbing, she managed to find time to remarry not once but twice, finishing up as Mrs Aubrey Le Blond, the name by which she is best known. It was during her final marriage that she achieved fame as the first woman to lead a climb without a guide. Eight years after her first ascent of Mont Blanc, she climbed Piz Palu with a woman companion – an expedition thought to be the first 'women's rope'.

There were many notable women climbers at that time and though not all of them responded to the imperative of the Alps, all had to cast off the same deadening weight of social prejudice before even attempting their courageous ascents. Some met obstacles so great that they were forced to consider desperate measures, such as marriage.

Freda du Faur was an Australian who spent her summer holidays in New Zealand and fell under the spell of the snow peaks of South Island, returning there to learn the techniques of mountain climbing so that she could make an attempt on New Zealand's highest peak.

Aorangi, also known as Mount Cook, is 12,349 feet, and though not as high as the main Alpine peaks, it lies in the path of rain-laden ocean winds which can rapidly turn to ice and snow and so make it Alpine in character. It was first climbed in 1894, when, characteristically, a group of New Zealand climbers, hearing that an Alpine party had arrived to attempt the first ascent, began their own climb which was to end in triumph on Christmas Day. Some fifteen years later, Freda du Faur found herself the object of tiresome criticism which rose, at times, to a crescendo of public outrage. Her crime was that she climbed unchaperoned. Had she been married it might not have been so bad, but for a young unmarried woman to go off up into the mountains alone with a guide was totally unacceptable. So determined was she to climb, however, that she eventually had to bow to public opinion and hire in addition to her guide a porter who would double up as a chaperone – two male companions, apparently, being less unseemly than one. She bitterly regretted having to do this, not least because of the extra cost involved. 'I almost succeeded in wishing that I possessed that useful appendage to a woman climber – a husband. However, I considered sadly that even if I possessed one, he would probably consider climbing unfeminine and so my last state might be worse than my first . . .'

The choices were indeed difficult but she stuck to her ambition and eventually succeeded in traversing all three peaks of Mount Cook – the first woman to do so. It is ironic that women pioneers encountered social prejudice in places where pioneering was the name of the game. Despite the fact that women had already got the vote in New Zealand, attitudes had changed little: 'I don't want to pose as a martyr,' wrote Freda du Faur, 'but merely to point out the disadvantages of being a woman pioneer even in the colonies, where we are supposed to be much less conventional than elsewhere.'

Society had tried to make her pay the price for being the first unmarried woman to want to climb Mount Cook. Fortunately, it was a price that her generous spirit was prepared to pay.

There were other women pioneers, however, who remained impervious to criticism of their sex. While Elizabeth Burnaby was cycling round France, Fanny Workman was hopping on her safety bike (solid tyres and no gears) to cycle to Spain, Morocco and eventually Bombay, with her husband pedalling furiously behind. In 1898, when she was forty and he fifty-two, they set off for the Himalayas. Their aim – like most travellers they felt the need to justify their pleasures – was to study architecture.

The daughter of a Republican senator, Fanny was educated privately and sent off to Europe for finishing touches to be added before she married an Ivy League man. She was lucky to find a partner who was as devoted to travel as she was herself. She was also fortunate enough to be able to employ a servant to travel ahead of them and sort out their sleeping arrangements, but despite such luxuries the going was often very tough. They cycled long distances and despite appalling roads, they managed on one occasion to cover eighty-six miles in a day. They were beset by robbers, yapping dogs – and punctures. In one stint alone they mended forty.

That first visit to India in 1898 sparked off an insatiable hunger for ice and snow, and over the next thirteen years Fanny made six major expeditions to the Karakorams, following in the paths of explorers such as Younghusband and Conway. She became the first woman to climb the 21,000-foot Koser Gunge and three years later, on an expedition across the Chogo Lungma glacier, she claimed to have broken her own record by scaling the 22,568-foot Mount Lungma. Crossing the glacier was no easy thing to do in a long skirt and without oxygen but she persevered – an unlikely sight with her face masked by a scarf and an incongruous *topi* balanced precariously on her head.

Fanny's enthusiasm for her own exploits frequently led her to make claims that have not stood the test of time. Much of the area she and her husband William climbed was unmapped and she made frequent, if understandable, errors – mistaking a mountain here, miscalculating a height there. But such was her forceful personality that she rarely listened to her critics, assuming that they were wrong and she was right. She had established herself as the leading woman climber of the time and was affronted if challenged. On one memorable occasion, another American climber, Annie Peck, claimed to have made an ascent in Peru that was higher than Fanny's. Amazed at the woman's audacity, and certain that she must be mistaken, Fanny sent an expedition of French engineers to Peru to survey the disputed peak. They returned with the news that Fanny's reputation remained intact. (The audacious Annie Peck, a classical scholar, was still climbing at eighty-two.)

Fanny's major and undisputed triumph came in 1912 when, at

the age of fifty-one, she led an expedition to the 46-mile-long Siachen Glacier. Ill at ease with the local porters, unable to understand either their language or their demands, the Workmans hired Alpine bearers and guides whom they found it easier to deal with. The expedition to the Siachen Glacier was well supported by money and equipment both from the Royal Geographical Society and the Survey of India, for it was the Workmans' intention to map the area. The glacier, the most inaccessible in that part of the world, was a nightmare to cross. High winds constantly threatened to sweep away both camp and climbers. The river, which had to be continually crossed and recrossed, had turned into a torrent, flooded by melted snow from the glacier above.

The caravan consisted of the Workmans, their team of surveyors and porters, plus a large quantity of grain, sheep and photographic equipment. On the glacier, one member of the team crashed headlong into a crevasse and though rescued did not survive his ordeal. Garbled reports of the incident, including one of Fanny's death, eventually reached Europe and over three hundred obituaries appeared in papers throughout the world, the extent of the publicity amazing even Fanny.

Once at the top of the world, Fanny Workman was determined to stay there. Her singular way of planning her expeditions made her unpopular with other climbers and surveyors and her obviously intractable nature led her into frequent disagreements with her porters. The women's altitude record which she set, however, remained unbroken for twenty-eight years and for that alone she deserves to be remembered. Her achievements did not go unremarked; she made sure of that. In 1904, the Sorbonne invited her to give a lecture on her travels – the first woman to be so honoured – and the following year, in London, the Royal Geographical Society invited her to address its fellows. Only one other woman had had that distinction – the redoubtable Isabella Bird Bishop. Fanny also wrote nine books on her travels, including six on the Himalayan journeys. In them, she publicized her achievements and made clear her intention in so doing:

> When, later, woman occupies her acknowledged position
> as an individual worker in all fields, as well as that of ex-

ploration, no such emphasis on her work will be needed; but that day has not yet fully arrived and at present it behoves women, for the benefit of their sex, to put what they do, at least, on record.

But although on record devoted to the cause of women, there was, in her own particular brand of feminism, a strange coldness in her nature which detracted from her declared sympathy for her sisters. Her response to the plight of other women seems mechanical and to lack the fire and the indignation expressed by some of her contemporaries.

*   *   *

The first blast picks me up from flat on the glacier and carries me twenty feet through the air. Next comes tons of snow and ice driven by eighty-mile-an-hour winds. Miraculously my hat is still on my head and I snatch it to cover my face and breathe through. Every bit of exposed skin is abraded by the driven ice and hurts like hell but I just keep breathing. As the wind dies to about twenty miles an hour, I look out to pure white . . .

The climber, a member of the first all-women's team to attempt to climb Annapurna, had encountered the first of many avalanches that were to come hurtling down the mountain, relentless and unswerving. Her glasses had become caked over with snow but she could hear, above the roar of the avalanche still thundering down the mountain, the screams of one of the film crew. Two others had been buried in a foot of snow and were clawing their way out. Another member of the film crew had disappeared altogether but was found six feet down in a crevasse, where a snow bridge had miraculously saved her from falling into the bottomless void.

In their high and solitary world, engulfed by choking snow and invaded by fear, they recalled the farewells they had made a few months earlier to husband, lover, child and parent when, riding high on the hope of success, they had set out in August 1978 to become not only the first women but also the first Americans to climb the 26,500-foot peak of Annapurna I.

Mountains are strange, majestic places, their summits repelling and at the same time beckoning those who dare to look up to them. Mountaineers bolster their courage with the language of challenge, which conceals their underlying unease. They speak of attacking and assaulting a mountain, of its summit falling to a climber and of the climber conquering its peaks. Mountains are invested with a power of their own, projected on to them by climbers needing to make sense of the sudden crash of snow, the unexpected splintering of ice, the fearful slithering towards the precipice of death. When a companion dies, they speak of the wrath of the mountain and when they themselves narrowly avoid death, they speak of the generosity of the mountain spirit. Mountaineers themselves are often at a loss to explain the magnetism which wrenches them from the safety of home and, significantly, only stumble across a reason – if that is what it can be called – after they have achieved their aim.

Monica Jackson left her husband and two children to take part in the first British Women's Expedition to the Himalayas in the 1950s:

> What strange compulsion was it that induced two sensible women to give up their jobs and a third to part from a beloved family, to subject themselves to extremes of discomfort and possibly to risk their lives creeping up and down singularly lonely, alien and desolate wrinkles on the earth's surface? If there is any precise answer, I do not know it. We certainly did not go in search of excitement though excitement sometimes came our way, nor to pit ourselves deliberately against more formidable hazards than we had hitherto faced. I think we, in common with most mountaineers who go to climb in the Himalayas, went there on a sort of pilgrimage.

Women mountaineers often find themselves dogged by Catch 22, for in order to join an expedition a climber must show some previous experience, and to gain experience, one must become a member of an expedition. So rarely are women chosen for major expeditions, even today, that when they are selected they make the headlines, as Julie Tullis did when she became the first woman selected to join the prestigious 1985 British Everest Expedition.

It had always been firmly stated that women were unsuited to

101

high-altitude climbing. They were not strong enough to carry the necessary loads, they lacked the aggression and the drive needed to keep going. They didn't gel together as a group in the way men did and worse, far worse, if a woman went on a high-altitude climb she could upset the 'easy masculine companionship which is so vital a part of the joy of an expedition'.

The Himalayas remained a closely guarded male enclave for many years. The area contained the highest mountain in the world – and the most difficult to climb. Some of its mystique would undoubtedly be lost if women, with their well-known frailty, were to attempt to climb it. Nevertheless, attempt it they did. After Fanny Workman's, there was a lull in Himalayan climbing expeditions. World War I intervened before, in 1934, Hettie Dyhrenfurth brought to a definite conclusion the argument that had erupted twenty-eight years before between Peck and Workman. As part of an international expedition to the Himalayas, she climbed to 26,370 feet – making a new high-altitude record for women. Finally, in 1975, a Japanese woman reached the top of Everest, proving conclusively that women were capable of making long, dangerous and highly technical high altitude ascents.

Annapurna is the collective name for a large range of mountains in the Himalayan region of Nepal. To reach the massif, you first travel to Kathmandu, load up with provisions, hire porters and Sherpas and take a bus to Pokhara – at best a five-hour trip but with stops and punctures, it can take seven or eight. After that, there's a ten-day trek to base camp, followed by the reason for the whole mad idea – a fifteen-mile climb, much of it vertical, to the summit. For the American expedition, it had to be done in the six weeks remaining before the monsoon hit Nepal.

At 26,540 feet (8078 metres), Annapurna I is the tenth highest mountain in the world, and holds a special place in mountaineering history as the first 8000-metre summit to be reached. In 1950, Maurice Herzog made the ascent with his companion Lachenal. The climb was arduous and almost ended in disaster. Both climbers had to be lifted off the mountain for Herzog was suffering from severe frostbite after losing his gloves at the summit. Down in the lowlands whipped by the monsoon rains, he was put on board a train bound for India, where the team doctor hacked off his gangrenous toes and fingers and hurled them out the carriage window. Since that momentous triumph, there had been only one attempt made by women climbers on an 8000-metre peak, and that was unsuccessful.

In 1959, the distinguished French climber Claude Kogan, heading a group called Feminine au Nepal, set out to climb Cho Oyo. Included in the international team was Dorothy Gravina, now a strong-bodied and energetic woman of eighty. She was delighted though surprised to be included in the team as she felt her age (she was then fifty-four) might have been seen to be a disadvantage. In climbing, as in other areas of life, however, age can be an advantage, bringing to a team experience and skill gained over the years. Dorothy Gravina had begun climbing seriously when her sons had grown up. She was always driven, she says 'by an awful urge to get to the top of everything. I simply like summits. There is the view spread out below, always mystifying and uplifting.' She knew men would say they were no good and she was determined to prove them wrong.

> We started the climb in September and went on into October. October had been a lovely month and we were all happy, especially for Claude as she had put so much into planning the expedition. Her husband had died a few years earlier and she was wearing a cross of his which she intended to lay on the summit in his memory. She and another member, together with two Sherpas, went on up to Camp 5 to begin the final climb to the top. During the night, we heard an avalanche but thought nothing of it. They were coming down all the time, but next morning I was a bit worried about the weather and sent a Sherpa up with a note to Claude telling her she ought to come down, if only until conditions improved – but it was too late. There was nothing remaining of their camp, absolutely nothing. I had to take over the leadership of the expedition. Somehow the others seemed to expect it of me. Everyone was so dispirited and despondent that I decided we should all withdraw from the mountain. Ever since, of course, I've regretted it. It would have been a fitting

tribute to have continued up to the summit and completed what Claude had set out to do, but the will to go on was not there among the other members of the team, especially the French who were grieving. I told the Sherpas when they found the bodies to hurl them down into a deep crevasse where they would lie undisturbed forever.

Annapurna means 'the goddess rich in sustenance', or 'the Harvest Goddess'. In fact, as we have seen, far from sustaining its climbers it shows an alarming potential for destroying them. By the time the American team set out, thirteen parties had already tried to make the ascent of which only four had been successful. Nine climbers in all had been lost over the years on this mountain alone. The US team hoped that theirs would be the first American success.

What strand of fate bound these women together and led them inexorably towards this challenge? The youngest was a 20-year-old geology student and the oldest celebrated her fiftieth birthday on the mountain. For the most part, they were middle-class professionals. Their leader, the admirable Arlene Blum, has a doctorate in physical chemistry. She had earlier been rejected by a major expedition on the grounds that her sex made her un-suitable. It was just the spur she needed and within a year she had gathered together a group of climbers and helpers all sporting tee-shirts with the expedition's immortal legend: 'A Woman's Place is on Top – of Annapurna.' Among the team were a teacher, a phy-sicist, a computer scientist and an eye surgeon. Some had partners, some were single. Some had children and one fell in love in the middle of the whole thing. Above all, they were individuals, outspoken, assured and healthy – women in their prime.

The expedition was first conceived of in 1972. At that time, despite Claude Kogan's attempt, no woman had reached 8000 metres but between the conception of the idea and its realization, two major climbs were made. In 1974, an all-women team from Japan had climbed to beyond 8000 metres and in 1975, another Japanese woman had got to the top of Everest, a staggering 8848 metres. Small and slight, Junko Tabei was thirty-six when she left her small daughter at home and set out as deputy leader of a

Japanese all-women ascent of the highest mountain in the world. As the Japanese team made its perilous way up the mountain, a Chinese team was approaching it from the north side. Climbing without oxygen, it placed nine climbers on the summit including a Tibetan woman, Phantong – one year older than Tabei and mother of three children. Chairman Mao commented: 'Times have changed, and today men and women are equal. Whatever men comrades can accomplish, women comrades can too.' 1975 had been a good year for women climbers on Everest.

While the US expedition continued with its planning and fund-raising, other teams strove to get to the top of Annapurna I. Four Japanese and a Sherpa were killed in one avalanche and two members of an Italian expedition were carried to their deaths by another. A Spanish team and a Dutch team got to the summit but an Austrian team failed, with the loss of one member. It was a jittery time for the US women's expedition.

Why were they doing it? Not to prove that women could climb high mountains. With a simplicity that defied contradiction, Arlene Blum pointed out that that was something of which they were confident before they began. Instead, in common with Fanny Workman, her hope was that more people would at last realize what women could accomplish in general.

There are, of course, certain areas in which women climbers are at a disadvantage: muscular development in arms and legs must be built up for arm strength, in particular, is vital. The Annapurna team had devised a weight-lifting programme and one member had walked up a steep hill each day carrying sixty pounds of bricks in her backpack. Their fitness was tested regularly and it is interesting that despite the wide disparity in years, the older members were no less fit than the younger. But high-altitude climbing with a team demands skills and reserves that must come from sources other than the physical. 'The determination needed to keep melting snow for water and cooking,' wrote Arlene Blum, 'can ultimately be more valuable than the skill to climb steep ice.'

There are decisions to be discussed and agreed upon. With a group of women committed to cooperation rather than competition, decision-making takes time. Experienced members will have strong views on routes and on strategies which may be in conflict with those of others. Routine jobs must be done whatever the weather or the mood. A network of relationships will form and reform, shifting the balance between the group, and caught in the middle of it all is the leader.

Arlene Blum soon found that her feminine upbringing was not necessarily the most useful when it came to leadership. The moderate, soothing approach was not always the most effective. What did it mean, she wondered, to be at the head of ten tough-minded women? She soon found out because they told her. They wanted her to be strong and decisive but to allow them to contribute to the major decisions – a tall order.

The physical demands, of course, cannot be underestimated. Right from the start, the fight was on. There were the ubiquitous leeches lying in wait for unwary members who went in search of what the team, even in the open spaces of the Himalayas, referred to as the bathroom. There were Sherpas who went on strike and a cook who mistakenly added iodine instead of soy sauce to the spicy fried rice. Within hours, the whole camp was writhing with diarrhoea. There were disagreements and illnesses and above all there was the weary knowledge that they would have to reach 21,000 feet before the real climb began, for getting to base camp would be a major journey in itself. The larger the team, the greater the support it can offer, but the correlating disadvantage is that more equipment and supplies must be carried and more porters and guides hired to convey the baggage to base camp. To save on energy, food must be bought *en route* and financial negotiations with impoverished villagers can be protracted and wearing. Heavy equipment such as oxygen, often used by climbers when they reach 25,000 feet, only adds to the burden of the porters. The constant rush of avalanches was the most dangerous aspect of the Annapurna ascent. They can break away at any time of the day or night and can cover a distance of 7000 feet in a few seconds. They are fearful things at any time but for Arlene Blum on Annapurna, they held a special dread, a dread which entered both her waking and her sleeping hours. She had been introduced to climbing by a young student who was himself in love with the icy heights. An avalanche took him out of her life forever.

While making their ascent, the US team picked up some

depressing news:

> Every few minutes that afternoon we heard another
> avalanche. Until now, I had been able to ignore the sound,
> but after the day's near catastrophe, I jumped up each time
> I heard that all-too-familiar roar to make sure it was not
> coming towards our camp. At 6 p.m. base camp radioed up
> the tragic news that three Japanese climbers had been
> killed in an avalanche on Dhaulagiri, across the valley,
> raising to six the toll of climbers who had died this month
> in avalanches in Nepal . . .

Were they frightened? Undoubtedly. One member descended
to a lower camp to think through her fear and then came up again,
ready to continue. It was one of the strengths of this all-women's
expedition that individual members were able to withdraw in this
way, although Dorothy Gravina feels that there are certain dangers
inherent in such a team: 'Women,' she says, 'do not have the same
sort of group loyalty as men and this can be risky and disruptive.'
Arlene Blum, however, felt that one of the factors which contributed to the relative calm of the expedition was that members
were not pressurized and did not feel compelled, for fear of losing
face, to push themselves beyond their own limits.

Even at the eleventh hour it was possible to withdraw. Piro
Kramer, an opthalmologist from Seattle, had almost reached the
summit when she found her right index finger was frostbitten.
Immediately, she rearranged her priorities. As a surgeon, she could
not risk losing her finger and without further thought, despite the
fact that she was one of the three lucky ones chosen to make the
final climb to the top, she withdrew from the ascent. The last part
of the climb had been more demanding than anything any of them
had attempted before. The two remaining women and their Sherpas
had been climbing since six in the morning and by the afternoon
the altitude was beginning to break them: 'I try to regulate the
pace so I am breathing six times for each step and I try not to slip
back in the unstable footsteps . . . We put on the masks and I feel
better momentarily. But soon I'm back to six breaths per step . . .'

And so in October 1978, two months after the expedition bus
had left Kathmandu, at half past three in the afternoon, when

businessmen were finishing a late lunch and children were watching the hands of the clock move slowly towards the end of the school day, Irene Miller and Vera Komarkova together with two Sherpas reached the top of Annapurna 1 – a place where time is relative.

Their triumphant stand at the top had to be short-lived for night was coming, their oxygen was running out and one member of the team was rapidly losing her strength. Coming down, they met the two members who were to make a second attempt on the summit. The parties spent the night together and next morning went their separate ways, Alison Chadwick-Onyszkiewicz and Vera Watson going upwards – to their death. Sometime during that day, they slipped and fell a thousand feet into oblivion.

There has been a trend in recent years to climb without oxygen and to manage without the back-up support of Sherpas and porters. Annapurna I had been climbed without oxygen in 1970 by Whillans and Haston and five years later the Tibetan woman, Phantong, reached the summit of Everest also without oxygen. The trend is in part due to the enormous cost of funding expeditions, which puts high-altitude climbing well beyond the reach of many mountaineers. Money, however, is not the only consideration. There are now more and more climbers who simply want to get to the top on their own, without benefit of artificial aids, and without the help of a retinue of porters. The rewards, they feel, are greater because the achievement itself is greater.

Although she is a mountaineer who prefers climbing without oxygen, Lin Rutland is aware of the extra strain this imposes:

> You become lethargic and lose the will to carry on. Each step is made by an effort of the will. Without porters, all the hauling of loads has to be done by the team which means yo-yoing up and down the mountain ferrying supplies from one camp to another, using up precious energy that should be conserved for the final ascent. A woman lucky enough to have a reserve of fat must start to draw on it now in order to keep her muscles in shape; otherwise they too will begin to fade.
>
> Women find it easier to acclimatize because of their ability to build up red blood cells, but other things may

work against them. Pre-menstrual tension can make a woman very tired and prone to germs. Vitamin supplements help but nothing can make up for the loss of nourishing food which eventually means that periods will stop altogether.

Lin Rutland is a cheerful, down-to-earth woman in her thirties whose life is devoted to the mountains. She is one of the relatively few travellers and explorers who docs not come from the social and financial security of a middle-class background: born into a working-class family, she seemed all set for a predictable future of shop work, marriage and child-rearing. Her father, a soldier, disappeared from the family scene while she was a child and she was raised in a council house, one of four children who were always short of clothes and pocket money. As a teenager, she found the discos and the dance hall held little attraction, and the prospect of a job in Boots the Chemists was as unexciting as it was inevitable. Then, unexpectedly, the whole course of her life changed. Invited to join a weekend group going trekking in the Yorkshire Dales, she desperately emptied her pockets in the hope of finding the price of a pair of walking boots. Unable to scrape together the three pounds, she came to a never-never arrangement with the local shopkeeper.

The weather was dismal and the going tough. If the climb had not nearly destroyed her feet the new boots would have done so. Yet for Lin, the weekend was a resounding success. A future in Boots receded like a bad dream and within a few years, she had married another climber, spent her honeymoon climbing the Matterhorn and later, in 1979, achieved the British women's altitude record by climbing to the summit of Annapurna III as part of a team of seven – six men and herself. The climb is technically demanding and one by one the other members of the team dropped out until there was only herself and one other left to go it alone – despite the fact that at the start of the climb there had been irritating slights on her climbing ability. Her partner was fit, fitter than she was in fact, and she found the ascent as demanding mentally as it was physically. However, they reached the 25,000-foot peak without the help of either Sherpas or oxygen. Descending to base camp, she found her stamina and reserves of energy once more came into play; her partner now found the going far harder than she did and moved considerably slower.

Sitting in her small house near Lake Windermere, the winter rain beating drearily against the window panes, she spread out on the floor the photographs and press cuttings of her climbs and attempted to explain:

'I'll tell you what you have to do to make yourself safe when you're on your own,' she says, as matter-of-factly as if she were explaining how to sew on a button. 'You dig your ice axe into the snow and tie a rope to it, then you tie yourself to the other end of the rope. Going across a crevasse there's usually two of you but if you're on your own you have to make do. You find a snow bridge and cross it, praying it doesn't collapse under you.'

The eye measures, the brain calculates, the foot reaches forward, the hand grasps and the spirit is restored. Excited by a rare harmony of mind and body, the climber experiences a spiritual exhilaration close to perfect happiness.

CHAPTER 6

Queens of the Desert

Jane Digby had, as a young girl, tried to fit in with the dictates of upper-class England at the beginning of the nineteenth century: she dutifully married the man chosen for her, graced his table, and bore him a son. Her passionate nature was such, however, that she allowed herself to fall deeply in love with a visiting diplomat. The scandal and divorce that followed shook society to its foundations and she fled – a scarlet woman whose reputation was to follow her to the grave. In the intervening years, she led a life that was notorious even by Regency standards. Another divorce, six children and many lovers, including both King Ludvig of Bavaria *and* his son, preceded her marriage to Sheik Abdul Medjuel el Mezrab. She was nearly fifty when they met, but with him at last she found happiness.

Now, twenty years on, she was fretful, afraid that her Bedouin husband had gone back to the desert to be with another woman. She had done everything she could to please him – had adorned his side, listened to his wisdom, ridden with his tribe and given herself to him under the stars of the Arabian sky. She counted the days and found it had been a month since he had last come to her room. What could be the reason? Her eyes still shone, her skin was pale ivory and her long hair hung in plaits. She served him as she had always done, bringing him water to wash his face, kneeling to wash his feet with her own hands. And still he stayed away from her bed.

Jane Digby el Mezrab was as passionately in love with her Arab husband as she had been when they had first met, and his frequent solitary disappearances into the desert – his first and only home – were a continuing source of grief to her. Jealousy was shredding her heart. Although he always denied it, she was sure he had taken another wife, as was his right as a Bedouin. She didn't know which was worse – the pain of knowing or the ache of doubt.

Once, when he had failed to return from the desert, she had threatened to leave their Damascus home altogether, and was making preparations to go when a horseman rode up with a message. 'A letter from Medjuel! Oh, what a moment! And that he was coming in a few hours. I nearly fainted.'

She mounted her swiftest Arab mare and rode out to meet him, only too eager to believe the diplomatic reasons he offered for his absence: 'Oh what sweet explanations and doing away with all doubts and jealous fears.'

She could now be calm – until his next disappearance. Since their first meeting, however, time had been making its demands even on her desert sheik although her eyes, still blinded with love, had failed to notice. Jane herself was now seventy-three and Medjuel only a few years younger. If he occasionally faltered in his love-making or failed to present himself at her bedside with the regularity of old, it was perhaps understandable.

They had met in 1853 on the caravan route to Palmyra, when Jane had enlisted the services of Medjuel as escort. As the caravan proceeded through the stultifying heat of the desert she was soon enraptured by the slow, rhythmic movement of the camels, described by Isabelle Eberhardt, another lover of the sands, as 'those creatures with their strange heads, half-bird, half-serpent'.

The caravan halted for the night and the low, black goatskin tents were set up for the evening meal. During it, Jane found Medjuel a handsome and entertaining companion. Courteous and educated, the sheik's son spoke both French and Turkish. When the party was set upon by nomad raiders, for it was inconceivable that a traveller as rich as the Englishwoman should escape their attentions, Medjuel shielded her with his own body. Later, he declared his love.

Brought up on the Byronic literature of romance and adventure, and, like him, unable to tolerate the alliance of discretion and deceit practised in the Regency drawing-room, Jane had, throughout some twenty-five years of travelling, managed to retain a spirit that was ever hopeful and receptive. What sort of man was it that could win and keep the heart of this impetuous, romantic woman? Medjuel was small for an Arab – slightly over five feet – with a dark beard and black hair curling under his *keffiyeh*. He walked erect and with grace and his eyes were as soft and as gentle as any woman's.

When Jane Digby died, the Christian community in Damascus placed Medjuel in the leading carriage of the funeral cortège. Trapped inside and unable to bear the silent, doom-ridden procession, he suddenly hurled himself from it and rushed headlong down the road away from the cemetery. Choosing to ignore his strange behaviour – he was, after all, a foreigner – the small English community continued with the service until the clergyman began to sprinkle a handful of earth on the coffin. As he did so, the hot, still air was shattered by the sound of hooves and the Sheik returned, thundering down the road on his black mare. He reined her in, stared in silent misery at the open grave, then turned and galloped away. Later, out in the desert within the comforting brotherhood of the tribe, he sacrificed a prize camel in memory of one of the greatest lovers of the century.

If Jane Digby went to the East hoping to find love, Margaret Fountaine went there determined to resist it, and never was an innocent woman more sorely or more frequently tempted. Respectable daughter of a respectable Victorian parson, Margaret's interest in collecting butterflies led her across Europe to Syria. The East still had its attractions, but with the new class of traveller forced to spend each penny carefully and wisely, a form of commerce developed between traveller and the local people, a development which detracted somewhat from the glamour and the mystery of the Arab world as Jane Digby had known it.

The industrious Victorian had a penchant for trading, preferably fairly, and was not to be hoodwinked by any wily merchant or hotelier. Margaret Fountaine was just such a Victorian and guarded her money well, perhaps all the more so since it had come somewhat unexpectedly in the form of a legacy.

By the time she reached Damascus she was a seasoned traveller, for she had taken her butterfly net to Sicily, Italy, Greece, France and Hungary. In her middle thirties, single and resolute, she was adept at hiring guides and at assessing both hotels and men – whether importunate or just plain ill-mannered: 'At Ain-Sofar, the hold-all was a terrific business to get out of, and no man offered to help me – the Syrians and Turks are not a gallant nation. However,

I ordered one of them to help me with it, and being told to do so he
lent a hand readily enough.' Once settled in Damascus, she took
on the services of a dragoman, Khalil Neimy, who would guide her
in her search for butterflies.

The Lebanese hills abounded in these delicate creatures and
though getting there could present problems, the joy of travelling
always made up for the discomfort. Riding out to see the cedars
meant a 5 a.m. start and 'before the great heat of the day had come,
we rode away across the great plain where camels were at work.'
Later, they rode 8000 feet up into the mountains where, although
it was June, they found snow still lying on the top. At the end of
June, Miss Fountaine decided to make the long ride from Damascus
to Jerusalem. With Khalil and a groom and three horses laden with
luggage and saddle bags, they set off. The ride presented its usual
complement of disagreeable events. There were fleas in the bed-
sheets, the Bedouin women they met were, she felt, polluting the
stream from which they had to drink, and the heat was so intense
that she fell asleep in the saddle. Yet there were compensations:
riding through the moonlit hills, finding rare and beautiful speci-
mens of butterfly – and Khalil, who had fallen in love with her.
He was twenty-four and she thirty-seven. Many men had fallen in
love with her before in the course of her travels and she had always
found the will to resist, but this time she felt herself surrendering.

> When Khalil came in next morning and folded me in his
> arms – while I feebly expostulated because I was still only
> in my night-gown and dressing-gown – my whole heart
> went out to him. He carried me in his arms across the room
> and laid me on my bed and when he lay over me the weight
> of his body was sweet . . .

Less pleasing was Khalil's occasional coarseness – due, she
assumed, to his humble origins. While she enjoyed seeing his eyes
dilate and his chest heave with passion, she felt it unseemly that he
should admire her legs. I love very much your legs, he would say,
trying to embrace her knees. She tried to raise his mind to a higher
plane by making him a present of the Bible translated into Arabic –
and then regretted it for the Old Testament was not always as
edifying as she would have wished.

114

They could never marry for Khalil had been forced into an early, unhappy marriage and his wife, like a character from a Victorian melodrama, had returned whence she came – to the streets. Miss Fountaine, however, accepted Khalil's ring, sensibly taking it to be valued by a Greek jeweller in Istanbul. They had, she said, 'escaped the cares and worries of matrimony, and maybe that satiety which is so often the unwelcome guest to the soft, downy pillow of the marriage bed . . . and we lived for so much more besides mere sexual intercourse.'

It was the beginning of an unorthodox partnership that was to take them all over the world: to South Africa where she went for a couple of drunken miners who offended her; to the West Indies; to America, and to India, where she bought Khalil a white suit so that he might look like a proper Englishman abroad. She was proud to belong to 'the most powerful nation on earth' but prided herself also on being able to stoop to the level of low company, for she was both practical and pragmatic. Above all, she shared with Jane Digby an infinite capacity to enjoy the new and the untoward, though she was never as unwise as the hapless Jane when it came to love affairs. For Margaret Fountaine, the freedom to travel came first and neither marriage nor man must tie her down. Instead, she travelled the world keeping her captive Syrian exactly where she wanted him – fluttering helplessly against her breast.

The women who travelled through the hot sands of Africa and to the deserts of Arabia were drawn there by many things: some, like Jane Digby, by mystery and romance; some by the solitude and magnitude of the desert, by the infinite scope of its nature; others by the inherent precision and balance found within the culture of Arabia. Archaeological scholars such as Gertrude Bell and Freya Stark searched the deserts for the stones and bones of a past time. Others prowled in search of adventure beneath the desert moon – said to shine more brightly over the Nile than anywhere else. There was Hester Stanhope who saw herself as Queen of the Desert and the sad Anne Blunt who wandered through North Africa looking for Arab horses, preferring the stinging whip of the Sahara sand to constant reminders of the infidelities of her wayward husband. And there were the women who needed to live on the knife-edge of danger – Alexine Tinné and Isabelle Eberhardt, the former killed by tribesmen, the latter dead at twenty-seven, consumed not by the blazing sun but by her own inner fire. Finally, there were those like Lady Mary Wortley Montagu and Isabel Burton who followed their menfolk on diplomatic missions. 'I want to live,' Isabel Burton told her mother. 'I hate the artificial existence of London . . . I want a wild, roving, vagabond life . . .'

She got her wish, in a manner of speaking, by marrying the most celebrated vagabond of the day – Sir Richard Burton. When he was appointed Consul in Damascus in 1869, she was enraptured : 'I am to live among the Bedawin Arab chiefs. I shall smell the desert air; I shall have tents, horses, weapons and be free.'

The East offered freedom on many different levels. There was time, for instance, a new and demanding concept which could not be measured by the clock at Greenwich but took its rhythm from the moon. Instead of church chimes, the muezzin's eerie call marked the earth's passage through the night. Daybreak took on a new dimension, when travelling out into the desert from Jerusalem or Palmyra meant a sleepy pre-dawn start. When night came, like the sudden shutting of a door, there was no drawing of curtains and lighting of candles. Instead, the company sat out under the stars, smoking and talking long into the night.

The East also offered, for women, the chance to wear clothes that were loose, comfortable, flamboyant and with a faint air of fantasy. In Damascus, Isabel Burton, by then a portly thirty-eight, dressed as an Arab boy in order to walk the streets more freely, and a portrait painted 150 years earlier shows Lady Mary Wortley Montagu resplendent in a flowing turban, hung about with feathers and jewels.

Lady Mary, arriving in Constantinople with her husband in 1716, found the women there 'freer than any ladies in the universe . . . it being their husband's business to make money and theirs to spend it.' Back in England, she had given her whole attention to the task of arranging clandestine meetings with her lover – a man of whom her father disapproved but whom eventually she was to marry. They arranged to pass each other on the steps of church, an opportunity for a whispered message, and exchanged long lists of mutual acquaintances in whose drawing-rooms they could try to meet. They used false addresses to which letters might be sent, employing every conceivable method of thwarting the conventions of the day.

· To the 27-year-old Mary, now a respectable matron with husband and family, the freedom of the veil was something she could only envy: it allowed Turkish women to come and go and no man dared accost them in the street. For who could know what lady – wife or lover – hid behind the veil? The streets of Constantinople, it seems, were thronged with women hurrying to assignations arranged for them by their Jewish go-betweens; with so much freedom to hand, Lady Mary concluded, perhaps wistfully, 'the number of faithful wives is very small'. Seventy years later, Eliza Craven found things not much changed. Arriving in Constantinople in 1786, she declared she had never seen a country where the women enjoyed so much liberty.

The demands which Georgian England made on its women were difficult to meet, and more difficult for some than others. They must marry young, bear children and remain dutiful wives to the end. Some succeeded. Others tried but failed. Eliza Craven obediently married at seventeen and bore her husband seven children, but by the age of thirty she found herself pensioned off by him with £1500 a year. In retrospect, it was probably the best thing that could have happened to her: she had been a young and spirited bride who must have found it difficult to bear the yoke of marriage. Indeed a contemporary magazine reported that she had been seen one night returning home late 'in great confusion and her clothes huddled on in a hurry'. When her husband bribed the men who had carried her chair, he found she had been at 'a certain famous house of carnal recreation in Covent Garden'. Following her divorce, she left England and in 1785 set off on a year-long journey.

'You will be much surprised', she wrote to the Margrave of Brandenburg, Ansbach and Bareith whose *belle amie* she was, 'when I tell you that I hate travelling . . .' He must, indeed, for her journeying had taken her not only to Constantinople but also to Moscow, St Petersburg, Amsterdam and Vienna, and had earned her the name of the Titled Wanderer.

For someone who professed to hate travelling she was remarkably professional about the whole business. On the back of her coach she strapped her side-saddle, for to ride astride would have been unthinkable. Inside the coach she carried her harp and a tea-kettle. Like many a woman traveller both before and after, she had been told her journey into the Crimea was dangerous. The air would be foul and the water poisonous. As a precaution, she tasted the local water, but although she found it good, she decided in the end to stick to fresh milk in which she usually melted some chocolate.

Like Mary Wortley Montagu, she was bemused by both the institution of the harem and the discreet use made of it by the heavily veiled women of Constantinople. If a Turkish husband returned home and found a strange pair of ladies' slippers outside his wife's room, custom required him to go away and not interrupt the visiting lady. It would be easy, she thought, for a man to disguise himself as a woman and visit his illicit lover. Prayer times too, she noted, could afford plenty of opportunity for plots whether of an amorous or political nature, for 'a figure wrapped up like a mummy can easily kneel down by another and whisper any sort of thing'. Turkish women, she felt, had nothing to complain of. Not all travellers viewed the veil in the same pragmatic way. Richard Burton found its main advantage was that it concealed all manner of nasty things like coarse skins, fleshy noses, wide mouths and vanishing chins.

The harem, of course, was a place of pilgrimage for foreign women who, later, were always questioned closely about it by their menfolk. Could it have been that these determined and strong-minded women were unconsciously attracted to the idea of captivity and the male strength it implied? They had made a stand against the conventions of the day but had rarely found a partner who could share their convictions or match their bravery. The apparent peace and quiet of the Turkish harem with its established order imposed by an unquestioned master must at times have seemed a safe and desirable haven, a place where a truce – even a temporary one – in the war of independence might be called. Such an oasis was, of course, little more than a mirage; the harem could be a seething cauldron of political intrigue where women jockeyed for position and babies were disposed of as minor inconveniences.

Nevertheless, the ladies paid their courtesy visits. Lady Mary Wortley Montagu, visiting the wife of the Deputy-Vizier, found the door opened for her by two black eunuchs. Passing through the courtyard scented by jessamine and honeysuckle where a white marble fountain played, she found the women clothed in damask and brocaded silver. She was offered a place of honour, seated upon white satin cushions, and deduced that Turkish ladies led a life of uninterrupted pleasure. In the baths, she found the women like Titian goddesses with their skins 'shiningly white' and their hair braided with ribbons and pearls, tended by beautiful young slaves.

Seventy years later, Eliza Craven was less impressed: on the whole, she found the Turks led far too easy a life, sitting round on cushions all day, smoking their pipes and marking the slow rhythm of time. For the Titled Wanderer, now in her mid-thirties with one lover in tow and another at home, the slow pace of Eastern life was wasteful. She had brought with her a sense of English industry; to her, idleness was the enemy of the soul and the apparent sloth of the Arab was incomprehensible. 'I wish to see a colony of honest English families here,' she said sturdily, 'establishing manufactures such as England produces and returning the produce of this country to ours.' She longed to wake 'the indolent Turk from his gilded slumbers'. In this attitude lay the difference between East and West.

She noted with approval that everything in the harem was clean and tidy, the cushions and curtains of pure white linen and the coffee, sherbet and sweetmeats pleasant. The inmates, however, were far from it. There was too much white and red make-up in evidence, too much black powder on the eyes. The young women had stooped shoulders brought on by sitting around all day doing nothing. Too many baths had aged their skin and smoking had blackened their teeth. Though she herself sported what she felt was quite a fine chemise decorated with many layers of delicate lace, it went unremarked among the gold-embroidered silk of the harem. Harem life, we are led to think, would have been much more acceptable had the ladies sat up straight, abstained from smoking and been taught to do something useful with their time.

* * *

Nearly thirty years later, Hester Stanhope arrived in Syria, concerned not with the boredom and inactivity of the harem but with adventure. From the start, her journey was packed with incident. In 1811, travelling between Rhodes and Egypt, her ship was wrecked. Two days later when she reached dry land, she took stock. Everything she owned, including her clothes, had gone down with the ship. Now thirty-four, of limited independent means, far from the restrictions of home and unfettered by the public position she had occupied as the Prime Minister's hostess, she could at last give expression to the flamboyant, strutting side of her nature which had been ill-contained within the clinging folds of her Regency gown. The moment of freedom had arrived. From then on, she decided, she would wear male dress.

Hester had grown up impetuous and imperious, used to having her orders obeyed and accustomed also to the talk and company of men. She had, a cousin said of her, the 'oddest mixture of cleverness and folly'.

Had she chosen to wear the garments of a Turkish woman, she would have had to adopt the veil which would not only have been totally out of character but would also have prevented her from mixing with men. Her Turkish costume was more colourful, far more dramatic than anything she could have worn in Regency England and it fitted well with her image of *enfant terrible*.

To reassure those back home – or perhaps to boast a little about her daring lifestyle – she described her clothes: a silk and cotton shirt, striped silk and cotton waistcoat, another waistcoat with sleeves, a short coloured cloth jacket, large breeches, boots and a sash into which went a pair of pistols and a short sword. A leather belt containing shot and gunpowder went over the shoulder and the costume was topped off by a many-coloured turban. At last, she had found a form of dress that suited her personality!

The shipwreck which she suffered in the Mediterranean was a portent of the life to come, for from then on she was surrounded by a jetsam and flotsam of people who came to depend upon her for their survival. At one time, her house in Syria was home to more than a hundred impecunious Arabs. Riding astride – quite scandalous in those days – she frequently took off on risky journeys into the Syrian desert. Warned not to ride into Damascus unveiled, she immediately felt impelled to do just that. Courageous, opinionated, flamboyant and imperious, she won from the Arabs their adulation, and was able to announce, without fear of rebuke, 'I am the oracle of the Arabs and the darling of the troops.'

They in turn must have wondered what to make of this strange being dressed in male clothes. Was she a man or a woman? She was indeed ill at ease as a woman and postured, instead, as the man she felt herself to be. Once settled in Syria, she set out to cross the desert to Palmyra, receiving *en route* a spectacular Arab welcome, one which brought her the approbation she so needed and sought. It was well-deserved, for she was among the first English travellers to go so far into a desert whose Bedouin inhabitants were normally anything but welcoming. Three previous Englishmen had been attacked and beaten and she had been told that a woman would never be safe alone, especially without a veil.

'I have been crowned Queen of the Desert under the Triumphal Arch at Palmyra,' she wrote in exultation, 'and, if I please, I can now go to Mecca alone – I have nothing to fear. I shall soon have as many names as Apollo. I am the sun, the stars, the pearl, the lion, the light from heaven, and the Queen.'

No wonder she should say she was 'quite wild about the people', adding, 'and all Syria is in astonishment at my courage and my success'. Modesty had never been her strong point. But behind this boasting, she was a sad character – she longed for acceptance and true affection, but always had to make do with the outward show of admiration. To the end of her days she failed to get close to the Arabs, try as she might. She died unlovely and unloved, a woman whose childhood and upbringing had been without the warmth which might have helped her find a softness which the Arabs could better have understood. She had had to be satisfied with a life of adventure – but of that, at least, there had been plenty.

Two years before Hester died her lonely death, in the year Victoria came to the throne, was born a woman who was to find in the desert adventure of a very different sort. Lady Anne Blunt had none of Hester's posturing and hectoring attitudes, but she was a fluent Arabic speaker and a fearless traveller: dressed incongruously in tweeds and an Arab headdress, she warded off desert raids by unfriendly Bedouin and slept in the overhang of a rock when her tent blew away in a sandstorm.

Daughter of the unhappy mathematician Ada Lovelace and granddaughter of Byron, Anne in her late twenties was plain, uncertain of herself and somewhat humourless. There was something in her character, however – determination, perhaps, linked with a hidden love of the bizarre – which attracted to her side Wilfred Scawen Blunt, diplomat, poet and womanizer. He was also attracted, no doubt, by the gleam of her inheritance.

Having tried desperately to give him a son and endured many miscarriages, Anne finally gave birth to a daughter whom she deposited two months later in the care of one of Wilfred's ex-mistresses, in order to set out with him on the trail of Arab horses for their now famous Crabbet stud. It was the beginning of a lifetime of wandering, interspersed with short periods at the family home.

It was an odd partnership between this stoical, studious heiress and the penniless, lecherous poet-diplomat three years her junior. Both had been solitary people when they met and married, and although they were close on an intellectual level, the relationship between the two was neither warm nor calm. It was only on their travels that they were able to establish a rapport that approached the companionship each sought. When that happened, however, they lived to the full their moments of shared joy.

There was also an element of fantasy in their travelling. In a marriage that was at best dull and at worst sorrowful, the chance to dress up and ride away together across the desert sands on camels or on their swift Arab mares must have appealed to the romantic side of poor Anne's nature – a side which she would have undoubtedly have inherited from her adventuring grandfather but which had been suppressed by her austere upbringing. For Wilfred their travels in the desert came as a welcome relief and he was only too pleased to substitute the real thing for the cloak-and-dagger games he got up to in England. Decked out in a black *keffiyeh* embroidered in gold, and striped silk gown, he added the finishing touch with a curved, Persian sword. Anne was prepared to settle, as always, for something less flamboyant, simply exchanging her hat for a *keffiyeh* and wearing a Bedouin cloak over her tweed travelling coat.

Wilfred and Anne Blunt

They must have looked a strange sight: 'When we arrived at the door of the Residency, the well-dressed Sepoys in their smart European uniforms barred us the door with their muskets. They refused to believe that such vagabonds, blackened with the sun, and grimed with long sleeping on the ground, were English gentlefolks or honest people of any sort.' When she wrote this, Anne and Wilfred had finally arrived at the end of their harrowing 2000-mile journey through central Arabia, from Damascus to Bushire in the Arabian Gulf.

Wrapped in furs against the icy winds, they had trekked across the wastes of sand where the nights were so cold that the sand next day was strewn with dead locusts. The locusts themselves were a daily feature on the menu and a traveller as tough as Anne – though she drew the line at roast hyena ('its stomach was full of locusts and fresh gazelle meat') – had no difficulty in describing how they should be cooked. Having experimented, she found that they were best boiled. Then, with the legs pulled off, they could be dipped in salt and eaten. Typically, Wilfred said they were as good as any *hors d'oeuvre* served in a Paris restaurant. She was not so sure.

It was a companionable time: as soon as they crossed the Mediterranean to Arabia, they seemed to find an oasis of tranquillity in a troubled world and pleasure in an otherwise arid relationship: 'It is strange how gloomy thoughts vanish as one sets foot in Asia. Only yesterday we were still tossing on the sea of European thought, with its political anxieties, its social miseries and its restless aspirations . . . and now we seem to have ridden into still water, where we can rest and forget and be thankful.'

Eventually, however, the private hurt of her husband's many and self-indulgent love affairs began to spread; she had gone into the desert to seek solace only to find, even there, his errant footsteps in the sand. The couple separated in 1896 and Anne settled in Egypt, where she eventually died at the age of eighty.

*   *   *

It is perhaps surprising that so few women travellers met their death as a result of their exploits; of those who did, Alexine Tinné was one of the most remarkable and indeed her boat journey along

Arrival at Gondokoro

the Bahr el Ghazal attracted the attention of the explorer of the day, John Hanning Speke.

Alexine was a Victorian heiress, daughter of a Dutch sugar trader based in Liverpool. Her wealth was astronomical and the money left to her in her father's will provided, through the interest alone, the handsome sum of £600 a year which was to pay for her education. By the time she finally came into her inheritance in 1856, at the age of twenty-one, she was a very rich young woman. She was also an energetic and curious person, and set off chaperoned by her mother and aunt to explore North Africa and the Nile. It was a source of fury to Sam Baker that while he waited in enforced idleness in Khartoum, anxious for the money to come through to finance his own Nile expedition, Alexine and her party should set off ahead of him.

'There are Dutch ladies leaving without gentlemen,' he wrote. 'They are very rich and have hired the only steamer here for

£1000. They must be demented! A young lady alone with the Dinka tribe . . . All the natives are as naked as the day they were born.'

Alexine and her party sailed up as far as Gondokoro and coming back down the Nile met the disgruntled Baker and his wife on their way to meet Speke and Grant: 'The White Nile is becoming a fashion tour,' he grumbled. 'There should be a public house built on the Equator where travellers could stop for a glass of beer . . .'

After the trip to Gondoroko, Alexine decided to explore the Bahr el Ghazal, a tributary of the White Nile. With money no object, she took five hundred porters, a train of donkeys and sixty-five soldiers. It turned out to be a disastrous journey. First her mother sickened and died, then her mother's maid and finally her own maid. When the stricken party returned to Khartoum, Alexine was greeted by her aunt, who herself was dead within weeks. Africa had taken its toll.

Unable to face Europe, Alexine settled in Cairo with a retinue of eighteen servants. She bought a yacht at Cowes for £1950 and sailed around the Mediterranean, dressing up her crew in Arab clothes and absorbing their wives into the household so that they became, for her, a surrogate family: 'Arabs, blacks and French wives all pigging together. It is certainly rather expensive but at least one gets a laugh for the money.'

In 1869, Alexine set off to cross the Sahara, the first European woman to make the attempt. Her plan was to travel south from Tripoli to Murzuch, turn east towards the mountains and Lake Chad, enter the Sultanate of Bornu in Sudan and pass on down to Khartoum. She had brought gifts for the Sultan including a microscope, ice machines, a sewing machine, disappearing ink, guns, tooth powder and an alarm clock which lit a candle when the mechanism was activated. She was never to reach her destination: coming out of her tent one morning upon hearing angry voices raised, she saw that a number of strangers had entered her camp. They proved to be veiled Tuareg horsemen. A quarrel had broken out between the Tuareg and some of her own caravan – a motley bunch of Dutch sailors, local tribesmen and freed slaves making their way home. Seeing one of her men fall bleeding to the ground, she put out her hand to try to calm things down – or could she have been making an imperious gesture of command? She was, after all, a rich woman used to being obeyed. Whatever her intention, the Tuareg were in no mood to talk. One of them brought his sword down on her arm, severing the hand. Then a shot rang out and she fell.

Dying in such a dramatic way, at the age of thirty-three, it was almost inevitable that a legend should grow up around the hapless Alexine. It was many weeks before the news of her death reached her family, and the accounts were garbled. She had not died, it was said, but had been captured by tribesmen and taken away to become an unwilling but prestigious member of the Sultan's harem. Whatever the truth, no trace of Alexine was ever found.

The desert also claimed the life of the wild, eccentric Isabelle Eberhardt, in circumstances that were both tragic and bizarre.

Isabelle, born in Geneva in 1877, was the child of a rich Russian woman who left her husband in order to set up home with her Armenian lover – tutor to her children and himself an ex-priest. It was an unconventional household in which Isabelle sought and found a kind of love in her brother, Augustin.

Flamboyant, restless, romantic, unstable, but above all brave and bright-eyed, Isabelle was inevitably drawn towards the dark mysteries of the North African desert. Dressing in male Arab clothes, she rode among the warring tribes of the desert enjoying their intrigues, smoking hashish, and taking numerous Arab lovers. Still seeking the stability that was missing from her childhood, she married one of these lovers but soon became embroiled in the border politics of Algeria. Her reputation for fearing nothing and risking all, her willingness to eat and sleep and live like a legionnaire and her readiness to fraternize with the Arabs made her an inevitable target for political extremists. Still only twenty-four, she found herself in the middle of an inter-tribe war and narrowly escaped death, her crime being that not only was she on the wrong side, she was also an infidel and worse – a woman.

With money running short, she found work as a reporter, covering the hostilities along the Morocco/Algerian border. She wrote, she said – making one of her many self-dramatizing statements – because, like love, it was her destiny. Time was running out, however. Tall, slim and striking in her gleaming white burnous and red boots, her young face had nevertheless been ravaged by drink, hashish and successive bouts of malaria. One October morning in 1904, after one such malarial attack, she retreated to her small wooden house in Ain-Sefra on the edge of the Sahara, planning to be reunited with her husband. The waters had recently been thudding down from the mountains and in the middle of the morning a sudden torrent rushed through the ravine, sweeping away houses, animals and people. Isabelle's broken body was later found trapped under a house beam. She was twenty-seven.

In total contrast to the attraction the desert held for this reckless, undisciplined Slav, the interest that Englishwomen took in Arabia at the turn of the century was prompted largely by academic and scholarly pursuits. Education of women had taken an upward turn, and many were eager to avail themselves of it.

Gertrude Bell was born in 1868 into a family of wealth and privilege, and she built on these fortunate foundations with skill and dedication. Her young and beautiful mother died when she was four and Gertrude and her small brother were left in the care of their grieving father until he remarried seven years later. She was a pretty, solemn child whose early promise of cleverness came to fruition when, in 1888, she became the first woman to gain a first-class honours degree in History at Oxford. Later, on a holiday visit to Teheran, she fell in love with a young and penniless diplomat, but the edict of her possessive father prevented the affair from blossoming and shortly after her enforced return to England, the young man died. The loss of this early love left a lasting emptiness in Gertrude Bell's life and much later the love letters she wrote to Dick Doughty, a man whom she loved but who wasn't free to marry her, have an air of sad desperation about them.

From the age of thirty onwards, proficient in Arabic and Persian, she immersed herself in archaeology, travelling widely in Syria and Asia Minor. Brought up in a house in which ten rooms were set aside for servants alone, it is hardly surprising that her caravan in Arabia should include a canvas bath and that her servants should be trained to lay out napkins and appropriate silver, even in the desert.

Her expeditions took her all over the country, and she travelled usually with a full complement of servants and up to twenty camels in the train. Despite these high standards, her letters of credit were not always honoured and on one occasion she had to sell some camels to raise the money she needed to move on to her next destination. She could sometimes go for three months without hearing English spoken and it is small wonder that, after a gruelling day's ride when necessity might demand a 2 a.m. start, she should feel drained and despondent. She wrote that she could feel '. . . nothing. Dust and ashes in one's hair, dead bones that look as if they would never rise and dance – it's all nothing and one turns away from it with a sigh . . .' Even the sight of Palmyra, whose people, nearly a hundred years previously, had given Hester Stanhope such a tumultuous welcome, failed to cheer. She saw it as '. . . a white skeleton of a town standing knee deep in the bleached sand . . .'

She was naturally of a melancholy disposition, and, like many desert travellers, felt at times that she had undergone a strange metamorphosis: 'I have seen and heard strange things and they colour the mind . . . don't tell anyone that the me they knew will not come back in the me that returns . . .'

There were some moments of peace, however, when, lying in her carpeted tent, she could enjoy the erudite talk of the Bedouin sheiks, their hawks unmoving on the perch, their greyhounds resting on the sand. Then, she felt the spirit of her beloved desert return to her something of what she had given to it. Her knowledge of the desert was so extensive that during the 1914–18 war she was invited by the British Government to become a member of its Intelligence Corps in Arabia – a singular and well-earned accolade.

She was glad to go. By 1915, her love for Dick Doughty was becoming intolerable: 'I can't sleep . . . out of your arms there is no rest . . . I flame and am consumed . . . Dick, it's not possible to live like this.' She was forty-seven and knew that happiness could again elude her. He too felt the pain. 'So many memories, my dear queen, of you and your splendid love . . . and the wonderful letters you wrote me from your heart to mine . . .' He was killed, in April, at Gallipoli, and the following November, Gertrude left for Cairo.

Ironically, although she worked hard for Arab independence and valued personal freedom so highly, she had no sympathy for the struggle women were engaging in in England to win some degree of independence for themselves. She was, as we have seen, a founder member of the Anti-Suffrage League. In his biography of her, H. V. F. Winstone writes: 'She was no early feminist: indeed she distrusted and disliked her own sex, seldom missing an opportunity to comment on their ineptness or their unfitness to engage in those activities which were better left to men.' It was a surprising attitude in a woman whose own independence makes her one of the foremost travellers and archaeologists of her time, but it was an attitude conditioned and nurtured by a male world in which a woman's achievements were recognized only in so far as they could be contained within acceptable female boundaries.

Freya Stark was another scholar who followed in Gertrude Bell's footsteps, travelling throughout Arabia and along the coast of the Red Sea to Yemen. Born in Paris in 1893, a restless and not altogether happy childhood formed the bed in which the seeds of adventure and travel were sown, so that when the opportunity arose, she was ready to take it. After training as a nurse, she was given the chance to go to the Italian front to tend to the war wounded but by her mid-thirties her real passion had emerged – a love of travel, allied to her growing love for all things Arabic.

She applied herself assiduously to the study of the language – an exercise which became a sort of baptism of fire, an apprenticeship, for she felt she could not truly understand and appreciate the archaeology of Arabia unless she was first proficient in its language.

Invited to Bagdad by the Prime Minister, she travelled the Crusader routes and mapped the Valley of the Assassins. When the war came, her knowledge of the Arab world was such that she was appointed to do propaganda work first in Aden and later in Cairo. These jobs were interludes, however, in her life of travel – this always remained her first love. She made a list of rules which the good traveller should observe, which included: to know how to use stupid men and inadequate tools with equanimity; to be able to disassociate oneself from one's bodily sensations; to be as calmly good-tempered at the end of the day as at the beginning.

Unlike her predecessor Gertrude Bell, whom she was not altogether sure she liked ('I am not very fascinated by her as a woman'), there is a cheery gaiety about Freya Stark that has persisted into her nineties. Like a learned and enquiring butterfly, she decked herself out in striking hats and *haute couture* fashion, the antithesis of women such as Stanhope and Eberhardt whose response to the desert was to dress and act like men. For Freya, there were no doubts about her identity as a woman.

After the war, she received and accepted a proposal of marriage from Stewart Perowne, her former boss in Aden. She was fifty-four and he forty-six. It was a union that lasted only a short while and she withdrew to Asolo again, the village in the Dolomites to which her mother had first brought her in 1901. A true survivor, she is now, beyond doubt, the First Lady of the travelling world.

*   *   *

Spanning two centuries, these women travellers found in the desert a spirit and a passion that belonged to another time, for the desert now is strewn with the weapons of war and the waterholes have given way to oil wells. The bandits have put on army uniform and the low black tents have settled dangerously near the towns. Women travellers too have changed, and are no longer prone to lose their hearts so easily, seduced by the sighs and whispers of the warm, desert night.

*A lady's mirror, drawn by Isabella Bird Bishop during
her travels in Japan.*

CHAPTER 7

To Follow or to Lead?

In the fortress town of Vidin, in what is now Bulgaria, a market was in progress. In the compound stood an attractive 17-year-old girl, her long hair done up in plaits. Around her, the confusing babble of Turkish traders mixed with the hectoring tones of an auctioneer calling out bids. In the crowd stood an interested foreigner whom, by his looks, she guessed to be English.

Sam Baker was a *Boy's Own* hero. Born in 1821, two years after Queen Victoria, he was the epitome of the sort of Englishman the Empire was sending abroad: physically courageous, patriotic and adventurous, without too great an interest in intellectual pursuits. Widowed at an early age and left with four small daughters whom he handed into the care of his sister, he cherished the ambition of participating in one of the great African expeditions of the day, but his solitary nature and gauche manner made him something of an outsider and on more than one occasion he failed to be selected. Now he stood, far from home, playing reluctant nursemaid to a young Maharaja who wanted to see the world. It was an altogether unsatisfactory way of life for an energetic, able-bodied man and it was probably frustration which drove him to take the next decisive step.

The year was 1859. In two years, the United States would announce its intention of banning slavery but here, in the Ottoman Empire, such acts of conscience were unthought of as long as the trade in slaves, particularly white ones, proved to be such a lucrative business.

The spectacle which Sam Baker had come to witness was indeed a slave auction and before it was finished he had purchased the pretty, blonde 17-year-old. It was a pathetic gesture of bravado. Rejected by his own heroes and unable to pursue the life of exploration and adventure that he craved, he chose on impulse to buy a slave so that over her life at least – if not his own – he could exert some influence. He had undoubtedly saved her from a sad future spent as a member of a harem.

Florence Maria Sass – Sam called her Flo – had been sold into slavery as a child when the Turks overran her Transylvanian home. They made a strange, lost pair, both cut off from home, family and country, he unfulfilled and nearing forty, she a solitary young girl twenty years his junior. Nevertheless, she proved to be the key to her saviour's happiness. She became his mistress, and the arrangement turned out so well that three years later he decided to take her with him to Africa. They would sail up the Nile and, with any luck, they would meet Speke and Grant who had gone in search of the source of that great river.

In 1862 they set off, taking twenty-one donkeys, four camels, four horses and ten tons of grain to feed the forty-five porters who were to complete the team. Though still only twenty, Florence had perceived, with remarkable insight, what her role must be: a combination of mistress, wife, hostess and life support. Only by combining all these things could she ever hope to repay Baker, and for the rest of her life she devoted herself to him, proving an industrious and loyal companion, and never once complaining about the hardships she had to endure.

She formed one of that amazing band of women who, in marriage, gave themselves completely to their husbands. Their loyalty was a state of mind, simple and absolute. If called, they followed – through malarial swamps and rain forests, desperately trying to make a home of sorts wherever they could and whenever they found time to do so. They followed their men not because of what lay at the end of the journey but because that was where their duty lay. It would be wrong to think of these women as meek and biddable. Hidden deep within them was an ambition to share with their husbands whatever life had to offer and it was this – their hidden strength – that kept them going.

Florence was motivated as much by gratitude as by a sense of duty, and she turned her mind to making her gratitude felt. Camping along the banks of the Nile, she turned even a thatched mud hut into a comfortable dwelling, managing to create the very thing that Baker had always wanted – a place where he could belong. To

The Bakers travelling by camel

him, it was a form of paradise: 'In the course of a week, we had formed as pretty a camp as Robinson Crusoe himself could have coveted; but he, poor unfortunate, had only his Man Friday to assist him, while in our arrangements there were many charms and indescribable little comforts that could only be effected by a lady's hand.'

For Florence, of course, there was a price to pay. She suffered badly from the heat and on one occasion succumbed to such a bad bout of malaria that her death was expected daily. Carried through the forests – they could not stop for fear of attack from hostile tribes – she hallucinated, passing from one shadowy world to another, never sure of where exactly she was. When eventually they stopped she was lifted, unconscious, and laid in a hastily erected tent. Sam, with leaden heart, ordered his men to start digging and it was to the sound of hoes and spades preparing her grave that Florence finally regained consciousness.

Choosing to ignore the advice that he should not take a young girl any further up the Nile because of the unhealthy marshes and hostile tribes, Baker pressed on southwards, driven by the hope of meeting Speke and Grant who, he had heard, were now on their way back down the river. With nothing to eat or drink but wild spinach and tea made from wild thyme, they made their slow and cautious way upriver. Finally, at Gondokoro, their determination was rewarded. The explorers appeared, and Flo, hostess to Baker's heroes, presided over the dinner table with pride. Sam had at last been admitted to the brotherhood of explorers but it is to his companion that some credit must go for easing his way on this journey, the fulfilment of his ambition.

There were many other women travellers who suffered equally willingly and often in silence by their husbands' side. The image of Queen Victoria, dutiful wife and noble mother, hung like a spectre over the women of the nineteenth century. Her doleful devotion to family life and her elevation of Albert to a position of sanctity that few husbands could ever achieve laid a heavy burden on lesser wives. In a pious hope that they would one day emulate this royal ideal, women were trained from the start to look to a man for guidance and approval, first to their fathers and later to their husbands.

Such a girl was Mary Moffat. Daughter of Robert Moffat, a missionary of considerable standing in Africa, she was twenty-three when David Livingstone, seven years older, arrived at her father's mission station, to try, as he said, to make an open path for commerce and Christianity. Moffat, his chest covered by a huge white beard, was the personification of patriarchy, devoted to both his family and his evangelical work. He welcomed Livingstone into his home, noting that the young man had been 'smitten with Mary's charms'. In Livingstone, Mary would have seen a younger, more exciting version of her father and would have perceived early on that a union with him would be blessed by her father's approval.

Livingstone himself had been contemplating marriage for some time and had even thought of advertising for a 'decent sort of widow'. Mary, at that time, was sturdily built with a serious look and a heavy jaw. With her dark hair severely scraped back from her face and in a lace bonnet of the period, she was yet another image of the sombre Queen.

To Livingstone she appeared dutiful and compliant – as good a woman to marry as any. She wasn't romantic, he told a friend, but she was matter-of-fact and strong and would be all that he wanted. He went through the courtship rituals and then wrote a pompous, self-important letter to his superiors in England: 'Various considerations connected with this new sphere of labour, and which to you need not be specified in detail, having led me to the conclusion that it was my duty to enter into the marriage relation, I have made the necessary arrangements for union with Mary, the eldest daughter of Mr Moffat . . .' To a friend, he confided carelessly: 'I am, it seems, after all to be hooked to Miss Moffat.'

They were married in 1845 and the following year Mary gave birth to her first child, a boy. Within months she was on the road, trekking through Bechuanaland with Livingstone on his missionary work. The next year she was pregnant again and Livingstone expressed irritation at having to delay some of his plans in order to wait for the child's arrival. In 1849 the third child was born and the following year, with Mary again pregnant, the family set out on a major missionary trek. There had been misgivings about taking three small children into an area that was rife with malaria and, indeed, the two older children were quickly stricken with fever. Livingstone, for once, was forced to put duty to family before duty to religion. It was a rare gesture for he now felt his mission in life was divinely inspired.

Later that same year Mary gave birth to a daughter, but the child lived only six weeks. By now, the heavy strain of childbearing, travelling and home-making was beginning to show. Whenever the family was settled long enough in their house in Kolobeng, Mary played her role as missionary wife to the full, attending to the local people's needs, running a local mission school and seeking to lead an exemplary life in the hope that her example might lead the local Africans towards Christianity. With the birth and death of her small daughter, she developed a paralysis of the face, a symptom of the nervous strain under which she lived. Within five months of her bereavement, the family was again on the move –

Mary Livingstone

back into malaria country. This time Mary, morbid and heavy-hearted, wrote to her mother: 'I must again wend my weary way into the far Interior, perhaps to be confined in the field.' It was a cry for help from a stricken woman.

Mrs Moffat did what she could, writing to Livingstone and castigating him for the pressures to which he was subjecting her daughter, but the family had already embarked on what was to be the worst journey so far, a trek through the sinister and arid land between the Makarikari Depression and the Okavango swamps, a land of 'sand, drought and dreariness'. Devoid of living things, empty of life, the place had the stillness of death about it and when the party ran out of water it was hardly surprising that Livingstone should notice his wife weeping with the agony of worry. She must also have shed tears of exhaustion for, with three young children to care for, the past four months' trek had almost destroyed her. On top of everything was the fact that she was pregnant yet again. Like an 'Irish manufactury' was how her husband ungraciously described her many pregnancies, choosing to ignore the fact that they were the result of his own sexual energy.

In September of that year, 1851, under a camel thorn bush, she gave birth to her fifth and last child. A week later, Mrs Moffat's outraged letter reached Livingstone. He was now burning with a compulsion, which he saw as his God-given duty, to continue deeper into the interior, encouraged by his recent discovery that beyond the rivers and deserts lay a land of water and rich vegetation. His family had become a distinct hindrance and Mary's increasing paralysis offered a welcome excuse for sending them all back to England. Accordingly, in April 1852 the pathetic little group, hastily kitted out in respectable clothes (too smart for a missionary family, Livingstone thought) was put on board a boat for home. They didn't meet again until Livingstone returned to England in 1856 – to a hero's welcome.

Whatever sadness she may have felt about being parted from her husband – and who could know if in fact she would ever see him again – the four years gave Mary some respite from the endless pregnancies, the nervous illnesses and the debilitating treks through arid, soulless deserts. Of the eighteen years of her marriage, those four years in England were the only ones when her health was not put at risk. In 1862, she returned to Africa – and to her death.

Travelling with Livingstone on the Zambezi, she caught a fever during an enforced wait in the unhealthy river delta. When her condition worsened, they took her off the boat and laid her on a makeshift bed – a mattress spread across three teachests. A week later, she lapsed into a coma and died, taking on in death, her husband noticed, the 'very features and expression of her father'. She was forty years of age. They buried her under a boabab tree and within a week, Livingstone was making plans for the next part of his expedition.

Mary Livingstone was forged on the anvil of wifely devotion, a life-convict branded both by her womanhood and by Christianity, and made to travel through what was undoubtedly, for her, a vale of tears. Only one voice was raised on her behalf and only one voice dared to speak the awful truth. Mary, said her mother, was a sacrifice ready to be offered up.

In the history of African travel, wives take on a shadowy existence, brought temporarily into focus when needed, their image blurring and eventually fading when they are no longer relevant. Like old forgotten photographs, they gather dust in history's drawer, their diaries and letters home the only record of the iron will which so often sustained their menfolk's lives.

In 1882, Edward Hore set out from London, bound for Africa. With him he took his young wife, Annie, his expedition's guinea pig. If she survived the journey into the interior then he could send back favourable reports to his superiors. Edward was not himself a missionary, but as a scientist was employed to assess the viability of certain routes along which missionary groups might travel. In particular, he needed to discover if such routes could be travelled by women since, increasingly, women were travelling to Africa to set up mission hospitals and schools.

For Annie, not long married and leaving England for the first time, the journey was of paramount importance. Not only must she survive for her own sake, but upon her survival depended her husband's career. And there was another even more vulnerable member of the party whose survival would be the final feather in Edward's scientific cap. The Hores' small son Jack was only three months old when his parents packed him in his Moses basket and set out for Zanzibar. Their aim was to trek from the coast to Ujiji on the shores of Lake Tanganyika, a distance of about 830 miles.

It was less than fifty years since the first missionaries had travelled to Africa and the risks were still great. Malaria remained the greatest killer of men and women alike. Mary Kingsley had not yet made her historic journey to West Africa, proving conclusively that women could survive the deadly, steaming heat of Africa's river swamps, and Mary Slessor had been in the dark continent for only six years. Preceding Annie on the eastern side of Africa had been Florence Baker, but she had had the good fortune to have an experienced hunter and explorer as her companion and one, moreover, who was as justly proud of her ability to pour tea as he was of her handiness with a rifle. To Edward, ostensibly at least, Annie and her baby represented little more than a test of endurance, a scientific experiment and one which he was determined to make work. Certain that Annie would be unable to make the journey unaided – she had, after all, the baby to care for as well – he modified a wicker bath chair by adding poles and adjustable wheels. Jack's Moses basket was kitted out with a steel frame so that it could be hoisted on the back – like today's backpack. The party set out with four bearers carrying Annie's chair.

The first attempt to get to Ujiji failed. Annie developed liver trouble, the rains came down and the whole venture had to be abandoned. The family split up, Edward to press forward on his own and Annie and the baby to wait in South Africa for the next summons. It was two years before Jack saw his father again. By then, the boy was nearing three. Gone was the Moses basket. In its place was a pram converted into a miniature palanquin.

The second attempt to reach Ujiji was dismal and frightening, though this we can only deduce from Annie's diary, since self-pity had no part to play in the dutiful wife's survival kit. With dogged determination she kept to her bath chair, clinging to it even when, on fording a flooded river, only the heads and hands of the unfortunate but faithful bearers were to be seen. Jack fell dangerously ill and his death became a distinct and awful possibility.

By now they had acquired a donkey and Jack would ride with no one but Annie, so she had to find a way of simultaneously holding the reins, supporting Jack and protecting him from the elements with an umbrella. In his fevered sleep, his small three-year-old body weighed heavily on her aching arms and perhaps it was an awareness of her own sad, sorely-tried state that made her look more closely at that of African women.

Both Annie and Jack survived the ninety-day journey to Ujiji, thus crowning with success Edward's mission. Annie continued to lend weight to its success by writing home glowing accounts of the mission station and the improvement in her son's health since settling there. The local women and girls, she noted, held a most degraded position and she herself provoked much amusement because of the interest she took in these second-class citizens. Annie was a thoughtful woman, capable of making wise judgements on what she saw. Her insight into the dangers that the 'civilizing' influence the colonizers might have on Africa denotes an attitude of mind that is both perceptive and sympathetic, and not wholly representative of the thinking of times. She noticed, for instance, the creeping consumerism encouraged by the new wave of traders who followed closely on the heels of the missioners. There was the incongruity of 'almost naked savages' drinking from glass tumblers (today's plastic cups) and the 'wildest native orgies' taking place by the light of paraffin lamps. The creed of commerce allied to Christianity was making itself felt.

If Annie felt lonely or dispirited during those early years of marriage, there is little hint of it in her journal. Just as Edward had a job to do in Africa, so Annie had a mission in life – to be his wife and perform her duties ungrudgingly. To have shown disloyalty to Edward, or to have displayed a lack of faith in his judgement would have been to strike at the very *raison d'être* of her existence. During the African experiment, Annie Hore's light shone bright and brave – a foil to her husband's venture. The job completed and her purpose served, she fades into the background, forgotten and unsung.

*   *   *

Even more forgotten have been those gallant women who followed their husbands out into the unknown world of the colonies.

In 1788, at the age of twenty-one, young Elizabeth Veale married one John MacArthur and sailed the following year to Botany Bay in New South Wales where her husband had the job of guarding the convict settlement. The sea journey was arduous, and made more so by the fact that not only did she have to cope with a teething baby, but she was about to give birth again. Sadly, her newborn baby died during the voyage. On the plus side, however, the journey lasted only six months, significantly less than some other voyages embarked upon in those years. (In 1792 the 73rd Regiment had sailed from England with 1024 convicts on board but by the time they docked in India, thirteen months and thirteen days later, 261 men, sixteen women and four children had died.)

Elizabeth was the first Englishwoman of status to reach the colony and a portrait shows her looking very elegant, in a black dress which revealed pale shoulders, and with girlish curls. She was far from being helpless, though. 'Having no female friend with whom I could discourse', she turned to 'a little easy science'. She gave birth to another seven children and at the same time made a name for herself in the local government circle. When her husband ran into political trouble and had to return to England, she took over the running of the wool farm he had built up and managed it for the eight years of his absence. It was, in fact, due to her business acumen that Elizabeth Farm became the first great Australian estate.

A year after Elizabeth's death, Charlotte Godley sailed for New Zealand with her husband, John Robert Godley, an Anglo-Irish lawyer who hoped to develop that country as a Christian colony. They sailed from Plympton on the *Lady Nugent* with their two-year-old son, who found the four-month sea journey so irksome that his mother had to send back to England for more dissecting puzzles to keep him amused. For the adults there were entertainments in the way of theatricals and lectures by John Godley. If the weather got too hot the men could be hosed down on deck but there was no such relief for the women, who were expected to remain in their cabins. The ship's doctor, Charlotte wrote home, was often tipsy though he did stay sober enough to deliver a baby. When they encountered another vessel at sea there was a good deal of celebration: letters were exchanged with boats going in the opposite direction and on one occasion some young men even rowed over for tea. In fact, Charlotte's morale improved so much that she sent home to England for her silk stockings.

Once in New Zealand, the working women had a hard time of it. The Reverend Vicesimus Lush, visiting New Zealand in the 1850s and asked what he had noted most, replied: 'The workworn hands of the women.' Some couples had landed with little more than thirty shillings in their pockets but though prices were much higher than in England (shoes cost four times as much, for instance), it was a place where you could exist on your wits and live in hope of something better round the corner. The early settlers learned to make a poultice from the pulp of roasted apples mixed with tobacco, and made biscuits from egg yolks, sugar and baking ammonia which they called 'men's promises' – because they were so easily broken.

Many wives were cheerfully prepared to do what they saw as their duty by following their husbands to the other end of the earth, but there were the usual bright exceptions to this rule, and none braver than Polly Munger, better known as Mrs George Black, who in the excitement of the Klondyke Gold Rush chose to defy her husband Will.

Born in Chicago in 1866, Polly's businessman father had announced, 'I am disappointed. I had expected a boy.' She was cossetted, however, by her father's money and at the age of twenty-one had a small, smart wedding on Lake Geneva. Her husband, Will, was employed by the railway with a salary adequate to cater for their comfortable lifestyle. Ten years later, both their marriage and Will's job had dulled somewhat, and when the Klondyke gold appeared they both saw it as a welcome answer to the boredom of their social round. Together with Polly's brother, Richard, and group of friends, they decided to set out in search of their fortune. Polly equipped herself with a large supply of Jaeger combinations and some Russian leather boots. Just before they left, however, Will was recalled to the family business in the Sandwich Islands. There were, he wrote to his wife, just as many opportunities there, and the weather was better, too. Would she join him there instead?

Polly's heart was set on the Klondyke, however, even if it meant the end of her marriage. 'The North Star, my lodestar, beckoned me. It lured me onwards. My whole being cried out to follow it. Miserable and heartbroken as I was, I could not turn back.'

She wrote her farewells to Will and was never to see him again. Her two small sons were in the care of relatives in Chicago – there were no further barriers. In June 1898, she set out from Seattle with her brother and a team of six to steam the 1000 miles to Skagway. The ship was greeted at the dock by a painted, feathered and ruffled lady – one of the 'lilies of the field', and by Soapy Smith, the local desperado. The men pitched their tents while she, a lady, was given a tiny shanty. Ahead of them lay a 42-mile walk over the 3000-foot ice-bound Chilkoot Pass, which would lead them down to Lake Bennett. Crossing the Chilkoot was hell, especially dressed as Polly was in full bloomers, buckram collar and tightly boned corset. After a particularly painful fall in the snow, her brother, exasperated at her apparent weakness, called out, 'For God's sake buck up and be a man!'

Once over the Pass and in Canada, Polly met up with a smartly dressed lady in raincape and tweed hat – *The Times'* colonial editor. Eventually the party reached Dawson, where the Klondyke flows into the Yukon, and there they found a makeshift city of tents, shanties and log cabins. They started to build a log house, and Polly at last had the opportunity to produce the silver, the linen table napkins and the bolt of cretonne she had brought all the way from Chicago.

The winter closed in and with it came the terrible realization that she was pregnant – out on the Yukon, without a husband and far from family or help. The local priest could provide a bed and the services of a doctor in his hospital – at a cost of $1000. Unable to find that sort of money, she gave birth to her third son alone in her log cabin. She was thirty-three. Dawson at that time was a town on the edge of the world, where a gambler could lose $5000 at a game of stud poker and a girl could roll a man and get $250 for nothing. The saloons were peopled by women like Diamond Tooth Gertie, Lime Juice Lil and Spanish Jeanette, and they all dropped in to admire the fatherless baby laid in a cradle made from a packing case. The table napkins had long since been sewn up into baby clothes. Months later, her father turned up to bring her home, on the understanding that she would never return to the wandering Will.

There was no danger of that – her short taste of freedom had been so delicious that after only a few months of living in her parents' comfortable home she once again felt a yearning for the hard but satisfying life of the Yukon. 'What I wanted was not shelter and safety but liberty and opportunity.' She returned to Dawson, went into partnership with a couple of mill owners and married a local solicitor with political leanings, George Black. At the age of seventy, when other old ladies are thinking of settling down to a 'sunset life' of knitting, she got herself elected to the Canadian House of Commons, only the second woman ever to do so.

The idea of the dutiful wife accepting without question the

Lady Mary Wortley Montagu

Lady Hester Stanhope enjoying eastern hospitality

Alexine Tinné at her house in Algeria

M. S. BLANCHARD celebre aeronauta
al momento del volo...

May French Sheldon goes calling in Africa

Madame Blanchard,
he celebrated aeronaut

Fanny Workman remains
dignified in difficult
circumstances

Alexandra David-Neel with Yongden

Mary Kingsley

Margaret Fountaine

Beatrix Bulstrode astride a particularly
motheaten camel in Mongolia

Isabelle Eberhardt

Amy Johnson and Amelia Earhart, pioneers of the sky

Ann Davison

Gertrude Bell outside her tent at Babylon

Christina Dodwell in conversation

Arlene Blum

Dervla Murphy

Bettina Selby

plans of her husband was taken to its limits when Ella Wallace, living in Montreal, received a telegram in April 1938: 'If you wish to join me at Cape Dorset this summer for two years I shall be pleased. Think well. Fools rush in. Charge expenses to me with Hudson's Bay and Company. Extra clothes etc unnecessary. I shall not be able to receive a reply. Tom Manning.' For reply, she bought a ticket on the only boat going north that year.

Tom Manning was leading a British/Canadian Arctic expedition and was making a study of fish and geese in the region. Ella married him at Cape Dorset with a Hudson's Bay employee John Buchan, now Lord Tweedsmuir, as best man. Tom borrowed a wedding coat from an Inuit friend and the brass wedding ring was forged from an engine fitting. The honeymoon bed – Tom, after all, had not known whether or not Ella would be on the boat – consisted of two sleeping bags ripped up to make a single one and topped by an evil-smelling deerskin.

There had been some uncertainty as to whether a woman could, in fact, join the expedition. The Arctic, it was felt, was no place for a woman – a white woman, that is. In the end, a compromise was reached. Ella could stay and do some survey work for the Canadian Geodetic Service. Tom had prepared her for life in the Arctic but, as always, the reality was another thing altogether.

Before setting out on their honeymoon trip – a journey up the west coast of Baffin Island – Ella had to sew up shoes, mitts and sleeping bags from caribou skins; the caribou steaks, they ate. Ella noted the Inuit women chewing the shoes to soften them up after the hard night's freezing, but though she tried it herself she found the taste totally unpalatable. For the first few months of the expedition, they were accompanied by an Inuit helper, but from then on they were alone, without radio or plane contact. Their snowhouse often melted and dripped and had to be patched with bits of paper which themselves became saturated. Night closed in at 3 p.m. and temperatures could drop to minus forty. It took two or three hours to melt a day's supply of water, and a shortage of seal oil meant that fires could only be lit at certain times. Copies of *The Times*, years old, were read with avid attention as they ate their way through a monotonous diet of jam, milk and Bovril.

From the time we broke camp in the morning – we usually got off at half past eight with the first glimmer of light – until we were within the snowhouse at night, we were enveloped by a thick milky gloom of frost crystals. Sometimes, it was clear enough to distinguish between snow and ice and sky and the flat, unvarying horizon [which] swept around us in a great empty circle; then the mist would close about us, limiting visibility to a few yards, shrouding and hemming us in in an impenetrable veil of frost.

*　　　　*　　　　*

As women emerged in increasing numbers from their cages, they could be heard to question and to query the hitherto accepted dictums of the dominant sex. Women have no automatic response to the group, no unquestioning loyalty to an emblem. If the Light Brigade had consisted of women there might never have been a Charge. To the confusion of men used to having their orders obeyed, women have often demanded to know the reason why. '. . . men . . . do tend to accept orders in an emergency and get on with whatever they are told to do to solve the particular problem at the time. Girls (*sic*) tend to need reasons for doing things. They seem to have this need to discuss what it is they have to do before they actually do it . . .' One can only sympathize with the army-trained expedition leader who found himself mystified by this female demand for a rationale.

The phenomenon of the woman traveller following wherever her man may lead is not one that we are likely to encounter today and it is significant that when women lead women, the emphasis shifts from autocracy to democracy. Women on the whole tend towards cooperation rather than competition and the women's movement has been instrumental in developing those skills by which women give each other support: the sharing of concerns, the practical assistance and, above all, the talking through of problems. Such exchanges, which are central to women's philosophy of mutual self-help, are sometimes dismissed by men as idle chatter, gossip and women's talk – real men don't do it.

As we have seen, the very strength of the US Annapurna expedition – the determination of its members to discuss their difficulties – proved to be a major headache for its leader. A scientist by profession, Arlene Blum was used to sifting through every bit of evidence before reaching a conclusion and with ten members all wanting to make a contribution, there was plenty of evidence to be sifted. A further difficulty was the way in which she, as leader, felt herself isolated by the democratic structure of the group. Even before the team left the States, her position was challenged by an older woman and though she survived the challenge, she found her decisions constantly called into question. Democracy, she found, is easier to preach than to practise. 'Although my upbringing and experience had taught me to be moderate and soothing, I was learning the hard way that these traits are not always compatible with effective leadership.'

The problems of leadership are no less difficult when the group consists of only two, for the difficulty lies not with the size of the group but with the fact that women are unaccustomed to being in positions of authority.

Wildlife film-maker Cindy Buxton set off for the islands of the South Atlantic accompanied by her assistant, Annie Price. Sub-zero temperatures were aggravated by chilling winds blowing off the glaciers, making filming at times almost impossible. Cramped together in a small hut measuring twelve feet by ten, the two women had only one another for company and at times that was one too many. Their personalities scraped against each other like chalk on a blackboard and some *modus vivendi* had to be worked out if the film were to be completed.

Cindy Buxton is a forthright, independent-minded person whose exemplary good manners would never allow her to behave in a manner other than courteous. Yet, with Annie, isolated both geographically and by her position as leader, she found herself facing the same problem as Arlene Blum: how to impose her will on another woman without being despotic. The American climber had a declared commitment to women and had used the services of a clinical psychologist to help in planning and guiding group discussions and in analyzing their possible responses to stress. To Cindy Buxton, the feminist issue is of no specific importance and she chose to rely simply upon her own common sense and her determination to get the film finished. Her unfamiliar role presented problems for both of them for she and Annie had been friends since their convent schooldays. In the one and only confrontation they had, Annie was confused. Was Cindy friend, partner or employer? She was soon to find out:

'We both glared at each other, rigid with anger. After a few moments, Annie silently and somewhat dejectedly crossed the tussock grass till she was standing in front of me and then we had the real row – no holds barred . . . I don't think we spoke to each other much for the rest of that day. I'd never had to give anyone orders before and I had to learn how to do it with grace.'

It was one solution to a difficult problem. Later, on South Georgia, they found themselves united by the threat of hostile Argentinians who chose that year to land on the other side of the ice-bound, desolate island.

CHAPTER 8

❖❖❖

A Question of Duty

The heavy mantle of duty has lain upon the shoulders of women throughout the ages. Daughters, wives or mothers, they have each served their time. Moulded by society to be the carers, they have looked after children in their infancy, parents in their old age and husbands throughout their marriage. But what gaiety breaks out when, released from these responsibilities, they cast off the cloak of duty and set out into the bright day. 'Just off,' wrote Mary Kingsley, 'to skylark and enjoy myself in Africa.'

Mary Kingsley belongs to that group of women travellers – the unmarried daughter caring for her parents – whose years of enforced imprisonment were like a secret granary of ambition in which were stored, year after year, the hopes and longings for another existence. But before we look at the dutiful daughters, we might spare some time for the women travellers who, in their middle years, decide that there must be more to life than marriage.

After twenty years of matrimony and after bearing him fourteen children, Margery Kempe sat down under a tree one midsummer's day, in 1413 to be precise, and told her husband John she had had enough. Henceforth, she intended to lead a life of amazing sanctity. There would be rigorous fasting, no sex and a pilgrimage to Jerusalem. Aghast, John played for time. Could they, he wondered craftily, continue to occupy the same bed if he promised not to bother her? The answer was a firm no and to make it absolutely clear, she put on the widow's ring of celibacy, donned a white cloak and set off on her marvellous adventure in which she was helped across the Alps by an Irishman with a crooked back, guided round the Mount of Temptation by a kindly Saracen and subjected to thrilling visions of 'white things before the eyes, flying thickly all about her on every side, bright lights by day and night'. During her two-year journey to Jerusalem, she stopped off in Rome for a

149

few months, staying wherever she could find a bed, taking a nursing job to pay her way – an early hitchhiker, living on her wits.

What woman could settle back into the humdrum routine of marriage after excitements such as those? Not Margery, certainly. Like her Victorian sisters who were to follow, she conveniently fell ill as soon as she got back to England. Dying of boredom perhaps – or trying to manufacture an excuse for setting off on another pilgrimage? Whatever the illness, she was off again, this time to Santiago de Compostela.

Hers is the first record we have of the women – and there have been many – who realize that they have reached a point in their lives when neither their husbands nor their children need them. It is a time for dusting out the mind, shifting round the furniture of a marriage, and taking a look at life from a different window. Change is the only answer. It is a strategy that has been used by women throughout the ages.

In 1665, at the age of eighteen, Maria Merian married. Twenty years later, dissatisfied with the whole structure of her life, she reverted to her unmarried name, left her husband and, taking her two young daughters, went to live in a commune where she pursued her career as a noted entomological artist. At the age of fifty-two, she set out on the perilous sea-journey to Surinam.

The unrest and the need to push back the boundaries of the narrow, female world has not been confined to the matron; indeed the frustration felt by the single Victorian woman was every bit as great as that of her married sister. Mary Taylor, energetic and un-married, found life in England unsatisfying and without future, and finally set off in 1844 to spend some time in Wellington, New Zealand. Her friend and confidante, Charlotte Brontë, was mysti-fied, not so much by the going but by the destination: 'Mary has made up her mind she cannot and will not be a governess, a teacher, a milliner, a bonnet-maker nor a housemaid,' she wrote. 'She sees no means of obtaining employment she would like in England, so she is leaving it. I counselled her to go to France likewise and stay a year before she decided on this strange, unlikely-sounding plan of going to New Zealand . . .' In Wellington, ironically, Mary Taylor was to lead a life not very different from that which she might have led in England, but at least it was one of her own choice.

Other mid-life crises propelled women towards travelling, sometimes in desperation, sometimes in search of solace. Beatrix Bulstrode, the daughter of a clergyman, married a doctor who died in 1911. Two years later, she set out to explore Mongolia. A photograph of the time shows her resplendent in long skirt and formal hat, sitting on top of what appears to be the most motheaten camel in the land. Not surprisingly, for the Mongolians were rebelling against the Chinese at the time, she was refused a passport to travel in the area. She was undeterred; indeed, if anything, more determined than ever to reach her destination. She set out by train from Pekin to travel round the back way, via Siberia, to Urga, exchanging her train for a little two-wheeled horse-drawn contrivance known as a Pekin cart. Such undertakings cannot progress without excitement and she was almost immediately imprisoned by an unscrupulous museum keeper who saw what he thought was an opportunity to make some easy money from the foreign lady. This lady, being the sort she was, however, escaped by devious means – to be greeted by her terrified servant: 'Mississee, make talkee one bad man shutee up – Chlist!' Beatrice commented with equanimity: 'I'm afraid that he believed this to be quite a polite expression of amazement.'

On the train she travelled second-class in order to meet as many people as possible. She was making the journey, she said, to 'revert awhile to the primitive'. Using chopsticks, she said, was rather like playing golf – largely a game of chance and temperament – and the local food she found a trial, objecting to the practice of eating from a bowl which had previously been 'wiped out by the fingers of some dirty old woman who the moment before had been employed in feeding the fire with the horse or camel droppings'.

She met up with an Englishman from the Chinese Maritime Customs Service who, like her, wanted to see what was happening in the warring areas, and they continued on together, she ready for every eventuality: 'Underneath my Burberry I slung the Mauser pistol and a large Colt revolver.' These she wisely concealed in a jug which she topped up with walnuts when going through customs.

She noted the low status of Mongolian women: '. . . if anything in the life of the country can be called drudgery at all, it certainly falls to the lot of the women', though she noted also that youth had its compensations: 'What they do not know about flirtation is not worth knowing and the young woman who is unable to attract two or three lovers to her side is, they say, generally looked down upon.'

She was a formidable woman and not one to argue with; one Chinese gentleman who chose to do so found himself grabbed by his pigtail: '. . . I administered the severest chastisement I have ever given, boxing his ears soundly several times. The crucial question had arisen. Was I to lose face or was he?' The outcome could never have been in doubt. All in all, it was a memorable journey made even more so by the fact that although she found Edward Gull, her travelling companion, a 'peppery little man', she enjoyed his company enough to marry him later.

Agnes Deans Cameron, born in British Colombia in 1863, never married and led a vigorous life as a schoolteacher, but after twenty-five years of it she felt she wanted that little extra that life had to offer. The Thomas Cook man in Chicago was unable to help: 'Well, Miss Cameron, I guess you've got us. Cook's have no schedule to the Arctic.' So she spent two years planning and saving for the 10,000-mile round trip from Chicago up through Winnipeg, along the delta of the McKenzie River to the Arctic and back home again, a journey which lasted six months. Agnes was a no-nonsense lady – hair pulled back, Mountie hat plonked on top, she dressed in a long skirt and many-pocketed safari jacket.

One sunny May day in 1909 she set off with tent, typewriter, cameras (with film wrapped in oilcloth), tin wash basin and her young niece for company. They stopped off at Winnipeg to purchase a hatchet and a copper kettle before boarding a train northwards, Agnes yelling exultantly, 'All aboard for the Arctic Ocean!' The going was rough – only twelve years had passed since the Klondyke Rush and accommodation, when they were lucky to find any, was usually in log huts, the 'Waldorf Astorias of the wilderness'. At other times the excitement and beauty was almost too great: '. . . it is too wonderful a night to sleep.' Their travelling companions were traders going up to the Hudson Bay and missioners returning to their flock. Shooting the rapids was dangerous but thrilling, the boat beneath them like 'an elephant drawing his feet together to take a water fence'. She travelled, she said, 'for fun' but also 'to come near to the people, our fellow Britons. We want to see what they are doing, these Trail-Blazers of Commerce.'

In fact, Agnes Cameron was far more interested in what had gone before, carefully recording the almost unbelievable stories she was told of the terrible winter of 1841 when, driven by desperation and starvation, women apparently deserted even their children, and families were reduced to eating one another. She heard of women far more daring than she who had travelled the icy wastes on their own: an Indian woman who made a solitary thirteen-day trek on snow-shoes, her only source of heat and life the small fire she managed to keep alive in the kettle she carried with her; Mrs Ray who travelled by dog-sled from Hudson Bay to Winnipeg with her children in order to put them into school there – her husband, a fur trader, was unable to leave his post. She watched children playing football with a walrus bladder and noted that babies, at the age of two, were weaned off the breast straight onto a pipe. (Beatrix Bulstrode observed Mongolian babies happily puffing away at the age of one.) She found seal's brain 'delicious' and enjoyed too raw entrails 'which our hostess draws through her fingers yard by yard in pure anticipatory delight, each guest being presented with two or three inches of the ribbon-like *pièce de resistance*.' A reindeer parasite eaten either raw or cooked was found to be a 'mellifluous maggot'. At one wedding she danced the Red River Jig, but she found it less a musical event than an endurance test. As always with such women, the really exciting moments are played down: when she encountered a grey wolf she found he had no yawning maw, no bloodshot eyes; he was just a creature who turned tail and left. The trek northwards was not a route often travelled by women and in fact she was the first white woman to get to Fort Rae on Great Slave Lake. She did, however, meet a few others *en route*: at a mission station there was Sister Thomas of Canterbury who climbed a ladder to wave goodbye with a table-cloth; and at Fort McMurray, the young Miss Gordon, the only white woman for five hundred miles, plying her fur trade among the Indians. Up in the Arctic Circle, she unexpectedly found a few brave and indomitable pioneers growing potatoes, cabbages and turnips.

Her journey was packed with adventure, and her account of it with warmth, for she was motivated by both curiosity and compassion. Three years after her return she died, at the age of forty-nine.

Much more recently, women like Bettina Selby, Christian Miller and Sabina Shalom have absented themselves from their marriages, commuting temporarily into the unknown. At forty-seven, Bettina Selby packed a slow-burning candle, safety pins, two water bottles and a few other things into her saddle bag and set off on the journey which for many years she had promised herself to make: 'The family all knew I would go. It had been talked about for years – that I would cycle to India one day. When a convenient moment presented itself – between teaching jobs – I sold the car, bought the bike and went. I wasn't running away from domesticity and making a feminist point. I was simply impelled, pursued by an idea which I had held for a long time. It just wouldn't go away.'

When Christian Miller decided to ride across America, east to west, on her folding bike, she was fifty-seven. Her daughters were grown up and could manage without her. The journey was prompted not so much by the fact that they no longer needed her as by the fact that she needed to get away from them. And she had spent the previous seven years nursing her mother through an illness from which she had recently died, and wanted time to be alone, to reassess and readjust.

'I'd travelled quite a lot, even right round the world a few times, but it had always been civilized travelling. This time, I wanted to get lost, so lost that no one and nothing could reach me, neither phone calls nor business letters. If I'd been younger, I'd have gone somewhere like Tibet but as it was, I chose America because I knew I could get lost in it . . . And I chose to go by bike because it meant I could see literally every inch of the way.'

She is a small woman, gentle but determined. So determined, in fact, that when she landed on the East Coast with her bike, she actually cycled eastwards at first, so that she could then turn round and begin the journey proper from the water's edge. She chose the east–west direction so that she might follow the route taken by the early settlers. Being a lone cyclist and a woman presented no particular problems. Like many solo travellers, it was the cities rather than the wide open spaces that prompted in her feelings of loneliness. The sensation of oneness with nature was lost. In the big cities, too, she sometimes felt fear – the fear of violence.

Christian Miller took nearly six months to cycle across America, sleeping in her tiny tent at the side of the road when needs be, or treating herself to a bit of luxury from time to time by staying in a hotel. Eventually, she reached the Pacific Ocean. Beyond lay Hawaii but she had come to journey's end. She had no need to travel any further. She was ready to go home.

*   *   *

If we can spare some thought for women who feel themselves trapped in the doldrums of the middle years, we can perhaps feel even greater sympathy for those women for whom the choice of marriage, let alone escape from it, rarely presented itself – those single women who, in a Victorian era which set such store by the security and respectability of marriage, were pitied if not actually despised.

It is significant that these women travellers, with minds hungry for knowledge, took mental sustenance from their fathers who were often their only contact with the outside world. And in some instances, the father's unrealized ambitions to write lived on through the daughter, whose own travel writings formed a final rounding-off of the relationship.

'My father,' said Marianne North, 'was the one idol and friend of my life.' As a child – she was born in 1830 – he used to take her with him on rides about the countryside: '. . . plunging into the forests, over hills and valleys where we met pretty roe deer, hares or foxes and [where we] gathered great bunches of lily of the valley . . . so calm and peaceful.' Hers was a gentle, untroubled childhood. Her father was MP for Hastings in the days when a man could be elected to Parliament by 'ten Freemen one of whom was himself'.

In 1847, he took the family travelling round Europe for three years during which Marianne took singing lessons, listened to Mozart, floated peacefully up the Elbe and travelled by slow train to Prague – an idyllic youth. When she was twenty-five, her mother, on her deathbed, 'made me promise never to leave my father'. It was a promise to which she kept faithfully. First her brother married, then her sister, leaving her father as the centre of her life. Frail and infirm, his deafness meant he could hear no one but her – or so he would have her believe. All around, she heard her identity confirmed in her role of dutiful daughter. 'The one strong, passionate feeling of her life,' said her sister, 'had been her love for her father.' But throughout those years, she had nurtured another passionate interest, one which could have no real expression until she was free to travel and explore the world. As a child, she had persuaded strange fungi to grow in jars in her room – until the appalling smells had revealed their presence to the rest of the household. Later, she perfected her drawing skills by going to Kew to sketch the many rare trees and plants brought back by travellers and explorers. But it wasn't until her father's death in 1869 that she felt free to travel. His death had left her devastated – ' "Come and give me a kiss," he had said, "I am only going to sleep." He never woke again and left me indeed alone . . . I left the house at Hastings for ever . . .'

Two years later, at the age of forty-one, she set out to travel to America where she was amazed to meet a female reporter, a black politician and a woman who had been divorced eight times. Astounding as these strange beings were, they were nothing to the marvellous plants she discovered on her travels through Japan, the West Indies, Java and the Himalayas – to name only a few of the places this splendid woman visited. So famous did she become as a traveller that it was she who was invited to tea in London with two other illustrious travellers, Isabella Bird Bishop and Constance Cumming-Gordon when the offending remark about 'three globe-trotteresses' was made. Once free from the heavy duty imposed upon her by her mother, Marianne North pursued her work with determination, giving to it all the energy she had lavished upon her father during those many years of caring for him.

Two years after Marianne North's death, Mary Kingsley found herself freed from a similar bond. Up to the age of thirty, she had led a life of exemplary familial devotion, caring first for her parents and then for her brother. During her childhood, she had seen her father only intermittently for he was frequently away, employed as companion/physician first to the Earl of Pembroke and then to Lord Dunraven. His sporadic returns were marked by the rows which suddenly erupted, precipitated no doubt by his low tolerance of domestic responsibilities. He brought to Mary's childhood, however, the news that the world beyond was a thing of wonder, as she listened to his stories of storms in the Mediterranean, of sailing in the South Seas, of hunting with Buffalo Bill, of his visits to Cape Colony, to Newfoundland and to Japan. He lived in a world of shipwrecks and cannibals, and he returned to England each year with an increasing volume of notes which one day he planned to turn into a book.

Despite these stories, his frequent absences from home meant that as a small girl Mary hardly knew her father, but in adolescence she took on the job of sorting through the notebooks, collecting and annotating his anthropological researches and pursuing the subject herself the better to be able to do her work. Although two thousand pounds were spent on her younger brother's education at Cambridge, it was not thought worth spending anything on Mary's, apart from some private German lessons which would help her with her father's work.

Mary Kingsley had led a lonely life. From an early age, she had been required to be self-reliant and resourceful. If something went wrong in the house, she had to mend it, flipping through the pages of the *English Mechanic* to find out how to do it. She was the epitome of the unmarried daughter, at the beck and call of others to such an extent that she felt ill at ease if not performing a service for someone. '. . . I always feel I have no right to associate with people,' she said, 'unless there is something the matter with them.' With her father away for such long stretches, she became her mother's 'chief officer' and on his return, her father's 'underworker'. One cannot but feel sympathy for this slim, pale young girl, toiling away in the service of others, stealing whatever moments she could to have a quiet read, working her solitary, unguided way through Huxley and Darwin.

When, after twenty years of roving the earth, her father came back for good, it was to a home organized and managed by Mary, for her mother, broken under the strain of poverty and marriage to a frequently absent husband, had lapsed into a state of mental malaise. To Mary had fallen also the job of looking after her brother, who showed signs, if not of illness, at least of being 'delicate'. It was not an altogether unhappy household, however, for her father's personality and entertaining talk enlivened it, even in his declining years.

Mary continued with her tasks, both domestic and secretarial, but the first increasingly took precedence over the second. As they aged, her parents made more claims on her time and nursing skills. Her mother was a 'cruelly exacting invalid', she said, and imprisoned in the family house, even the immediate world of Cambridge, where they lived, must have seemed far away and unattainable. In 1892, when she was thirty, during an unaccustomed break from the drudgery of home, a telegram summoned her back with the news of her mother's death. Within six weeks, her father too had died.

With no image of herself other than that of housekeeper and nursemaid, she took on the task of caring for her brother Charles. 'I have always been the doer of odd jobs and lived in the joys, sorrows and worries of other people,' she wrote. When he decided to travel to the East, her moment of freedom had arrived and she embraced it with fortitude and courage. She found herself 'for the first time in my life . . . in possession of five or six months which were not heavily forestalled.'

If the long years of loneliness and service could be seen as a period of apprenticeship, then, in retrospect, they could be invested with some meaning:

> It was years of work and watching and anxiety, a narrower life in home interests than ever and a more hopelessly depressing one for it was a long, losing fight with death all the time. And then, when the fight was lost, when there were no more odd jobs anyone wanted me to do at home, I, out of my life in books, found something to do that my father had cared for, something for which I had been taught German, so that I could do for him odd jobs in it. It was the study of early religion and law and for it I had to go to West Africa.

With the £8000 legacy left to her by her parents, she set about planning her journey.

Mary Kingsley had been her father's amanuensis, her mother's constant companion, and had been forced to live in her brother's shadow. She had reason to feel aggrieved at the way in which she had been called upon to sacrifice her precious years of youth in the service of others, yet hidden within the chrysalis was a spirit whose shining generosity and infectious humour has still the power to dazzle even from the printed page.

Maiden ladies, spinsters, unmarried daughters – the negative image of the single woman has faded somewhat since then but the role of dutiful daughter still remains for those women called upon to fill it.

It is an indication of her tremendous powers of endurance that someone like Dervla Murphy could act so ruthlessly – and so wisely – in order to survive the exacting demands of her invalid mother. For as long as she could remember, her mother had been an invalid, confined to a bath chair. Though limited physically, she was nevertheless a warm and invigorating woman who during her younger and relatively healthy years stimulated her daughter's curiosity and encouraged her to explore the world on her bike, on journeys which took her to Germany, England and Spain. It was only in later years that illness turned her mother into a querulous tyrant who sought to keep for herself every precious moment of her daughter's time.

An only child, the whole burden of caring for her parents fell on Dervla and she tried to devise a pattern of living that would allow her to perform her duties with honour and generosity but within which she could hold safe her own, individual soul. For a woman to whom freedom of the spirit is as vital as physical freedom, it was a difficult task. From her father, a librarian, she had inherited her love of books and the household chores were often performed while reading, with a book propped up on the table or draining board. Her father was something of a scholar but his ambition to be a writer remained unfulfilled, a continuing source of disappointment to him as the rejection slips piled up. When, at the age of sixty, he fell ill, she nursed both parents, surviving on little more than whiskey and cigarettes until his death.

It was the next eighteen months of caring for her mother that were to take their toll and when, eventually, the task became too much for her, she left to work for six back-breaking weeks on a

German farm where thoughts of home and her abandoned mother were dulled by the welcome drug of exhaustion. Later, after her mother's death, she thought about her motive in forsaking her at that time: 'If I wished to lacerate myself I could argue, plausibly, that I killed her by deserting her that August. But if this is so, I did it under the guidance of my own instinct of self-preservation. Jungle law operated. One of us had to be sacrificed and the fittest survived.'

Once released from her duties, the feeling of liberty, she wrote, ran through her body like a mild electric shock. She was at last free to set out on the journey the dream of which had been stored in her heart since she was ten. From the long years of caring and serving, she drew forth the iron will that had been forged, tempered and honed on the love that existed between herself and her parents. It was this will, fuelled by a slowly uncoiling spring of energy, that took her through snowbound forests and across raging torrents to her longed-for destination – India.

In publishing her account of these last anguished years, she was aware that she was following behind the ghost of her father:

> Walking through St James's Park, I thought of all my father's rejected novels – all the years of work, hope, disappointment – a cycle of frustration endured without bitterness... And so, on that sunny June day by the duck-ponds, the acceptance of my first book seemed less a personal triumph than the fulfilment of an obligation to my parents.

There are many women who hold in the palm of their hand the key to the world. Unseen, it lies within the tight knot of their clenched fist – a fist which is often clenched in fear – fear of the unknown, of truth or of pain. But most of all, there is the binding fear of what the key represents – the knowledge that, above all else, the naked will to survive supersedes the needs of others.

Once a traveller has found the courage to acknowledge that, then the fist uncurls and the world awaits.

CHAPTER 9

◆●◆

Escape or Compromise?

'I would gladly be as you are,' Jane Digby wrote to her mother, 'but I cannot change my nature. I am different. How different I hardly realized.'

She had returned briefly to England in 1856 at the age of forty-nine. It was nearly twenty years since she had last visited the country that was once home. The grim and inhospitable climate was in sharp contrast to her own feelings, for she had recently fallen in love and was missing not only her Arab husband, Medjuel, but also the warmth and brightness of Syria. As she celebrated her fiftieth birthday in England she expressed amazement at the new joy she felt: 'Here I am still with a beating and burning heart.'

She had very little chance of regaining the approval of her family, however, for she had cut the ties irrevocably after the scandal of her youth. In a society where pretence and outward appearance counted for more than the honest searching of the soul, she had had little choice but to leave. Now back in England to visit her ageing mother, the subject of her recent marriage to an Arab sheik was carefully avoided. The plea to her mother for understanding was as sad as it was pointless, for they lived in two different worlds. When the time came for Jane to make what would be her last farewell to England, her mother remarked that it was such a pity she had to go before the Boat Race.

Her departure from England this time was not a flight into the unknown but a joyous return to the land and the husband that between them offered the happiness she had spent a lifetime searching for. So pleased was she to be returning to Syria that she stopped off in Paris to buy a piano, some books, and a selection of gifts for her adopted Bedouin family.

Forty years earlier, Lady Hester Stanhope, equally desperate, had set out to search for a new and more exciting life beyond

England's restraining shores. Did these women carry with them a sense of regret that they had to abandon family and home in order to live the sort of life they craved? Jane Digby certainly did, for though she had spent thirty years searching for love and happiness she still hankered after a kind, understanding word from her mother. It was never forthcoming.

By the end of the nineteenth century, things had changed a little. Where before the only hope lay in escape, it was now no longer necessary for women travellers to cut the umbilical cord with such finality. Compromise was possible and Victorian women could now come and go; this they did, often in the company of their husbands, for travelling was something that could be shared.

The fact that family life might suffer a little from these jaunts, that children might have to manage without dear Mama and Papa for months on end, did not cause undue concern despite the emphasis laid on family life, for the rich and the eccentric can usually manage to do as they wish.

Lady Anne Blunt, as we have seen, felt no compunction in leaving her daughter with a former mistress of her husband's, while she went off with Wilfred for frequent sojourns in Arabia. For Fanny Workman, equally, there was no conflict between the needs of her young daughter and her own desire to travel – she simply put the girl in a boarding school and took off with her husband first around Europe and later to the Himalayas. In Fanny's many books, there is no mention of the girl and it came as a great surprise to Fanny's friends to learn of her daughter's existence.

The idea of maternal bonding was not then invested with the same importance as it is today and it is worth noting that several travellers, among them Alexandra David-Neel and Freya Stark, had relatively unhappy childhoods. Ella Maillart and Sheila Scott both felt lonely during their early years, when they were frequently left to their own devices, but feel that this experience gave them a degree of independence which they might not have gained had they been the focus of their parents' attention. They had been forced to learn the skills of survival from a very early age. It is significant also that none of these women had children: 'Looking after myself is responsibility enough,' said Ella Maillart.

Some women travellers, of course, make sure that the opportunities for marriage which arise are inappropriate.

Hester Stanhope, though she took a young, energetic and ador-ing lover as soon as she had left England, insisted from the start that they should never marry. The difference in their ages – she was in her mid-thirties, he in his twenties – would create problems, she felt. It must also have occurred to her that it would be unwise to tie herself down to one of the very institutions from which she had fled. Her male attire, pipe-smoking and love of horse-riding suggest that she might have found the duties of motherhood ex-tremely irksome. She did not see herself as a mother; indeed, she had no one to model herself on for her own mother died when she was very small, and she had never been close to her stepmother.

Isabella Bird Bishop too rode away from the possibility of marriage after she had formed an unorthodox relationship with Jim Nugent, a dangerous and violent frontiersman whose intelligence intrigued her and who could sing as good a song as he could write a poem. He charmed her with his wild ways, and despite his strange, battle-torn features, or maybe because of them, she fell for him: 'One eye was entirely gone, and the loss made one side of the face repulsive, while the other might have been modelled in marble. "Desperado" was written in large letters all over him.' But, despite that, 'his manner was that of a chivalrous gentleman, his accent refined, and his language easy and elegant.'

Jim, always on good behaviour when in the company of so obvious a lady as Isabella, eventually lost his composure and de-clared his admiration for her. It was, he said, killing him. What was a respectable woman to do? Here she was, at forty-one, far from the sobering influence of her Victorian home, in danger of falling for the seductive talk of a trouble-shooting Irishman. 'I was terrified', she wrote home. 'He is a man any woman might love but no sane woman would marry.' And there, nestling in the heart of this Victorian lady, was the key to her own survival. For above all else, Isabella was a sane woman.

It was not that she wasn't used to tough men. She had lived in the company of trappers, settlers and miners during her months in the Rockies and her presence among them had made them 'pull themselves up'; while she had been around there had been far less 'low, mean and vulgar talk'. Jim, however, was given to black

Isabella Bird Bishop

moods which he tried to alleviate with the help of the whisky bottle and that was something which Isabella, brought up in a vicarage, could not tolerate. She had urged him to give up the drink but he had been unable to and now it was all too late. He wept, as strong men will, and Isabella was filled with sadness for she recognized the poignancy of the whole situation: 'He has excellent sense for everyone but himself, and, as I have seen in him with a single exception, a gentleness, propriety, and considerateness of manner surprising in any man, but especially so in a man associating only with rough men of the West.'

She had made up her mind, however, to keep her head and heart intact, for life with Jim would have meant staying in the Rockies and she had her sights fixed on Persia, Japan and China. So she turned away, keeping in her memory that last view of Jim with his 'golden hair yellow in the sunshine slowly leading the beautiful mare over the snowy plains back to Estes Park, equipped with the saddle on which I had ridden 800 miles'.

Back in England, she turned down a proposal of marriage from a quiet but persistent suitor, Doctor John Bishop. She still wanted to travel, and also felt that she could not abandon the faithful sister who had kept a home ready for her in Scotland whenever she chose to return to it. It wasn't until her fiftieth year and with her sister dead that she accepted the doctor's hand but even then could not help remarking, with regret, that this would mean she would be unable to make her planned visit to New Guinea. Widowed not long after, she continued to travel, embarking, at the age of seventy, on a thousand-mile trek on horseback across Morocco. Romance, marriage and bereavement could not hold her – only death.

The choices facing the woman traveller today have changed little – only the packaging is more attractive. Women are still seen as units on the baby production line and the industry of childhood, upon which so much of today's domestic economy depends, has turned parenting into a crushing duty. Love is measured by the cost of the pram, the size of the bicycle, the number of toys at the end of the Christmas bed. Faced with this reality, it is perhaps not too difficult to understand why marriage and motherhood do not figure on some women's list of priorities. Because society still favours the family, however, those women travellers who have remained childless must somehow justify themselves. We question them about their reluctance to marry and find it difficult to understand how they can manage without the prop of a partner or without the identity that comes with motherhood. In a society geared to couples, we imagine they must be lonely and wonder how they feel about growing old without a family to care for them.

Sheila Scott was married for a short time, but now lives alone in a small, neat London flat where everything is efficiently to hand :

> I can think of nothing better than being married to some-
> one whom I respect, who was my friend and who I would
> definitely enjoy going to bed with but frankly, I haven't
> had time for marriage although there have been a lot of
> men in my life. Some have stayed in my life for four or
> five years, and that in a way is like a marriage. Really,
> though, I'm leading the wrong sort of life for marriage –
> unless the man was also in the adventure field. I never
> made a definite choice not to marry, it just happened but,
> of course, once I started making record attempts then
> flying did have to come first. And finding the money was
> always a priority. You know, people always think I lead
> a glamorous life, smart clothes, hair done, make-up and
> so on, but that's the public image. I spend hours sitting
> on trains, travelling to women's groups to talk, and then
> hours back on the train again. When I was making all my
> record flights the man I was with had to put up with all
> this and I realize now how fabulous he was. I mean, I'd
> get home late at night and have to say, Well, I can't now,
> darling, I've got to be up in four hours to catch the train.

Current contraceptive methods and a greater degree of financial
independence mean that women travellers nowadays have some
choice in the matter of whether or when they have children. Once
produced, however, there is still the problem of what to do with
them. Fifty years ago, a traveller such as Naomi Mitchison could
happily set off for Russia, leaving her two-year-old in the care of a
nanny. 'Really, you needed a rest after breastfeeding a baby for six
months,' she said. You don't, of course, but it's a good excuse.

Nowadays, few mothers would breastfeed their babies for that
length of time and in any case it would be greatly frowned upon
were a mother to leave her young child in the sole care of a nanny
for any length of time, assuming of course she could afford such a
thing. Naomi Mitchison may be the last of that era.

In a manner typical of the highly individual people which most
travellers are, they find their own solutions to the baby or partner
problem, and although many say they have made no conscious

choice, for others the choice has been quite deliberate.

Dervla Murphy, determined and forthright, gave birth to a daughter without first taking the precaution of either getting married or acquiring a visible partner. Seen in the context of a conservative and rural Ireland, it was an unusual step, to say the least. Although the arrival of Rachel put a stop to her travels for a few years, the two were off together at the earliest opportunity. When Rachel was six, mother and daughter journeyed through India, the only concession to Rachel's youth being that while her mother walked, she was allowed to travel by donkey.

And though the child-conscious world shook its collective head in horror when the amazing Rosie Swale gave birth to a twelve pound son on board a boat with nothing more than a bit of string and a pair of scissors in attendance, she remained unperturbed and set off later with her two babies to sail 26,000 miles round the world in a catamaran. The experience of giving birth without benefit of modern technology later proved to be a life-saver. Thirteen years after she had sailed round the Horn with her family, Rosie returned to the Cape, making a hazardous solo trek down through Chile. Setting up camp one night, with just her horses for company, she was alarmed to hear groaning noises outside the tent. Climbing out nervously to investigate, she discovered a woman lying among some nearby bushes, about to give birth. The woman had been on her way back to her village but was obviously not going to make it. Hastily turning her tent into a delivery ward, Rosie sterilized her scissors and scrabbled around for any bits of string she could find. The baby arrived at dawn and the village, when it had been located, turned the whole joyous event into a fiesta, naming the baby – Rosie.

Rosie Swale was not the first woman to combine motherhood with adventure. As long ago as 1886, Henrietta Slocum, wife of the famous Joshua – the first person to sail solo round the world – accompanied him to South America, taking her two young sons along in the 35-foot boat. They were all later shipwrecked and only succeeded in getting back to New York when Joshua managed to fashion a canoe out of the wreckage – but that's another story. Forty years later, Julie Tambs became the first woman to give birth in a boat, first to one baby and then a second, while attempting to sail around the world. In fact, as Rosie Swale discovered, a boat is not the worst of places to raise a small child. There is no shortage of water and at times it is even warm enough to do the family wash. In the hotter zones, clothes can be minimal and nappies can be dried in the sun.

Few women travellers have expressed any deep regret at having to choose between children and travelling because their choices, after all, have been freely made. Society continues, however, to exert its pressures on women to marry and produce children and though these pressures can be more easily withstood today than they were a hundred years ago, they still leave a residue of unease at the back of the mind. Christina Dodwell acknowledges her feeling that, although they made absolutely no demands on her, she might be failing her parents by not settling down and presenting them with grandchildren. The marriage of her sister and subsequent arrival of children relieved her of what she previously felt had been an omission on her part. But while babies may be dealt with somehow or other – they have, after all, little choice in where they go or indeed how they travel – the problem of a companion is a different matter altogether.

Some women have felt it both impossible and unfair to expect a man to fit in with their lifestyle. 'I couldn't,' says Dervla Murphy, 'ask a man to sit around while I go off for months on end.' And nor could Sheila Scott. These two women, travellers and explorers in their very different ways, are certain of their priorities. A man, however companionable, would always come second and it is perhaps this attitude, so different from that of many women, conditioned as they are to finding fulfilment in marriage, that sets the woman traveller apart.

The need for separateness is an important element in her make-up – a need which would be threatened by marriage. As the traveller moves from space to space, she sees herself in many different contexts and gradually assembles the bits and pieces of her experience until she has a complete if fragile picture of her own self. It is this identity – which is both psychological and physical – which the woman traveller cherishes, for it forms the window through which she sees the world. Threaten that, and you threaten her existence.

The trouble with some men [says Sheila Scott] is that after they've known you for a while they want to change you, which is ridiculous because they met you as a pilot or an author or a mountaineer in the first place. But they very often can't compromise, although women, of course, have had to from the word go. I'd never want to change someone like that. It can't be done.

The Murphys and Scotts of this world, however flexible they like to think themselves, can rarely compromise over their essential determination to lead the sort of life they have chosen for themselves. Tough and resolute, there is nowhere else to be except out front, alone.

Other women have allowed themselves to be carried in the wake of their partners, with all the compromise this inevitably entails. Though divided by over a hundred years, Isabel Burton and Virginia Fiennes both found that being married to explorers meant only one thing: they must go too. And this decision involved personal sacrifices which less determined women would have found impossible. 'Pay, pack and follow' was Richard Burton's order to his wife when, in 1871, he was dismissed as British Consul in Damascus. It was the end of a dream and Isabel obeyed, for what else was there to do? As a teenager with a weakness for self-dramatization, Isabel Arundel had fallen in love with Burton when his fame as an explorer was at its height. To the passionate young teenager, he was a daring, attractive adventurer. Those who had met him were haunted by his dark looks and mysterious eyes – eyes that so captivated Isabel: '. . . the most remarkable part of his appearance was two large black flashing eyes, with long lashes, that pierced you through and through.'

Disguised as a beggar or as a wandering gypsy, he had hung about the bazaars of India, spying for the British Army. Later, again disguised, he had entered the forbidden city of Mecca. And later still, in 1858, he had made his way through the rain forests of Africa to uncover the secret of the Great Rift Valley: Lake Tanganyika.

Isabel, suffocated by the manners and restrictions of Victorian England, was, she knew, destined to marry him. The fact that

Captain Burton, making his dangerous way through life, was unaware of this destiny was neither here nor there. Their first brief
meeting had been at a carefully chaperoned party where they had
waltzed together and she had later declared to her sister: 'That man
will marry me.' But then he was gone – to Mecca, India, Abyssinia,
without any thought of the young Victorian girl waiting with
determination for his return. Meanwhile, she began to prepare
herself for the role of traveller's wife, doggedly learning to fence
and shoot, pitch a tent and ride astride a horse.

Many nerve-wracking years were to pass but eventually he
found her again, as she fully intended he would, and in 1861, when
he was forty and she thirty, they married, against the express
wishes of her parents who had opposed the liaison from the start.
They had wanted their daughter to marry someone better than a
bearded, wild-eyed explorer; they did not see him in the same
light as their wilful, romantic daughter: as a man who was strong
and daring, who spoke Hindustani, Persian and Arabic and who
had been touched by the mystery of the East.

The role of devoted wife was one she played with gusto, paying,
packing and following whenever she could. But the West Coast of
Africa was impossible, they told her – death for any white woman.
(Nearly fifty years later, they said the same thing to Mary Kingsley,
but then she was not a follower.) Isabel could go only as far as
Madeira for the odd rendezvous with Richard; then she must
return home to the safety of England. Later, she followed him to
the dank swamps of Brazil, playing the role of British Consul's
wife with patience and dignity. But all the while she was biding
her time, for she knew they both deserved better things.

Eventually, her hopes were fulfilled: Richard was appointed
to Damascus. It was the culmination of a lifetime of anticipation.
Since the fateful waltz at the age of nineteen she had seen no
future for herself other than one devoted to Richard, and for
twenty-nine years of marriage, until his death in 1890, she gave
herself to him completely. She had hoped for a child at first, a son,
of course, but when none appeared – Richard was away for long
stretches at a time and was often quite debilitated when he returned
– she decided it was all for the best. Human nature generally and
women in particular are adept at making do.

A hundred years after Isabel Burton dramatically resolved to follow wherever her adventurer should lead, Virginia Fiennes, a far more retiring wife, found herself accompanying her husband, Ranulph, round the world in a way that Isabel would have envied. At twenty-three, when she married Ranulph, Ginnie Fiennes hadn't been sure if she would be part of his exploring life, but within a few years she had been absorbed into the planning of the Transglobe Expedition and ended up playing a vital role as the team's radio communication link.

It was a vast undertaking for the expedition was gone for three years in all, cut off in the dark Antarctic winter for eight months and later in the Arctic for five, the radio its only contact with the outside world. Seven thousand feet up in the Antarctic base camp, she found herself assembling a kilowatt transmitter that had seventeen different components, fitting together the bits and pieces of the expedition's seven radios, and praying that the whole contraption would work. Locked in the Antarctic ice for months on end, there was no way out. Had someone fallen seriously ill, the only medical help available was via the radio link. While most travellers fear first for their own safety, Ginnie's fear was that she might let the expedition down, and that didn't bear thinking about. 'When you're travelling across Africa, perhaps through the Sahara, you can always drive a hundred miles and you'll find a phone box or you can send a telex or there'll be a local fellow who'll run with a message but in the Antarctic we were four hundred miles from anyone. No aircraft could get in for eight months and if anyone fell ill, that was it.' There was no way of knowing if the link would work until it had been fitted together. One faulty connection and the whole thing was useless.

Ginnie Fiennes is quiet and unassuming and seems surprised that anyone should think she has done something out of the ordinary. Pouring out the coffee in her neat, suburban London home, she talks so matter-of-factly about the hazards of the expedition that you feel there really isn't much to living dangerously. Her gentle self-effacing manner, however, conceals an iron will, for in marrying an explorer Ginnie Fiennes had to shuffle all her own plans to the bottom of the pack.

Had her life taken a different turn, she would have done something with children, perhaps been a teacher or run a kindergarten. One can imagine her doing that, keeping a tidy home and tending to the family pets and the garden, supervising the children's homework and organizing an annual holiday in the Dordogne. It wasn't marriage that got in the way, so much as the sort of marriage she had entered into. She and Ranulph first met when he was twelve and she was nine. Fourteen years later they were married and any thoughts she might have had about following a career of her own were discarded. Her attitude to this is stoical, a characteristic which must make her an excellent partner on an expedition.

'We haven't got any children – the expedition came at the wrong time really. My best time for having children coincided with the expedition. We kept thinking we'll be going and coming back and then we'll have children but it always got put off.' Staring down into her coffee cup, she smiles almost apologetically and adds, 'One can't have everything I suppose.'

It's a phrase she uses a lot and her clear acceptance of her subsidiary role is unusual in a world where women now strive so much to assert themselves. She had known from the start what marriage to an explorer would mean: 'If the husband comes back after being away for six months, you've got to spend all your time looking after him, helping him, making the house clean and tidy, cooking the food . . .'

They had started planning the Transglobe Expedition in 1972, eighteen months after their marriage. The idea had been Ginnie's in the first place and it was an idea that was to dominate their lives for the next ten years – seven years of planning and then the three momentous years spent crossing the world from pole to pole – the first people to do so.

> If I'd had children by mistake during the planning or during the expedition, I'd have had to withdraw, it's as simple as that. We were a very small team and we all had a great deal to do and I would have felt I was letting Ranulph down. Besides, [and here the veil slips slightly and a look of pleasure lights her face] Ran wanted me to go because he knew we work together so well. We're almost telepathic at times. He'll be out on the ice and get an idea

172

and I'll be in my hut and call him up with exactly the same idea. It's grown over the years, like a marriage, I suppose.

So seriously did Amelia Earhart treat the question of marriage that she drew up what must be a unique marriage contract; one which, like its author, was well ahead of its time. Having finally agreed at the age of thirty-two to marry her publisher, George Putnam, she presented him on their wedding morning with a document which must have shaken him a little. 'You must know my reluctance to marry,' it said, 'my feeling that I shatter thereby chances in work which mean so much to me.'

Deciding to marry when she did, just a year before her solo flight across the Atlantic, was, she felt, the most foolish thing she could do, and although she knew it might have its compensations she didn't feel like looking too far ahead. Nor did she set too much store by fidelity.

> In our life together I shall not hold you to any medieval code of faithfulness to me nor shall I consider myself bound to you similarly. If we can be honest, I think the differences which arise may be avoided. Please let us not interfere with each other's work or play nor let the world see private joys or disagreements. In this connection, I may have to keep some place where I can go to be myself now and then, for I cannot guarantee to endure at all times the confinements of even an attractive cage. I must exact a cruel promise and this is that you will let me go in a year if we find no happiness together. I will try to do my best in every way . . .

Putnam, delighted that she had finally decided to marry him, accepted her terms, writing later that it was always a matter of great wonder to him that she had agreed to the marriage. They seemed well matched: Amelia placid with a certain poised gentleness, he full of drive, eager to promote what some people felt he saw as his latest acquisition. Putnam admitted to a certain jealousy over his wife's fame and on one occasion attempted to emulate her by making the first ever flight to Bermuda which ended, as he ruefully said, in disaster.

The carefully drawn up battle lines in what Amelia called 'the kingdom of the home' seemed to ensure a degree of quiet happiness. That they were financially independent of each other helped, she thought, and she employed others to do the housework believing that it was uneconomical for her to do household tasks when there were others more skilled. In this way, she was free to do what she was best at – flying.

Putnam recalled his last sight of her as she walked out across the tarmac to her plane on that fateful day when she set out, hoping to be the first woman flier to encircle the world: 'She looked very small and feminine – a little girl seeking to do in a very large world what had not been done before.' Her letters back to him before her disappearance were full of frank affection touched by a certain wistful loneliness for, though surrounded by the flashbulbs of the world, she stood – and died – alone.

Other travellers too had to come to some agreement when the subject of marriage was discussed. When that great romantic, Jane Digby, fell in love with her Arab sheik, there had to be some compromise for Medjuel el Mesrab, as a Muslim, had the right to take up to four wives. Always courteous, however, he agreed to limit himself to one – Jane – but she never felt secure for, having already divorced another in order to marry her, might he not perhaps discard her with equal ease? It was more than her passionate and fiercely jealous nature could endure, for who knew when he might revert to his Muslim ways? They drew up a contract in which he agreed that should he take an Arab wife, he would not cause Jane distress by telling her. The British consul thought the idea preposterous and advised her that any such contract, even a marriage contract, would have no validity in English law. But to no avail. Jane accepted Medjuel's word, for this was her final and finest love.

Perhaps strangest of all marriages, however, was that of Alexandra David-Neel. Born to an unhappy union between a French journalist and his Belgian wife, Alexandra spent her childhood trying to escape from her misery. 'I craved to go beyond the garden gate,' she wrote, 'to follow the road that passed it by, and to set out for the unknown.'

She ran away from home on numerous occasions, once going

all the way to England. A small legacy from a godmother set her on the road to India and gave her a taste for the unknown but earning a living was still a priority. Finding she had a good voice, she joined the Opera Comique Touring Company, becoming their *première chanteuse*. In 1903, however, she turned to her father's profession, journalism, and while in Tunis, decided at the age of thirty-six to marry an engineer, Philippe-François Neel. It was a dismal mistake and five days after the marriage they parted for good, he sailing to the south of France and she making for Paris. Writing to her husband two months later she said: 'We have made a singular marriage, more out of malice than tenderness. It was foolish, without doubt, but it is done.'

There followed recriminations and accusations. He was suspected of having returned straightaway to his mistress. Despite this unpropitious start, the relationship continued, at a distance, until Philippe's death forty years later. It was a childless union, of course, but Alexandra had no regrets about that. Parenthood, she felt, would have merely repeated the mistakes of her mother who had given birth to the child of a man she didn't love. There had been a big age difference between her parents and they had waited sixteen years for a child to arrive. By then, the marriage was over. It was a terrible lesson but she had learnt it well. She would provide no children for Philippe. Telling him about her mother's tragic marriage she said: 'See, my friend, that which sometimes awaits those imprudent women who look to maternity for consolation from an ill-matched union.'

Instead, she became a mother of a different sort. Her companion on her arduous journey to Tibet was a young Sikkimese priest, Yongden, and she later adopted him officially as her son. It was a maternal role that did not make too many emotional demands upon her. Philippe too found an easier role to play: he became his wife's agent. During her years of absence from Europe he carefully and faithfully collected and edited the notes of her journey and sent typed copies of them on to publishers and newspapers. He looked after the renting of her house while she was away and bought furniture for it when needed. He kept and sorted all the letters she wrote to him – over 3000 pages in all. And, amazingly, it was Philippe who financed her journey to Lhasa. She was aware of the uniqueness of their relationship and wrote warmly to him at times: 'You are the best husband one could dream of, I acknowledge it without hesitation, and it is for that reason I am tormented by a situation that is extremely painful for you.'

There was nothing she could do about it, however. She could change neither herself nor the circumstances in which they both found themselves. For her, there could be no compromise.

In the introduction to her enthralling book, *My Journey to Lhasa*, published in 1927, there is no mention of the shadowy Philippe. Perhaps he was, as some critics have commented, nothing more than a meal ticket. When he died, however, she mourned: 'I am desolated . . . I have lost the best of husbands and my only friend.'

CHAPTER 10

◆◆◆

Risks and Dangers

The boy's pupils were dilated so that his shining eyes, reflections of the dark river, seemed almost black. His lips were folded inwards to control his fast breathing, for he had been running. There was sweat at the edges of his hair. His eyes, swimming with intensity, were fixed on my face. Neither of us blinked. It was very quiet.

At last my arm moved slowly to find the bright wrap. I pulled it across my body and sat up. At the same time he hunkered down with his weight resting on his calves, face towards the ground so that I could only see the top of his woolly head.

'Albert, you have been running,' I said lightly.

'Wa, yes. I like it, running.' He ran a hand down his bent face from brow to chin, as though to wash it. Then he sprang up and adopted a relaxed pose.

'I feel hot now. I like to swim.'

'Where do you swim?'

'I show you, come.' He turned away and began walking at once. I followed, tying the wrap as I went.

The part of the river he took me to was broad and deep. A shallow waterfall ran across it tumbling fast white water down smoothly worn rocks. Above the fall was a long stretch of slow flowing river overhung with pale tee trees whose graceful, leaning branches were perfectly echoed in the mirror clear water. Below, there was a wide round pool, upon which floated a sprinkling of shining bubbles, escaped from the turmoil of the fall.

'Not that one,' he said, pointing to the lower pool, 'might be croc there.'

Kicking off his black undershorts he dived in above

the waterfall. Brown ripples lapped the bank and splashed up against the root of a tree. His head appeared on the other side, the invisible oil in his hair chasing off glittering droplets in chains.

'Swim!' he called. 'Swim!'

I stepped across the few dry rocks at the top of the waterfall and as though drawn irresistibly down, allowed my body to fall into the water. Pushing away from where the stream pulled towards the edge of the fall, I lay on my back, the folds of my wrap drifting before me. It was like floating in liquid satin, feeling the caressive resistance of the water whispering at my bare back.

With a splash Albert's head appeared at my side.

'Take your dress off.'

'No.'

Unrelaxed my legs sank down and I trod water, facing him.

'Take it off. I wont do it to you.'

The dress was already half dragged off by my paddling legs. I turned away, and keeping my body under the water, unwound it and hooked it over a branch. Albert disappeared and a few moments later I felt his arms clasping me around the waist from behind. Slowly I turned round, my hands gently pressing his shoulders away. His hands were grasping my hips, pushing my upper body out of the water so that his upturned face was below me.

'Are you frighten?'

'No.'

One of my thumbs was in the dip of his collarbone. I shook my head, aware, as from a distance, that I was speaking the truth.

'No,' I said again, and it was telling him no to everything.

'Please.'

'No, let me go. Let us swim.'

His eyes were rich with his plea but he let me go, first quickly imprinting a child's kiss to one side of my mouth.

He dived and stayed under the water for a long time and
then swam upstream once strongly and back again. I got
out and retrieved my wet dress.

On the way back he was mostly silent, contemplative.
Once he said :

'What if I rape you?'

Luckily for Lucy Irvine, a present-day castaway on a desert island
off the north coast of Australia, the question from her unexpected
visitor was speculative. Or was it? There can never be any way of
knowing how a potentially dangerous moment is likely to turn
out, and all a woman can do is sigh with relief when the danger
has passed. The anger comes later.

Although rape must be considered an occupational hazard for
the woman traveller and explorer, it is a hazard that should be
kept in perspective for it is only one of many and, as Dervla
Murphy has noted in her eminently sensible way, 'Rape must be
exceedingly disagreeable yet at least one is still among those
present next morning.'

Sexual assault comes in varying degrees, making demands upon
the person which range from irritating chatter to physical attacks,
and can leave a woman either mildly amused or wildly irritated.
When the all-woman team from the United States set out to climb
Annapurna, the Sherpas passed the time by drawing phalluses in
the snow, and then watching for the women's reaction. Eventually
tiring of it, one of the women asked them to stop. 'Yeti make
pictures in the snow – not Sherpas,' they protested, as innocent
and knowing as naughty schoolboys. Any woman who has visited
Jerusalem will be familiar with the pint-sized bottom-pinchers
who ply the crowded narrow streets of the old Arab quarter and
who are far from representative of the courtesy and kindness to
be encountered among Arabs generally.

For the woman traveller, offers of fulfilment and promises of
delight are always to hand ('You come with me, I make you very
happy') and may be accompanied by extravagant claims to inside
information as to what women from particular countries like in
the way of entertainment. At Benghazi airport, alone and late at
night, Sheila Scott was suddenly cornered by a mechanic who

informed her, categorically and with intent, that 'Englishwomen like Arab kisses'.

Such hazards, however, could be more appropriately described as aggravating discomforts, on a par with fleas and sweaty clothes, which tend to pale into insignificance beside the mortal danger in which the mountaineer, the single-handed sailor or the solo flier finds herself. Of more immediate concern to any traveller are the niggling, everyday infections caught from exposure to the elements, and from moving between extremes of heat and cold. Mountaineers can find themselves short of oxygen or, failing to acclimatize, may fall victim to mountain sickness. Fliers and sailors can suffer from lack of sleep and everyone can be hit by the tummy bug, brought on by unfamiliar food or polluted water. A relatively simple thing like a toothache becomes a major setback, and as for a broken limb!

Strange insects including the malaria-carrying mosquito abound, waiting to bite. In the West Indies, there is a fly called the doctor fly: if it bites you, you have to see the doctor. In the undergrowth, leeches hang about waiting for a convenient piece of flesh to which they can attach themselves. No respecter of persons, they will go for any part of the body unwisely presented to them. 'Irene,' wrote Arlene Blum in her book about the Annapurna climb, 're-turned from the bushes shaken. While she had squatted, four slimy leeches had crawled onto her bottom. She had managed to pull them off before they could attach and begin to suck her blood, so no damage had been done except possibly to Irene's psyche.' Squat high if you have to squat, had been Irene's advice after that.

For some travellers, the obstacles they encounter have more significance than the destination for which they are heading, and each one conquered gives an exhilarating substance to the day. For others, hellbent on arriving at journey's end, the hazards they meet on the way are merely incidental. Danger in myriad forms – pirates and highwaymen, plague and disease – was ever present for the unwary traveller in past centuries: to travel at all was to court disaster. Nowadays, though most of those dangers have gone, they have been replaced by others. High-altitude flying, for instance, with its attendant discomforts of oxygen tubes and extreme cold, brings with it the danger of blacking out. The health hazards which attended the travellers of earlier days can now be largely avoided by the judicious use of drugs but the possibility of being captured by hostile, or even friendly, locals has not lessened. If anything, it has increased as politically-conscious guerrillas learn the value of hostages.

We should spare some sympathy for women travellers of the last century who risked not so much their lives as their reputations when they set off along the exciting road to freedom. A hundred years ago, they could expect to find and did indeed find themselves protected by the very fact that they were women, but there were, of course, occasions when men fell short of the high standard of behaviour demanded of them. Then, it seems, all a woman had to do was remonstrate with the uncouth fellow and he would immediately be covered with shame. In her excellent book graciously entitled *Hints to Lady Travellers at Home and Abroad*, which she wrote in 1889, Lillias Campbell Davidson advises the reader how to cope with some of the more distressing aspects of nineteenth-century travel:

> Much has been said about the danger of women, especially young women, travelling alone, of annoyance from impertinent people or obtrusive attention from travellers of the opposite sex. I can only say, that in any such case which has ever come within my personal knowledge or observation, the woman has had only herself to blame. I am quite sure that no man, however audacious, will, at all events if he be sober, venture to treat with undue familiarity or rudeness a woman, however young, who distinctly shows him by her dignity of manner and conduct that any such liberty will be an insult.

What happens if the man is not sober is obviously too awful to contemplate and if you think that when it comes to annoyances, Lillias's mind may not be dwelling on anything as crude as rape then you would be right:

> Real annoyances from fellow travellers should never
> be endured. I mean such uncalled-for breaches of polite-
> ness as smoking in a carriage not dedicated to that pastime
> when there are ladies, the use of bad language, quarrelling
> or small indulgences of that sort. A remonstrance [she
> adds kindly] will often have a good effect.

She may well have been right. Her views were shared by that
most ladylike of travellers, Margaret Fountaine. Always ready to
be courted and complimented by the numerous men upon whom
she graciously bestowed a smile, she displayed an amazing capacity
to be mortally offended should that smile be misconstrued. While
collecting butterflies in Corsica in 1893 she found herself accosted
by a wild, gypsy-looking fellow who offered to carry her basket.
Such encounters she always viewed with interest, for who knows
to what intriguing romance they might lead? It was possible that
his dark gypsy looks added a delicious thrill to what was, for an
upright English woman abroad on her own, a most improper
meeting. In any event, she allowed him to carry her basket but
soon found out that his manners did not measure up to his looks
for he made an indecorous grab at her as she was climbing over a
stile: 'What providence preserved me, as I was completely in the
power of this man, I can never tell, only that I believe there is a
special and direct protection over a pure and high-minded woman,
which no man however base can break through.'

To a man from a different culture, unused to such things, the
appearance of a lone female traveller could easily be misunderstood, even in the old days when women were ladies and men, if
they could not be gentlemen, at least knew their place. Miss
Fountaine for one seems to have been constantly warding off the
amorous attentions of strange men who seemed totally unaware
that she was protected by an impenetrable veil of purity.

Few women were as adventurous as to travel entirely on their
own; so lowly a position did the Victorian servant hold that to
describe a woman as being a solitary traveller often meant merely
that she was unaccompanied by someone of her own social class.
If she were not accompanied by a sister or a companion, she would
most probably have had a paid guide and possibly a maid. Indeed,

Lillias stipulated that 'for one or two ladies starting a riding tour alone, a groom is an absolute indispensible'.

Amazing as it may seem, when Fanny Workman set out to climb in the Karakorams with her husband, she took forty-five porters, plus another fifteen to carry supplies for the first forty-five – although by the time they had reached the mountains, most of the servants had deserted. Interestingly enough, it seems that the Americans with all their liberal democratic ideas were not as successful at managing their bearers as the British, who knew all about protocol and the class system and were able to both accommodate and turn to their own advantage the complexities of the caste system too.

Just twenty years ahead of Workman, Nina Mazuchelli, together with her husband – an army chaplain – and a friend, had set out on a pleasantly conceived trip to explore the southern Himalayas, taking with them seventy servants whose job it was to lay carpets in their tent and set the table for dinner using the correct silver and appropriate glass. They also had to look after the many cows and chickens which had been brought along to provide fresh milk and meat on the journey. Although a perfectly healthy young woman, Nina was carried by a team of porters in a special device: a reclining chair suspended from poles by leather

Nina Mazuchelli travelling in style

183

Nina, strapped into her chair, being carried up a mountain slope

straps. This system worked well until the party started up a 600-foot incline. Then she had to be strapped into a bamboo chair which was in turn strapped to the back of a porter who, bent double, carried his burden to the summit.

One cannot be too critical of Nina's way of travelling, for her clothes would have made climbing very difficult. Though crinolines had disappeared, she wore a dress with a voluminous skirt which concealed numerous petticoats, drawers and a corset. On top of it all, she wore a hat and shawl and her only concession to the fact that she was climbing a mountain, and quite a severe one at that, was to exchange her high-heeled boots for a pair of moccasins.

On this journey, Nina, though not threatened by indecorous locals, did have to face danger of a different sort: the possibility that they might not survive the sub-zero temperatures of the mountains. That was something that took them by surprise and as they climbed higher and higher the biting cold gnawed at their bones. Four thousand feet up on a desolate, treeless glacier, their faces blistered and cracked in the snow and they were forced to keep their clothes on all night. Some of the porters deserted when, panic-stricken, they realized the guides had lost their way. With eyes inflamed by snow burn, and the glare made even worse by mountain mist reflecting the snow, many of the bearers had to be led along blindfold. Nina's coiled hair tumbled down and froze solid during the night. There were many mouths to feed and inevitably, when they got lost, their food stocks began to run down. What had started out as an entertaining jaunt up to the foothills was becoming a dangerous test of survival.

Nina's husband had to use his rifle to persuade reluctant mountain villagers to part with their own rice and goats, for these were the villagers' only supply of food and were worth far more to them than the silver with which he paid for them – for, as Nina recorded piously in case we should think badly of her husband, 'we are just and generous people.' She worried endlessly too about the danger to which she had unwittingly exposed her husband's friend who was a young man with a wife and family. Should anything happen to him she would feel responsible.

The reality which Nina had faced on the mountain gave her a different perspective on the life she normally led and, in common with many other travellers, she returned to the latter with great reluctance. She didn't really look forward, she said, to going back 'to live in a house with windows in it, to return visiting cards and to toilets and morning calls and to be obliged to wear one's hair up and to look spick and span and ladylike once more'.

No doubt she spoke for all those women who succumbed to the urge to flee from the soul-destroying monotony of Victorian life and who shared Lillias's hope that it would become 'the right of every woman who has the means to achieve it – of becoming in her own unescorted and independent person, a lady traveller'.

A few years later, in 1898, another woman traveller was to make a journey towards Tibet that was to have an ending so horrific as to be almost unimaginable. Yet only a few years later she was to return to try to do what she had failed to do the first time – to reach the forbidden city of Lhasa. She was to fail again, leaving the way open for Alexandra David-Neel to be the first woman to reach this most sought-after city.

Susie Rijnhart was a young missionary doctor from Canada who set out through China with her husband Petrus, also a missionary, to bring Christianity to Tibet. Aware that the journey would be dangerous, and that the message they intended to preach could bring them suffering and persecution, that tears and even blood would undoubtedly be spilled, they remained steadfast in their mission and were so certain of its success that they brought with them their 11-month-old baby. The party also included several servants and twelve ponies. Financed by donations and savings, they took enough food to last two years, sending some along in advance on a camel caravan to various points *en route* to await their arrival.

Almost from the start, the journey was doomed. Some of the servants deserted, some of their ponies were stolen and their plans were thrown into jeopardy when they ran out of food and subsequently lost their way. Nevertheless, they kept their hearts up by celebrating the good days, like the one in June when Susie baked a special cake to celebrate the baby's first birthday. It was the last day of happiness for this ill-fated family. Soon after, two more servants deserted and five more of their ponies were stolen. Then, a month later, on a clear sunny day, 16,000 feet up on a plateau, the small boy died. His death was sudden and unexpected, due probably to the fact that his tiny lungs could not cope with the altitude. His parents kept an all-night vigil by his still, small body but Susie wrote: 'We knew we clasped in our arms only the casket which held our precious jewel.'

Next morning, with the help of the one remaining servant, they made a coffin out of a medical supply box and put the child in it together with his toys. The custom in nearby Tibet was to expose the bodies of the dead to the elements and the wolves and fearful that this might happen should the body be discovered, they laid the box in a deep grave and concealed the site with stones.

With nothing now to keep them going except their religious faith and missionary zeal, they pressed on towards Lhasa as the icy rain, piercing their faces like slivers of glass, turned to snow. At the Tibetan border, however, they were turned away and left with no alternative but to journey back through China.

Camping near the Mekong River, they were set upon by bandits who came at them with sticks and boulders, killing one horse and stealing the remainder. Fearful that they might return, Susie and Petrus spent the night in the open to be woken next day by the sound of vultures gnawing at the dead horse. For three days they travelled through deserted countryside, seeing not a soul but still sleeping in the open for fear of attack. On the third day, they came to a nomad camp on the far side of the river. They could at last get help, perhaps buy some food, maybe even get another horse.

'What rejoicing it brought us,' wrote Susie. 'At last our difficulties were over.' How very wrong she was. They were forced to camp in the middle of a snowstorm which had blown up without warning and decided to wait until morning before making contact with the camp opposite. Next day, the weather clear, Petrus waded up the river towards the camp, waving to Susie as he disappeared round a bend in the river. It was the last time she saw him. When he failed to return, she had to face the horrific truth: he had been attacked and presumably murdered by the nomads.

Susie was now on her own, in alien bandit country, mourning the loss of both her small child and her husband. For two months, terrified and miserable, she made her solitary way back along the Tibetan/Chinese border, certain neither of her own safety nor, indeed, of her route, until, after 360 miles, she found herself once again among friends.

Eventually she returned to Canada but such was the determination of this amazing woman that, some years later when the sorrow of her terrible losses had partly healed, she remarried and with her new husband again set out for Lhasa. This time, she did manage to get across the Tibetan border but the gods were implacable and she died three weeks later, giving birth to a son.

Susie Rijnhart was a traveller driven to limits of endurance rarely experienced by other people. It is terrible but ironic that, although her physical and mental stamina were such that she survived the loss of both child and husband, escaped death at the hands of nomads, and made a gruelling solo trek back to China, she nevertheless should fall victim to that most tragic of female fates – death in childbirth.

Perhaps the greatest loss to the world of Victorian travel was Mary Kingsley, whose untimely death at the age of thirty-eight, in 1900, dimmed the brightest star that ever beamed across the skies of Africa. The traveller had little with which to protect herself against disease, and the women who went to Africa were especially vulnerable. Tales of the White Man's Grave, however, were no deterrent for travellers as determined as she and although the horrific stories she was told contained an element of truth, she chose to ignore them.

Mary Kingsley's sense of humour and her capacity to relish the bizarre came to her assistance when a government official, welcoming her to Accra, took her to look at a couple of newly dug holes. Her account, with its wit and timing, would be the envy of any raconteur. She wondered aloud about the easy accessibility of the graves:

'Why?' I queried laconically.

'Oh! We always keep two graves ready dug for Europeans. We have to bury very quickly here, you know,' he answered. I turned at bay. I had had already a very heavy dose of details of this sort that afternoon and was inclined to believe another thing. So I said, 'It's exceedingly wrong to do a thing like that, you only frighten people to death. You can't want new-dug graves daily. There are not enough white men in the whole place to keep the institution up.'

'We do,' he replied, 'at any rate at this season. Why, the other day we had two white men to bury before twelve o'clock, and at four, another dropped in on a steamer.'

'At four thirty,' said a companion, an exceedingly accurate member of the staff. 'How you fellows do exaggerate.'

While in West Africa, she had caught more than once what she called West Coast fever but she had always managed to make a recovery. In 1900, she went to South Africa to nurse soldiers and found herself looking after Boer prisoners in a hospital in Simonstown: 'I never struck such a rocky bit of the Valley of the Shadow of Death in all my days as the Palace Hospital, Simonstown.' Within two months, she herself was down with the wretched illness that was claiming the lives of so many prisoners, enteric fever, and realized that this time she was not going to see it through.

This indomitable woman faced her death in the same way as

she had faced life – head on. She asked those nursing her to withdraw so that she could die alone: 'It was hard', wrote the nurse who looked after her, 'for us to do this, but we left the door ajar, and when we saw she was beyond knowledge went to her.' Later, as she had requested, she was buried at sea.

Until as recently as the 1920s, there was no protection against yellow fever or typhoid and the health risks to travellers were enormous. Penicillin, the first antibiotic, was not discovered until 1928. Until then, quinine was used to fight malaria and morphine to dull pain.

Beryl Markham, who in 1936 became the first person to fly solo across the Atlantic from England to Newfoundland, belonged to that valiant group of early aviators who transported medical supplies around Africa, in the days when runways were lit by the glimmer of crude-oil flares and airfields were fenced off against zebra, wildebeest and giraffe.

In her poignant, poetic book about those early days, *West With the Night*, she describes the awful plight of the malaria sufferer whose sickness turns to something even worse – the dreaded blackwater:

> A man can be riddled with malaria for years on end, with its chills and its fevers and its nightmares, but, if one day he sees that the water from his kidneys is black, he knows he will not leave that place again, wherever he is, or wherever he hoped to be. He knows that there will be days ahead, long, tedious days which have no real beginning or ending, but which run together into night and out of it without changing colour, or sound, or meaning. He will lie on his bed feeling the minutes and the hours pass through his body like an endless ribbon of pain because time becomes pain then. Light and darkness become pain; all his senses exist only to receive it, to transmit to his mind again and again, with ceaseless repetition, the simple fact that now he is dying.

While death is the ultimate consequence the traveller must be prepared to face, it is something few waste their time in contemplating any more than they are concerned about the lesser consequences of accidents or injuries. It is from the position of comfort and safety which the armchair traveller enjoys that the hazards appear so breathtaking and alarming – and so deliciously thrilling. We shiver in fear, gasp in horror and quickly turn the page in anticipation of fresh perils.

Our preoccupation with danger is one reason why travellers play down their more gruelling moments – unless, of course, they are seeking to capitalize on their adventures and feel the need to embellish incidents when writing about them. Many travellers, however, reject the idea of being pressured into making their journeys seem more perilous than they were.

Peter Fleming wrote of the affinity which existed on this subject between himself and his travelling companion, Ella Maillart: 'We were united by an abhorrence of the false values placed – whether by its exponents or by the world at large – on what can most conveniently be referred to by its trade name of Adventure. From an aesthetic rather than from an ethical point of view, we were repelled by the modern tendency to exaggerate, romanticize, and at last cheapen out of recognition the ends of the earth and the deeds done in their vicinity.'

And so the traveller's picture remains blurred for it is not they but we who project the image of danger, an image which is distorted and magnified by our own urbanized attitudes. To the unfree spirit, each beckoning bend in the road, each bright horizon represents an unknown which is threatening. To cope with it, we have to plan our movements, control our diet, monitor our thinking, confine our living space and do everything we can to lessen the possibility of the untoward and the unexpected. We surround ourselves with a safe wall of behaviour, appropriate and carefully planned, and view with alarm the unprogrammed lifestyle of some travellers who strike us as irresponsible if not actually insane.

In Papua New Guinea, Christina Dodwell, edgy and despondent at being held up by the Laigap River, then in full flood, jumped at the chance of fording it in the company of four locals. Each of them had a raft made of three logs tied together with vines. Two loops secured the wrists to the raft and the legs were then to be used to swim with. Three of the men set off into the surging water and almost immediately one of the rafts broke up:

We watched horrified as the man was swept **away**, catching glimpses of him in distant wavecrests as he struggled to gain hold of one log. Finally we saw he had caught the log and was floating safely back to shore. Then it was my turn. Kom and Araz positioned my float alongside that of the strongest man and they held it steady, pointing it at a slight angle upstream. I slipped my wrists through the loops of the vine and called my last goodbye . . . Cold, calm terror gripped my stomach, far colder than the icy mountain water around my legs . . . Water was roaring in my ears, and my knuckles were white with the effort of gripping the float. Despite my kicking, I was being swept mercilessly downstream and knew myself to be powerless against the river's force. . . . Waves were washing over us and we were dragged into heaving rapids.

Christina Dodwell is an extremely fragile-looking woman whose long straight blond hair, soft voice and gentle smile give no hint of the iron will and tough physique that lies beneath. Her encounter with the Laigap was but a rehearsal, though she didn't know it at the time, for a far more frightening run at the white waters of the Sepik River which she made with an American team a couple of years later. Her drive to push herself, to extend the limits of both her physical capabilities and of her psychological commitment, is unconscious but when the next challenge comes, she is always ready for it.

Rivers – nature's own boundaries – crop up frequently in travellers' tales, and rarely are they docile. Never one to go round mountains if going over the top of them is at all possible, Dervla Murphy found herself high up in the Himalayas, the way forward blocked by a swollen river. A small black cow provided the solution. Hoisting her bike over one arm – she was travelling all the way to India on it at the time – she threw the other arm round the neck of the surprised cow and, clinging to her, made the crossing safely – though as far as the human partner was concerned, it was a journey of great pain for the thundering, icy water which swirled around them was, in fact, newly melted snow.

Rising to a dangerous and difficult challenge heightens the

mood, lifts the heart and helps us to face new challenges but there is a moment before that – perhaps only a split second – when paralyzing fear can freeze the mind and put the traveller's whole existence in jeopardy. Not many explorers seem to experience fear or if they do, few admit to it. Perhaps this is because a crisis calls for quick action, leaving little room for anxious thoughts. By the time the sweat of terror has made itself felt, the fear can be utilized and turned to advantage, sharpening the senses and bringing precision and clarity to the choice of action. 'Fear,' stated the aviator Sophie Heath in ringing tones, 'is a tonic and danger should be something of a stimulant.' Such sturdy thoughts are the very stuff of brave adventurers, enveloping them in a whiff of devilry – a challenge to the gods. But mindful perhaps of their own power to nurture life, women explorers sometimes find it prudent to acknowledge the presence of other, more nebulous powers, and have been known to offer up placatory prayers for deliverance from danger and for a safe return.

Lin Rutland, left behind at a Himalayan base camp because she was ill, began climbing on her own the following day in order to catch up. Solo climbing brings its own set of dangers of which she was well aware. Making her way up a gully, she heard a rumble which soon turned to a roar as a sea of rocks the size of tables crashed down, loosened from their bed of ice by the warmth of the midday sun. Totally unprotected and in the path of the rocks funnelling down the gully, she crouched low and prayed that her death would be quick and painless. The fall continued and rocks thundered over her, leaving her hair filled with ice and grit but – miraculously – she was unhurt. It was uncanny.

'I am not a churchgoer but I felt protected by God.' This feeling gave her what she called a seventh sense and she pressed on up the mountain across glaciers and snow bridges without using ice axe or rope: pure folly for a solo climber, some might say.

The acknowledgement by climbers of the elemental powers of the mountain they are seeking to climb is a wise move – and one always made by Sherpas – for the unknown must be treated with respect. Arlene Blum was well aware of the dangers facing her team; Annapurna I presented as many problems as it offered rewards. Small wonder that one day she climbed a few hundred feet above base camp in order to contemplate her lonely task as leader. There had been many deaths on Annapurna. Further down they had passed the memorial of stones erected to the memory of individual lives claimed by the mountain; though she wasn't to know it at the time, two more stones, representing members of her own team, would be added to the cairn before they left the mountain.

'I continued to gaze at the peak towering above me. The Harvest Goddess had a disquieting history. I said a quiet prayer. "Dear Lord, please protect us. Please don't let avalanches fall on us. More than anything else I've ever wanted, I pray that we return from this mountain together, alive and in harmony."' Not all explorers project their own inner faith onto a recognizable deity with its implication of another existence. For them, a vigorous life led here and now is a sufficient statement.

Death has claimed the lives of many brave women who could not be pinned down to the certainty of dying at home and in their beds. Alison Chadwick, who at one time had climbed higher than any other woman, died on Annapurna with Vera Watson, roped together in death just as they had been friends in life. Claude Kogan, foremost mountaineer of her time, died in 1959 leading the first international women's expedition to Cho Oyo. Fliers in particular have spiralled like bright butterflies from the sky, among them Harriet Quimby, the Duchess of Bedford and both Earhart and Johnson.

How these women died is important. Those older and wiser may shake their heads at the foolishness of courting danger, of throwing life away in such a reckless fashion. But the women who lost their lives in this way have exercised a small choice in how and where they died and taken death as they had taken life — their spirits whole and free. For those left behind and for succeeding generations they leave the certain knowledge that there is more to life than dying.

CHAPTER 11

❖

Survival Strategies

Like stealthy chameleons, travellers negotiate the nets and snares of border crossings, traverse deserts, ford treacherous rivers, edge down mountain glaciers, emerge from the skies, rise from the seas, and return eventually to the comparative safety of home, bewildered that anyone should have shown concern for their wellbeing.

How on earth, everyone wants to know, did you manage to survive? How indeed, for what do you do when you lie alone somewhere in Africa, paralyzed by the bite of a virulent spider? Or when your tiny plane, flying low over an endless sea, starts running out of fuel? Or when, sailing towards the world's most notorious Cape, you find yourself a thousand miles from base and facing mountainous seas? What if you are a solitary woman in an unknown land, forced to spend the night alone in a mountain hut with a man who eyes you speculatively and then proceeds to take his clothes off? And how can you tell if the water is drinkable, the plant edible? Like everything else in life, you learn by observation and experimentation and, more painfully, you learn from your own mistakes. The experienced traveller gradually builds up a store of knowledge which, to the outsider, looks like intuition.

Christina Dodwell, who has travelled widely in Africa, drinks the same water as the locals, a practice that would horrify many a WHO worker who believes implicitly that water from rivers and streams can kill. For Christina, water is medicinal and she will drink a gallon of it if ill. She is not foolhardy, however. 'You have to get used to it gradually, taking a little each day to start with. If other people are drinking it it's a good sign. I'd never drink smelly water from a desert well and with a river the best thing is to wade out into the middle because there it's running fast and clear.'

She is always welcome at the London Hospital for Tropical

Diseases because she brings back so many interesting bugs, though she has now built up such strong immunities that she only discovered she'd had the river disease bilharzia when the hospital told her they'd found the antibodies in her blood. But whatever it is she's had, she's survived it – which is the most any explorer can hope for.

The traveller's strongest weapon for survival is her own belief in herself and in her ability to reach her destination. Although many women have succumbed, far too readily, to the old myths about their inherent physical weakness, there have always been women who stoically refused to believe such myths and by their very disbelief have helped to demolish them.

Not all classes of women, in Victorian times, *were* considered weak. Those, whether in England or Africa, whose lowly position destined them to be servants were actually thought to thrive on hard, repetitive manual labour. In 1893, the same year that Kate Marsden published a book on her travels through Siberia, the well-known travel writer Richard Galton noted that '. . . there are few greater popular errors than the idea we have mainly derived from chivalrous times, that woman is a weakly creature'. With a breathtaking absence of reasoning of the sort often attributed to women themselves, he takes his argument further.

> It is in the nature of women to be fond of carrying weights; you may see them in omnibuses and carriages, always preferring to hold their baskets or their babies on their knees, to setting them down on the seats by their sides. A woman whose modern dress includes I know not how many cubic feet of space has hardly ever pockets of a sufficient size to carry small articles, for she prefers to load her hands with a bag or other weighty object. A nurserymaid, who is on the move all day, seems the happiest specimen of her sex; and after her, a maid of all work who is treated fairly by her mistress.

He goes on to advise that when in Africa, it is wise to take the wives or porters along on an expedition, pointing out that a woman on such journeys was as good as a man and certainly better than a horse or a bullock.

Richard Hearne, an American traveller of the last century, also found that it made sound economic sense to take women along on an expedition – though only a certain class of woman, mind you.

> Women were made for labour; one of them can carry or haul as much as two men can do; in fact, there is no such thing as travelling any considerable distance or any length of time in this country [Africa] . . . without their assistance . . . and though they do everything are maintained at a trifling expense for as they always stand cook, the very licking of their fingers, in scarce times, is sufficient for their subsistence.

The convolutions of the male Victorian mind knew no bounds, for while such men recognized that serving maids and African women could possess an abundance of strength and stamina, they carefully ignored the possible existence of such attributes in their own wives or daughters.

Perhaps some Victorian women were indeed unfit. Laced tightly into corsets and rarely able to take the sort of exercise which would strengthen limbs and muscles, they were given to fainting attacks which at least had the virtue of providing a means of escape from the deadening boredom of inactivity – an inactivity that was both physical and mental. Their apparent predisposition to fainting served to underline the idea that women were poor creatures whom it would be unkind to expose to violent activity of any sort. Even the word used to describe their fainting fits had an inconsequential, trivial ring to it. Whoever heard of a man swooning? The medical profession's method of dealing with the vapours was to prescribe the Rest Cure – during which the 'invalid' was expected to sit around doing nothing all day, a state of inactivity which produced the same tranquilizing effects as that of today's valium.

Some cures, of course, went wildly wrong. When, in her youth, Isabella Bird Bishop was found to be suffering from a succession of illnesses, a doctor suggested she make a long sea voyage during which, no doubt, she would be able to sit quietly on deck covered with a blanket and read a suitably edifying book. In fact, the journey had quite the opposite effect. It was her first taste of freedom and she loved it. Never again would she be happy sitting at home with her beloved but docile sister. She realized the need for compromise, however, and managed it by enjoying roistering good health when away on her various trips, doing what she most wanted to do, but bowing to convention when back in England in between by allowing the statutory female illnesses to manifest themselves. She was a part-time occupant only of the drawing-room couch. Although eighteen long years were to pass before she was completely free to travel as she chose, when the moment arrived she was gone, streaking out into the great unknown like a determined comet.

Nor was she the only woman who, to the consternation of the doctors, brushed aside the medical theories of the day and set off on journeys from which, had the gloomy and inaccurate predictions been correct, she might never have returned.

Fanny Workman, who in 1906 at the age of forty-seven set a women's altitude record that was to remain unbroken for twenty-eight years, had been told that one cold winter spent cycling in the plains of India was about as much as anyone could undertake and that even if she survived such a winter she certainly wouldn't be in a condition to climb any mountains afterwards. Stout and strong as she was, she spent not one but two seasons cycling and then went on to the Karakorams to undertake her record-breaking climb.

Neither Isabella nor Fanny gave undue thought to their physical safety nor paid too much attention to the prevailing opinion about women's frailty, believing only that what they set out to do they would accomplish – and therein lay their success. Even now, though women are constantly attempting higher peaks of endeavour, they seem rarely to dwell on danger and death – their unwelcome travelling companions – for were they to do so, Reason, that destroyer of dreams, could convince them they should stay at home.

*   *   *

'Do be reasonable,' someone said to 41-year-old American May French Sheldon at Charing Cross Station as she was about to set off for Africa in 1891. 'Do be reasonable and abandon this mad, useless scheme.'

She didn't, of course. Instead, climbing down through dense forest to the edge of Lake Chala, a volcanic crater on the side of Mount Kilimanjaro, she punted her way round its previously unexplored waters:

> I found myself attempting to penetrate through a girdle of primeval forest trees, tossed, as it were, by some volcanic action against the rock base, and seemingly as impenetrable as any stockade. With bill-hooks and knives [the bearers] cleared a slight opening through which I managed to squeeze, on emerging to find myself standing on a boulder which was balanced upon another boulder, and every moment's tarriance seemed to imperil my equilibrium; and as I dared to venture on uncertain surfaces which presented a footing, it required cat-like agility to crawl or slide down, sometimes landing in a bed of leaves, which must have been the accumulation of centuries and into which I sank up to my armpits, and had to be hauled out by main force by my men . . .

Had she listened to Reason, she wouldn't have found herself sinking waist-deep into mud, her long, full skirts heavy with evil-smelling sludge, but then nor would she have been able to wonder at 'the strange whirring of birds . . . the whisking myriad of monkeys . . . the hooting of white-hooded owls . . . the eagle whose feathers scattered like storm-flawn flowers from its beating wings'.

Reason, sweetly seductive, might also have convinced the 1978 US all-women Annapurna expedition to turn back when within sight of their goal – had they chosen to invoke it. Overawed by the power of an avalanche which had almost carried away six members of the team, Arlene Blum was baffled by the fact that everyone avoided any discussion on whether or not they should continue. Previously, there had been heated arguments about the level of democratic decision-making needed and now, when it came to talking about something important, something upon which depended the whole success of the expedition, the group had fallen silent. Alison Chadwick, at that time the holder of the women's high-altitude record, eventually explained: 'The problem with talking about it at all is that if we admit we are really worried and try to have a rational discussion, we would inevitably come to the conclusion that we should give up.' Sadly, as we know, Alison was one of the two members who later lost their lives on the mountain. Had she sifted the arguments and gone for the rational option, she might now be alive.

*   *   *

Most travellers and explorers face death at some time or other in their lives but rarely speak about it. It is almost as if, by ignoring it or belittling the moment, they defuse its threat. One glorious exception was the mighty flying grandmother, Mary, Duchess of Bedford. Flying along the coast of North Africa over a very rough sea with not a boat in sight, her single-engined Puss Moth, piloted by her personal pilot, developed an air lock. Losing height rapidly, it looked as if they would hit the sea and disappear for ever. Although the cockpit was open and they could have climbed out onto a wing, the chances of surviving were slim. There was no feeling of terror, she said, as people often imagined. Instead, she felt disappointed that the flight would be wasted and that no one would ever know what had happened to them. There was, however, not a lot she could do, so, leaving the drama to the pilot, she picked up the sock she had been working on and knitted her way through the crisis. 'I thought it quite an agreeable way of finishing up compared with most ends which are the lot of man, and certainly the one I had most desired.'

They survived that particular calamity but she got her wish in the end when, at the age of seventy-two, she flew her plane out of Woburn Abbey on a routine flight one day in 1937, and was never seen again.

Most travellers are not afraid of death so much as the manner of their dying. In a fuel crisis, Sheila Scott put her fear to good use by turning it into positive action: 'I had learned how to use the adrenalin that fear produces. I realized, too, I was afraid of being hurt, not of death itself.' Instant annihilation is preferable to painful mutilation.

When Ranulph Fiennes was recruiting for his Transglobe Expedition, the qualities he was looking for in his team were not physical prowess so much as good nature and patience. Above all, he tried to assess how individuals might react to stress and strain. The ability to be flexible, to be able to assess a situation clearly and calmly, but above all to have the stamina and the will to go forward – these are the qualities that must go into the traveller's survival pack. They are qualities, however, whose usefulness may be neutralized by fear.

Naomi James, sailing single-handed round the world, took the decision to turn back during a period of temporary defeat brought on by the looming terror of Cape Horn. Later that same day, her 53-foot yacht *Crusader* capsized, righted itself and then went on to behave like a she-devil, surfing madly along waves that were thirty feet high:

> I gripped the wheel desperately to keep the stern directly on the wave and hold her straight . . . The speed was impossible to gauge as there was nothing to judge it by and the water all around me was at deck level, seething and hissing as if on the boil. I started to cry from a feeling of helplessness at being out of control . . .

The following day, although she awoke sore, depressed and lethargic, she began to re-examine her decision to turn back. Having lived through the storm which capsized her, she realized she had eliminated her fear. Elated by this knowledge, she reset her course for the Horn.

For the majority of travellers, once they have established in their own minds the firm belief that they can succeed, the will to go forward takes over and the planning of a survival strategy is temporarily relegated to a position of lesser importance. To understand this process, you must also understand the way in which the idea for a journey first takes root. There is no one day when a traveller or explorer wakes up and says: 'Today I shall start planning a journey – will it be Africa, or the Atlantic? Shall I go alone or with some friends? Is it going to be a dangerous journey and am I properly equipped to deal with such dangers?' Instead, the idea for an expedition insinuates itself into the subconscious, weaving seductive tentacles round the mind of the traveller until it has taken hold and there is no going back. The time to think about danger has come and gone – the die has been cast and though Death may have the last throw it is only now that the moment has come for survival plans to be made.

Danger, of course, is not the only hazard the traveller has to face. In any journey, she may have to contend with boredom, fear, discomfort, loneliness, cold, heat, hunger, thirst, sleeplessness and illness. How each person copes with these will be dictated by circumstances and the character of the traveller. Boredom and loneliness are both strong emotions that can dominate the tedious section of a journey. The overland traveller and the mountaineer do not suffer too much from these, for there are always places to pass through, people to meet and routes to be planned. For the lone and long-distance flier or sailor, however, there are hours, maybe days on end when little happens, when the traveller is distanced from the world and its people. One sailor reads a book a day and Ann Davison coped with her boredom by setting herself mental tasks, though even that tactic proved difficult during a 3000-mile journey: 'You start on some profundity like the expanding universe and then think, bother, I thought about that yesterday.' And loneliness can be compounded by other emotions: 'Loneliness does not come from the physical state of being on one's own so much as from fear – the same old fear of the unknown.'

Sophie Heath, on her historic 1928 flight up through Africa, passed the time reading and eating chocolates, and indeed so engrossed was she in her book that she barely had time to put on her customary silk stockings and jewellery in order to land in Cairo in her usual *haute couture*. Her journey up through Africa had not been trouble-free but it had been made easier by the many friends she had in high places. Nowadays, with the deadening hand of officialdom lying on everything and demanding entry and exit visas in triplicate, some travellers take a pragmatic view of the bribes and back-handers which may – or may not – ease them on their way. Before hands are raised in horror at such corruption, it should be remembered that such transactions are really little different from airport taxes, surcharges, tipping and other often unexpected expenses – except that they are levied at a personal level.

More practical, perhaps, was the bartering which most nineteenth-century travellers relied upon. Mary Kingsley deliberately set herself up as a trader the better to get to know the locals and their way of life. She went into this, as with most things, with her eyes well open, avoiding 'being swindled as much as possible by giving great attention to trade matters'. She dealt in rubber, tobacco and cloth and once traded twelve of her fine Victorian blouses. For small change, she used fish hooks which she kept in her special trade box.

Christina Dodwell, desperate for a cigarette in the African bush, was forced into a hard bargain. Led deep into the forest by a young boy, she came to a solitary hut with a couple of tobacco plants growing beside the mud walls. The old lady who lived there was happy to sell a few leaves but money was out of the question for what use could it be put to? Instead, she indicated that she would accept Christina's sandals – her only pair. All manner of other tempting things were offered. Perhaps she'd like some pencils or maybe a box of matches? The old lady was adamant and the traveller made her way out of the bush happy at last to have her tobacco but not so happy to be barefoot, risking the bites of countless unknown creatures.

May French Sheldon also took along the usual collection of beads and cloth for bartering, regretting that she was unable to meet the needs of one chief who requested an umbrella and a saw – though she did promise to have them delivered at a later date.

It is indeed no accident that it has often been the practicality of woman's nature and her attention to detail which has enabled her to cope with unexpected eventualities. Clothing is one example: while a man will give little thought to the clothes he wears while travelling, a woman must give the matter careful consideration. Does she want to emphasize her sex or play it down, for instance? We shall see in the next chapter how women have used their style of dressing as a means of confirming or underplaying their sexual identity. Disguise too can serve a useful purpose, and although some who feel they must remain true to their own identity spurn this particular device, other travellers know their journeys would have been impossible had they not concealed their sex.

Both Annie Taylor and Alexandra David-Neel disguised themselves in order to enter Lhasa, for during the course of the Great

Game foreigners to those parts were distinctly unwelcome. Indeed, Alexandra was forced to leave the city in considerable haste when, having inadvertently witnessed a family row, she was ordered to attend the local court to give evidence – an event which would certainly have led to the discovery of her ruse. Until that point it had fooled everyone. Of average height with her hair normally worn in a matronly coil, the 55-year-old Madame Alexandra David-Neel could never have entered Lhasa had she not disguised herself as a poor beggar, supposedly travelling on a pilgrimage in the company of her equally poor son – Yongden, the young Sikkimese monk whom she later adopted. She blackened her plaits with Chinese ink, garnished them with strings of yak hair and rubbed her hands on the bottom of the kettle in order to render them as black and greasy as those of other poor people. Once, while eating with her fingers as was the custom, she noticed to her dismay that dirty streaks were beginning to show up in the curds – the Chinese ink was coming off. Shutting her eyes, she stuffed the rest of the unsavoury ink-flavoured food into her mouth before anyone could notice.

A dedicated scholar, she had spent over three years studying the dialects of Tibet and familiarizing herself with its religion and customs. By the time she set off on her journey, she was able to pass herself off as an ignorant old country woman whose inability to speak well could be put down to stupidity. So successful was her disguise that she was beaten in the street by a policeman for walking in a place reserved for the rich; she was delighted.

More recently, a young Englishwoman called Sarah Hobson travelled through Iran in the 1970s dressed as a boy. Detection could have meant serious trouble but so determined was she to learn as much as she could about Islam that she was prepared to add this risk to any other she might encounter along the way. The disguise worked and she managed to get into the all-male Islamic college at Qum, even attending some of the classes there. *En route*, through being treated like a young man she gained an insight into how a man might think and react. So convincing was the disguise at times that it almost became a reality and her journey took her not only to Qum but also to the depths of her own identity.

Nowadays, in the western world at least, clothes offer some

respite from the throttling restrictions of both class and sex. Clear-cut differences have been somewhat blurred and the uniform jeans and T-shirt need no longer impose an immediate sexual identity on the wearer. This works to the advantage of the woman traveller for apart from being comfortable, baggy trousers and a voluminous shirt may also provide a convenient gender camouflage. The experienced traveller, of course, will be aware of the confusion this combination may give rise to in the mind of a man not yet exposed to this particular stage of sartorial development.

For the mountain men of Bulgaria or Turkey, such an idiosyncratic way of dressing was probably proof, yet again, of the strange ways of those living on the other side of the mountain. Dervla Murphy, trekking through both areas in the late 1960s, found that her practical clothes – bush shirt and corduroy trousers (both worn many sizes too large in order to accommodate her as yet unborn daughter Rachel) provoked interest from both sexes: 'While hitch-hiking from Ankara to Van, I had to fight off eight would-be rapists in eleven days. This marathon was garnished by two lesbian invitations to bed – Providence perhaps felt that I risked being bored by all those over-excited males.'

Things still have not improved all that much. Bettina Selby, cycling to Kathmandu, found that neither the full weight of her forty-seven years nor her loose, utilitarian clothes were any protection against the interests of a motorcyclist who chose to accompany her:

> 'I like English women', he said with great enthusiasm. I said nothing but proceeded with warning bells sounding loudly.
>
> 'English women very sexy,' he confided.
>
> 'No,' I said, 'English women are not sexy.'
>
> 'You are not being sexy?' he queried incredulously.
> 'Not being sexy?'
>
> 'No,' I said with even greater firmness. 'No, I am not being sexy.'

On this occasion, she was left in comparative peace though other passers-by continued to enquire with monotonous regularity about her physical proportions.

Some travellers deliberately adopt a style of dress that is ultra-feminine – a long skirt, for example – in order to make it abundantly clear that they are women and not, therefore, likely to present a threat. And of course, they always have to bear in mind the customs of the country which, due to a number of complex attitudes related to religion, sex and marriage, differ throughout the world. In some Arab countries, they would prefer not to look at the soles of your feet and in Islamic countries, it is considered improper for a woman to have her arms uncovered. In Europe or America, women's breasts are taboo; in Africa, they aren't. In a mountain village in Lesotho, I watched a group of Basotho schoolgirls playing netball wearing the green, incongruous gymslips of an English schoolgirl and not much else. Whenever they jumped to shoot a goal, a beautiful brown breast would leap in unison with the ball and the owner would nonchalantly pop it back in again before going on to score.

Choosing neutral clothes will often dampen the ardour of a would-be lover but what about those potentially dangerous situations when a woman feels a brisk display of strength may be called for? The whole question of their response to violence has exercized the minds and emotions of women over the centuries. On the one hand there is a predisposition among women to create an atmosphere of calm and quiet – though whether or not this is inborn is hard to say. A woman will prefer discussion to confrontation, and a woman traveller will much prefer to talk her way out of danger, coping verbally with other people's anger rather than confronting them with her own. On the other hand, the instinct of self-preservation tends to give them a sturdy attitude towards aggression and make them tough characters to deal with – not at all the sort of collapsible female that some bullying official or ruffian might hope to get the better of. The earlier travellers thought little of arming themselves with guns, even when loath to use them.

Alexandra David-Neel's attitude typifies their dilemma. While travelling towards Lhasa, she and her companion Yongden were attacked several times but, though armed, she felt that she would do best to try and protect herself with reasoned argument: 'We each had a revolver,' she wrote, 'and that still better weapon in the East – and perhaps everywhere – the "winged words" of the divine

Ulysses and the artifices of the goddess Juno.'

Annie Taylor, travelling the same route some fifty years earlier, also carried a pistol – and a telescope, for keeping a watchout – but so great was her faith in her own good intentions that it seemed impossible to her that anyone should attack her. Was she not, after all, an ambassador of the Lord? 'I have found,' she said, 'that a woman is rarely molested if she makes it quite clear that she is doing her duty quietly and unassumingly.' It obviously had not crossed her mind that what she considered her duty might be in conflict with that of the ordinary Tibetan. She was wise to carry some form of protection for she was prey to robbers along the way, and even her own party of porters included some dubious characters, notably a quarrelsome wife-beater who eventually betrayed her to the Lhasa authorities.

Guns have more often been used to fire warning shots than anything else. May French Sheldon, who set out on a remarkable journey to Africa in 1891, was unperturbed when a shower of Maasai spears landed in warning at her feet. She replied with her own version of a war-cry accompanied by a couple of bullets which went winging their way over her assailants' heads. When her bearers later revolted, she terrified them into submission by bringing down a vulture with a single shot, amazing herself with her own accuracy. She later revealed that she had disciplined some of the more recalcitrant among her bearers by whipping them.

That she was willing, when pushed, to wield both gun and whip is ironic when one hears that she had initially been advised by an army friend to surround herself with as many women as possible in order to indicate her peaceful intentions. He had added gallantly: 'I feel sure that your invaluable tact and perception will pull you through much that a man would fail at . . .' Like many women who have never had the opportunity to exercise power over others, she had set out with firm ideas about democracy. Whipping, she said, was brutal and degrading – both to the bearers and to herself. Before long, however, she had changed her views. Circumstances, she found, alter cases, for her porters did not seem to share her democratic views: '. . . coaxing arguments and persuasive talks were disregarded and sneeringly laughed at, probably the more because I, though leader, was a woman.'

Fanny Workman, travelling in India at the same time, held similar views: 'Sedition in the case of coolies, as in that of other bodies of unthinking persons, is a contagious affliction . . .' She too dealt with mutineers by having them thrashed. It is only fair to point out that both these women took large parties of bearers with them – Sheldon had 130 porters – and their organizational problems must have been formidable. Moreover, the Indian porters were provoked into sullen rebellion as much by Fanny's obvious wealth as by her aggression.

It was Mary Kingsley, with her old-fashioned ideas about imperialism, who managed to strike up a working rapport with her guides. Her saving grace was her immense capacity to see the poignancy and warmth of those she encountered on her travels and this, allied to her sense of humour, prevented her from adopting stances which would have distanced her from her bearers. Even from the bottom of an animal trap – a position that could never be described as dignified – she managed to communicate with them with vigour and authority.

Mary Kingsley was of the female persuasion that preferred talking to shooting: 'We each recognized we belonged to that same section of the human race with whom it is better to drink than to fight.' However, while she herself preferred to talk her way through dangerous situations, she firmly advised others that they should keep their guns loaded and to hand. They should also, she said, keep a knife handy – not the hinged sort, since they were given to rusting up. Revolvers, she held, were an 'idiocy' though she would always shoot if she had to, adding that she was 'more inclined to walk round the obstacle than to become a mere blood-splotch'. Few of today's women travellers carry a gun, many believing that in fact they are safer on their travels than at home, in an industrialized jungle of muggers, motor cars and rapists. The few who do carry a gun do so more for the look of it than anything.

When, in 1977, Robyn Davison decided to make a camel trek 1700 miles across the desert of western Australia, she first got a job as barmaid in the notorious Alice Springs. With her long blond hair she must have seemed like a visiting angel to the hard-drinking men who propped up the bar, drunkenly weeping and peeing at the same time. A few were bold enough to follow her out of town when the bar closed down, mistaking her for other ladies of the night. To disabuse them of any idea that she was easy game, she kept a high-powered .222 rifle near at hand. It was never loaded for she was a peaceable person and no further educated in the mysteries of ballistics than knowing that you hold on at one end and the bullet comes out of the other.

When Ella Maillart inadvertently left her revolver behind while travelling towards Tibet (where she thought she might encounter some bears) she felt profoundly relieved. There was now no danger that she might injure somebody or something by mistake. Dervla Murphy, on the other hand, starting out on her valiant journey by bike to India, would have been lost without the .25 revolver she packed in her saddlebag. Within a month of setting out she had to use it. Travelling down through Yugoslavia, she hitched a lift for herself and the bike in a lorry which subsequently crashed into a tree. With the driver injured, there was nothing she could do but start walking. The winter of 1962–3 will be remembered as the worst for eighty years and her route followed a two-mile path through a snow-bound forest. With only a torch for light, she stumbled off along the snow-packed cart track and suddenly found herself attacked from behind by three wild and hungry dogs. One dog she shot through the head, another through the rib cage while the last one took the hint and disappeared. Now, over twenty years later and an experienced traveller, she has developed less violent strategies of defence and, though she has been known to lay about her with a hefty stick, feels like many others that trust is the key to enjoyable travel.

Fortunately, women travellers are resourceful creatures; they pluck the strategy for their own survival as if out of thin air, instinctively forming their actions round the mood of the moment. It is the immediate response, which by its nature can rarely be predicted, that so mystifies the armchair traveller. What made you think of doing that, we ask, or What on earth did you do then? When faced with a awkward situation, most travellers make it up as they go along.

When Rosie Swale was making her way down through Chile to Cape Horn, a man burst out of the undergrowth, grabbed the bridle of one of her two horses and disappeared back into the bush with it. It took an hour of stumbling about in the scrub before she came upon the man desperately trying to haul the horse out of the deep ditch into which it had fallen. Using the only weapon she had, she sprayed the man full in the face with an aerosol antiseptic and he fled, screaming, to trouble her no more.

Christina Dodwell, travelling on a river boat in Africa, found herself imprisoned by the captain in his cabin. His mind was plainly fixed on one thing. Unless you happen to have the ship's crew on your side, there's not a lot you can do in a situation like this. However, she did what she could, which was to make herself as physically undesirable as possible. This involved chewing large quantities of garlic and making unbecoming hawking sounds whenever the captain's libido rose to the surface. It did the trick – and she lived to tell the tale.

A very small part of May French Sheldon's luggage

CHAPTER 12

'Merely Feminine Curiosity'

One of the most intriguing aspects of this subject lies in the fact that not all pioneering women travellers are what might even loosely be termed feminists – nor have they been in the past. With a few shining exceptions, most women shift uncomfortably when the cloak of feminism is laid upon them, for the journeys which the majority have embarked upon have been personal odysseys made by individuals who simply happened to be women.

That they bring with them a woman's perspective is undeniable, but the women who have peopled these pages have been, each one, special and distinct, linked by little more than their sex and their hunger for exploration. To claim that they travel because they are women is to take away from them that most precious of qualities – their own uniqueness.

There is, however, another factor common to most of them, one which undoubtedly is an important influence in their lives and which facilitates their setting off in the first place. This factor is their middle-class background.

Such a background may not always have provided the traveller with lavish financial resources, and may indeed have been a cage from which she longed to escape, but it has served to provide a degree of security and, in most cases, a fund of confidence with which the traveller can launch herself into a new world. Parental or family homes have often been available to which the traveller may return from time to time. Contacts abroad come ready-made, for the class net is cast worldwide and the hospitality formerly offered by diplomats and colonials is being replaced by that of UN personnel, World Bank officials and international aid workers. 'You get handed from one person to another', was how one traveller put it.

The snares which lie in wait for anyone making generalizations are numerous and on the whole deserved. But having made the observation that most women travellers are individuals first and women second, I hope I may be forgiven for advancing a few theories, not so much about women but about the social times which formed the backdrop of their lives and which have informed their views and attitudes.

There is always a whisper of doubt at the back of the mind – especially in these days when some progress appears to have been made along the road to sexual equality – that perhaps women's achievements in the field of travel are really no different from those of men. In fact, the uniqueness of their exploits lies not so much in the doing as in the *manner* of their accomplishment.

Travellers can be roughly divided into two types. There are those who set out with their sights firmly fixed on a distant destination. It may be an ancient city concealed in the deserts of time, a river whose source is unknown, a mountain peak which has retained its snowbound secret. The journey is a quest, the travellers searchers who cannot rest until they have reached their goal. They include the great explorers of the last century: Livingstone, Speke, Stanley, Doughty, Baker and Burton.

There is a second sort of traveller, however – those who weave in and out among the lives of people they encounter on the way, picking up, during their odyssey, a stitch here and a pattern there so that they return wearing cloaks embroidered with the rainbow of the world. It is this group which is dominated by women – the travellers who dawdle along the road, pausing to stop and stare and ruminate upon the idiosyncracies of life.

This difference in attitude is well illustrated by the remarkable journey across Chinese Turkestan undertaken by Ella Maillart and Peter Fleming in 1935. They had met in Pekin, both intending to travel across China to India. 'As a matter of fact,' he had told her coldly, 'I'm going back to Europe by that route . . . You can come with me if you like . . .' 'I beg your pardon,' she had answered, 'It's my route and it's I who will take you, if I can think of a way in which you might be useful to me.'

He was twenty-seven and she was thirty-one. Both were journalists and shared a liking for travel but there the similarities ended. Both his heart and his luggage were labelled 'England' and his eye was always fixed on the distant prospect of home. On the caravan across central Asia, he insisted on celebrating the Fourth of June, for he was an Old Etonian. The mystified Ella dined off tinned crab and curried rice and after dinner they lay in their tent drinking brandy and playing their three records on the gramophone. While he was untidy and impatient, she gave her attention to the details of daily living: when they made their makeshift pillows out of rolled-up sweaters stuffed with boots and field-glasses, her pillow was always neat while his was lumpy. When a woman with a noisy child joined the caravan, he felt sympathy for the crying child (a boy) while her heart went out to the distracted mother.

Ella preferred to travel slowly, to take her time, absorbing everything she saw, living for the moment: 'I liked to dawdle in my usual fashion, as if I had the whole of eternity before me.' He was restless, trying to cover two days' march in one, always straining towards home. They had a long journey – 3500 miles to cover – and the caravan moved slowly.

'Every night, Peter would repeat his refrain: "Sixty miles nearer to London." He did it to annoy me and I would tell him to shut up, for I wanted to forget that we had, inevitably, to return home . . . I should have liked the journey to continue for the rest of my life.'

When they did eventually draw near journey's end, he was far more pleased than she and planned to celebrate with smoked salmon. Despite the camel train, the curried antelope, the Chinese bazaars, and the magic of the Koko Nor, England had never been far away.

Idiosyncratic, languid and amusing, Peter Fleming was a far cry from the Englishmen who had set out on their travels a century before. The spur then had come from the national desire to increase trade, extend the empire and improve the living standards of those whose lands would soon be colonized. Entangled in the imperialist drive, however, was another, darker element, for those were times when men were required to present themselves as powerful figures of authority, setting out bravely into the unknown, bearing aloft the flag of their country on which was emblazoned their identity, confirmed in letters of gold. It is important to understand the ethos of Victorian exploration for the female-dominated struggle for equality at home was paralleled by the male-dominated struggle for Africa.

That shining continent, black and beautiful, was invested, by the threatened masculinity of England's patriarchy, with all the attributes of the devil woman, for what could not be subjected and controlled at home could at least be conquered and possessed in Africa. It is against this background of domestic power struggle and sexual confusion that the essentially male exploitation of Africa must be seen.

To appreciate the extent of the female personification of the continent, it is important to note the sexual connotations of the language of exploration. Armed with sword and knife, the hero/explorer penetrates the country's dark interior. Both attracted by the cool, inviting waters where he may drink and repelled by the dangerous, murky foliage, he plunges further and further into the moist undergrowth, unable to withdraw until he has possessed what he considers is rightly his. At last, at journey's end, exhausted but triumphant, he erects his country's flag.

Those were heady days. Mountains were assaulted and peaks conquered. Men thrust forward and took possession of virgin territories. It was undoubtedly a time of great excitement and exhilaration but it was a stage on which there was little room for women – until, that is, they decided to write their own play. Then, stealing on almost unnoticed, they brought to their part the things they were good at: an ability to listen, to empathize, to assimilate. They became observers, not of places but of people, and we owe them an eternal debt, for their records of sights and happenings complemented the scientific data remitted by male explorers.

Used to the minutiae of the household, they observed the trees within the wood, but because of this their observations were often dismissed as being trivial. The industrious Victorians wanted information about lengths of rivers, distances between valleys, suitability of soil for cultivation or for building railways. The customs and practices of the indigenous population were of secondary importance. Aware of this negative attitude and wanting to disarm their critics in advance, many women travellers adopted a self-effacing pose, unnecessarily belittling their aims and denigrating their achievements.

When, in 1891, the American May French Sheldon set out on her remarkable journey to Africa she disclaimed any scientific knowledge and said she was going 'simply to study the native habits and customs free from the influence of civilization'. This, however, was not good enough. The *Spectator* noted that since the journey had no scientific end it was motivated by a 'merely feminine curiosity . . . hardly a useful and laudable one'. Poor May! Even when she revealed that she had disciplined her recalcitrant porters by whipping them, the editor was unbelieving. Surely she wasn't strong enough to have punished the porters herself, personally? It was Catch 22. To have whipped the men herself would have been spirited but, regrettably, unladylike.

A book review in the same issue gives us an idea of the ideal woman. The heroine was '. . . graceful . . . pretty . . . sweet . . . and wholesome' and unlikely to have gone round whipping men, even if they were servants. There was also the fact that May was American and probably one of these New Women, for had she not left her husband in Naples while she went off on her own, jaunting through Africa?

'The horror,' continued the *Spectator*, 'is that the Lady Errant is not unlikely to encourage still further the feminine spirit of unrest and the uneasy jealousy that is forever driving the fair sex into proving itself the equal of the other. Isabella Bird Bishop has already shown what a woman is capable of in the way of pluck and courage.' Isabella by then was protected by the sober cloak of widowhood, was engaged in setting up a hospital in Srinagar and, best of all, was British.

But we should stay with May a little longer to learn what exactly the results of this 'feminine curiosity' were. Entertained by the Sultan of Zanzibar, she learned that his great regret was to have only three daughters and no sons. And he, in turn, discovering that she had no children, found it hard to believe that her husband did not have a few other wives hidden away who would provide him with the necessary family.

When travelling among the Maasai, she carefully noted the current market prices – five large beads for a wife but ten for a cow. In a playful moment, she showed a local chief how to cut a segment of orange peel into a set of teeth. Delighted, he withdrew and returned, bloody but smiling, to present her with one of his own teeth, just extracted, with a hole already bored through it so that she could string it round her neck.

May French Sheldon was a flamboyant dresser, suiting her garments to the occasion, for clothes are an important ingredient in the woman traveller's make-up, serving the dual purpose of helping her maintain her identity while at the same time giving out a clear message to those she meets along the way. In the late 1900s, the introduction of knickerbockers and divided skirts struck a blow at the very heart of patriarchal England. The corset, with its image of restraint and discipline, was giving way to a looseness of dress that might soon spread out into other areas of a woman's life. So radical were the impending changes that not only men but women too felt themselves threatened. To have sallied forth into unknown parts of the empire dressed in anything as preposterous as a pair of knickerbockers would have been unthinkable, if not actually treasonable. When Isabella Bird Bishop was reported to be wearing riding breeches in the Rockies she was furious and instructed her publisher to horsewhip the *Times* correspondent. She was, she said, wearing a skirt reaching to the knee and Turkish trousers gathered into frills which fell below.

Other travellers felt that as ambassadors of the empire they had certain standards of dress to maintain. Mary Kingsley believed in dressing in the African bush as she would for tea in Highgate. Wearing a heavy wool skirt, high-necked blouse with leg o'mutton sleeves and neat pillbox hat tied under the chin with a big black bow, she strode off through the forests, confident that she would be accepted for what she was – a well-intentioned, fair-minded English-woman who simply wanted to make friends with the locals. Nor was she at all bothered when the same locals turned up to tea dressed somewhat incongruously in her bartered blouses, adorned with nothing more than a daub of red paint and some leopard tails. The effect was startling if revealing but, as in Highgate, everyone knew exactly where they stood. Some of the bearers were even named after the clothes they wore so that apart from Passenger, Pagan and the Duke, there was also Singlet and Black Shirt.

In fact, the splendid Miss Kingsley had reason to congratulate herself on not taking the advice of the New Women back in London who had advocated male attire. Apart from being unladylike and smacking of the new feminism of which she did not approve, knickerbockers, not nearly as thick as her wool skirt, would not have saved her when she descended unexpectedly but majestically into an animal trap.

> It is at these moments you realize the blessings of a good thick skirt . . . save for a good many bruises here was I with the fullness of my skirt tucked under me, sitting on nine ebony spikes some twelve inches long, in comparative comfort, howling lustily to be hauled out.

A few minutes later, one of her bearers fell into a similar trap but, not wearing the sensible wool garments of a Victorian lady, he finished up 'a good deal frayed at the edges on those spikes'.

May French Sheldon, though not of the stuff of empire-builders, nevertheless had her position as a lady to consider. In her baggage she included clothes which she felt would be sufficiently regal to wear when visiting local chiefs, including a sparkling ball gown and blond wig. A contemporary picture shows her dressed to pay a courtesy visit looking like an Edwardian Lady Macbeth, her waist-length hair crowned with jewels and a ceremonial sword hanging round her curving hips. One chief was so taken with this apparition that he asked – and received – permission to stroke her thick, blond locks.

Clothes therefore consolidated the authority of these middle-class women who travelled far from home, where social changes were taking place of which they could not wholly approve. Maintaining the old standards of dress was both a comfort and a confirmation that some things, at least, need not alter.

Despite the fact that they were very obviously ladies of social standing (Mary French Sheldon was in the habit of sending an advance party to announce that she was a 'great white queen of limitless power come to make friends . . . and bringing many beautiful tokens of peace'), the two were often addressed as if they were men, Mary Kingsley being known as Sir and May as BeBe Bwana – Woman Master. That Africans were uncertain about the sex of these strong-minded women is hardly surprising when one considers that a similar if more complicated confusion exists in the minds of some women travellers themselves.

It is only in recent years that people have been able to recognize the existence within themselves of many differing and conflicting aspects of their personalities, some of which are characteristics more commonly found in the opposite sex. There are, said Eleanora Duse, a thousand women within me and each one makes me suffer in turn. In the past, characteristics were rigidly confined to one sex or the other. Man with the head and woman with the heart, wrote Tennyson firmly, and a friend of Mary Kingsley paid her the greatest compliment he could when he said : 'She had a brain masculine in its strength and in the breadth of its outlook.' As recently as 1946, a Cambridge don described Celia Fiennes' interest in the national economy as 'masculine'.

It is not altogether surprising therefore that when women, by virtue of their travelling, find the freedom to express another side to their character, one which hitherto has perhaps been unexplored, they sometimes feel confused about where exactly they fit in. Ann Davison referred to herself as a chap and Amy Johnson liked to be called Johnnie. As joint author with her husband, mountaineer Fanny Workman always used the umbrella pronoun he, even when it was clear she was referring to herself. And a present-day mountaineer, Lin Rutland, working and climbing with men, says : 'I live like a man and feel like a man.'

Perhaps the saddest though also the most daring of those women travellers who tried to come to terms with their identity was Hester Stanhope. Her adoption of flamboyant male Arab attire, about which she boasted in letters back to England, was a gesture misunderstood by many, including the men of Regency England who found it easier to dally with women of charm than talk to women of intelligence. Hobhouse, Byron's friend, when he met Hester on her travels, found her a 'masculine woman'. Byron, whose own role as London's black if romantic sheep might have made him more sympathetic to her, found this powerful and commanding woman merely puzzling and could only state crassly that he had discovered in her 'nothing different from other she-things'. Seated astride her horse, unthinkable in England, she rode out joyfully among her Bedouin – a woman for whom compromise was an enemy.

There are other advantages which a man may not enjoy –

and to the annoyance of some men, it may seem as if women have it both ways. We have seen how women, by virtue of their sex, were able to visit harems and report back to their eager but frustrated menfolk. While May French Sheldon was travelling towards Lake Chala, she entered a village where male rites, forbidden to women, were taking place. To her amazement, during the night she was approached by a senior woman of the village, wife of one of the elders, who took her under cover of darkness to a spot where she could witness '. . . a wild riotous performance by utterly nude fellows'. The sisterhood had extended its hand to the foreigner. In Papua New Guinea, it was the men of the village who permitted Christina Dodwell to enter their enclave and watch a taboo ceremony. They made her an honorary male for the occasion.

It is in the diversity of their views on issues relating to women generally that the individuality of women travellers is most marked. The history of the woman traveller and her journey towards self-identification mirrors the development of the female consciousness as a whole. With rare exceptions – Margaret Lucas was one – the early women travellers had little conception of themselves as women. Some, as we have seen, actually perceived themselves as men. With the beginning of the women's movement came the realization of self, of the universal need to express a hitherto submerged identity.

The movement found its expression during the last century in the articulate middle class on both sides of the Atlantic, but took firmer root in America than in England, for America had become home to wave after wave of energetic, immigrant women and was inevitably enmeshed in the fight for women's independence. When the *Mayflower* sailed from Plymouth in 1620, the company of pilgrims had included twenty-four women, nine of whom were dead by the end of that first harsh winter. For the survivors, life was hard, marked by the milestones of courtship, marriage, motherhood and widowhood. Frequently left on her own while her husband was away hunting or exploring new territory, the pioneer woman had to fend for herself and her family; this was no place for the fainthearted. By the time the women of the West had established roots and found some degree of comfort, there were plenty of causes to which they could devote their new-found leisure. The middle-class women of the cities, educated and articulate and with a background of non-conformism, soon became involved in the many political issues of the day.

Constantly divided over issues involving blacks, suffrage and prohibition, all of which jostled for position in the race for rights, American feminism was kept alive by the vigour of dissent within its own ranks and revitalized from time to time by the arrival of fresh groups of women immigrants, many of whom were already highly politicized by events in the countries they had been forced to leave.

Fanny Workman, born in 1859, eleven years after the famous Seneca Falls Convention on women's rights, grew up during a highly volatile period of feminism whose protagonists won battles that their British sisters were only beginning to consider fighting fifty years later. It was she who made history when photographed on a summit in the Karakorams in 1912, holding aloft a Votes for Women poster. Her writings express all the orthodox sentiments of the New Woman.

After witnessing the poverty of women in North Africa she wrote: 'It is to be hoped that light may fall upon the souls of men, that they may realize the great injustice practised on the weaker sex . . .' She urged other women to continue in their attempts at high-altitude climbing, citing herself as an example: 'I am not lightweight and am a slow climber, still my powers of endurance . . . have, for a number of years, been good.' She left money to four women's colleges and established a travelling fellowship at Bryn Mawr. She was, in many ways, an exemplary feminist. Hers was a brand of feminism, however, that was not wide enough to embrace everyone who might have laid claim on her sympathy.

Her bearers she treated with scant consideration as we have seen, grumbling about the money they demanded, beating them when they mutinied and threatening not to feed them until they had performed their tasks. When a woman from a local mountain tribe came to look and stare at these strange, rich foreigners, she felt uncomfortable to be confronted by this 'extraordinary' person who was 'not wholly normal'. In the end, she sent a servant to drive away this embarrassing spectre. Fanny, wealthy and middle-class, could afford to carry her banner to the top of the mountain, vociferously proclaiming the ideals of Seneca Falls, but her up-bringing had isolated her somewhat from the common experience and though she could observe and record the sufferings of her sisters she could not always empathize.

Fanny's views would certainly have been considered 'modern' in England: the first women's suffrage society in Britain was not formed until 1866 while in Wyoming, only three years later, women were actually given the vote. There were stirrings, how-ever. When Nina Mazuchelli made her near-disastrous journey up into the Indian Alps, there dawned within her the seeds of recogni-tion of her own individuality as a woman and a growing sympathy not only for her 'Oriental sisters' but also for the local country people: 'With our conventional English notions concerning the bearing of the lower classes to the upper, it takes some little time to accustom ourselves to the familiarity of these hill men . . .' When she found herself clearly occupying the lowliest place in the expedition's pecking order, after the District Commissioner and her husband, she was affronted, and not only on a personal level: '. . . there are limits to the depreciation of womankind in the social scale and on behalf of my Oriental sisters I object to the above order of things.'

In many ways, Nina, a dutiful wife cut off in exile from the support of home and family and existing officially only as an adjunct of her husband, arrived via her journey at a deeper con-ception of womanhood than Fanny Workman ever could despite her education and self-confessed feminism.

Many were opposed to women's suffrage, however; Mary Kingsley was one, and bitterly resented the label of New Woman which the press unwisely pinned upon her. She had no wish to be associated with what she described as 'shrieking female androgins', although she conceded that women in general 'were more honest and more unselfish and not an atom more fickle than men'. Never-theless, she felt that they were unsuited to play a role in parliament because their independent spirit would never allow them to sacri-fice their convictions on the altar of party politics. Instead, they should work at local level and seek to be effective from the outside. Something of a free thinker, being both a Darwinian and an agnostic, she was also a self-confessed 'old-fashioned imperialist' and when it came to votes, her priorities lay elsewhere. Like Gertrude Bell, who, as we have seen, actively opposed the women's suffrage movement, Mary Kingsley believed that a great woman 'either mentally or physically will excel an indifferent man, but no woman ever equals a really great man'. It was a sad attitude, conditioned and nurtured in a male world where women's achievements were recognized only as long as they could be contained within acceptable limits.

Given the relatively embryonic state of the women's rights movement in England, perhaps it is not after all so surprising that Gertrude Bell should not want to align herself with what she felt was a noisy, irrelevant group of women. Having gained entry to the coveted groves of study, she refused to be deflected by what she would have seen as side issues, devoting herself instead to a lifelong commitment to scholarship and eventually, in 1923, setting up Bagdad's National Museum.

By the 1920s, women had turned to fields other than politics where they felt progress had still to be made. Sophie Heath, British Javelin Champion for 1923, spoke regularly on the subject of women in athletics and eventually published a book on the subject. When she later turned to flying, she deliberately promoted in her style of dress a conservative image that would not alarm the critics of such unwomanly activities, and place them in possible jeopardy.

Across the Atlantic, Amelia Earhart was a diligent supporter of women in aviation who used her own achievements to promote the cause of women fliers. She had little interest in the small-town politics of feminism and confined herself to the area in which she was an authority, although she remained constrained by society's nervous attitude to liberated women. Like Sophie Heath, she was well aware of the importance of her image. The tough, butch look did more harm than good to the feminist cause. Both fliers lived during the era of the bob, when smart women demonstrated their disapproval of the frilliness of feminity by cutting off their long hair. Amelia was careful to trim hers but stopped short of the bob: 'I had tried to remain as normal as possible in looks in order to offset the usual criticism of my behaviour.'

Forty years on, women pioneers were still encountering opposition and criticism but through the lessons learned in the women's movement and by putting into practice the ideals of cooperation – which are at the root of feminist thinking – they found they could reach heights which many of their male colleagues had never even attempted. The ascent of Annapurna, though not without its critics, was a triumph for women – to which statement little can be added.

While the early travellers may have been concerned about their sexual identity there are still, today, women travellers who remain ill at ease with the concept of feminism, firmly disclaiming any sympathy, however tenuous, with the movement. Yet, at the same time, they cannot betray their sex.

'While I am no women's libber,' says Clare Francis, 'out to beat the men, at the same time I didn't want to let the side down.' While most women travellers acknowledge their sex as a factor in their motivation, few call themselves feminists and many avoid 'strident statements' (Arlene Blum) and disclaim any affinity with the 'noisy minority' (Christina Dodwell). But women travellers are a conundrum and may be judged as women, as travellers, or both for it is their actions, not their words, that speak the loudest.

Bebe Bwana's canvas villa

'The Will of a Woman'

All books, like all journeys, come to an end, but in the case of this book the end is merely a beginning for, if it has done nothing else, it may have opened the door to a glittering library of women's travel experiences.

It is no accident that the first travel book was written by, though not about, a woman, as was the first autobiographical travel book in the vernacular. Since those early days, women travellers, despite sexist thunderings and paternalistic admonishments, have remained irrepressible and uncontainable, finding their impetus and drive even in the very opposition to their journeys.

'What decided me to go to Lhasa,' said Alexandra David-Neel, 'was, above all, the absurd prohibition which closes Tibet.' To the traveller, a closed door is an affront, a border an insult. Perhaps Madame David-Neel more than any other epitomizes the spirit of the woman traveller, for once the invisible chains of society have been broken physical limitations remain little more than an irritant. In her mid-fifties, she declared: '. . . I took an oath that in spite of all obstacles, I would reach Lhasa and show what the will of a woman could achieve.'

It was – and continues to be – those women who have made solo journeys on limited funds who have truly managed to break free. They have been only too aware that the money which buys hotel rooms and comforts also forms a protective barrier round the traveller, isolating her from the very people she wishes to meet. When Livingstone set out on one of his expeditions to the heart of Africa, the bill ran upwards to £50,000. Mary Kingsley's second visit to Africa, on the other hand, cost £300.

This book can in no way be a complete review of women travellers – they are far too numerous and various for that. To add insult to injury, I will undoubtedly have omitted the one traveller most dear to the reader's heart and I hope I may be forgiven for this.

In selecting my subjects, I have tried to concentrate on women whose travels were or are the result of a compulsion, who travel either alone or in partnership because there is nothing else they can do. I have omitted, therefore, a great harvest of women whose travelling was perhaps incidental to their lives: the American journalist Elizabeth Seaman, also known as Nellie Bly, who, in 1890, travelled round the world in 72 days, stopping off in France to interview Jules Verne; Caroline Chisholm, who travelled to Australia from England in 1838 where she started her campaign on behalf of single, immigrant women; in the field of aviation, the American Fay Gillis Wells, the first woman to fly over Russia, who had to turn down an invitation to fly to Siberia with Wiley Post because she was just about to run away with the man she later married; on water, Emie Cole who, in 1966, at the age of ninety-two, sailed with her family from Africa to New Zealand. The list is endless, and indeed is one that grows from day to day.

'Some will think I have been uncommonly lucky,' said Alexandra David-Neel. 'I shall not disagree; but luck has a cause, like anything else and I believe that there exists a mental attitude capable of shaping circumstances more or less according to one's wishes.'

Propelled by courage and curiosity, informed by the memory of those who have preceded them, women travellers will continue to spin off out of the orbit of the mundane to claim the destiny which they have had some hand in shaping.

Bibliography

Addison, William. *The Old Roads of England*, Batsford, 1980

Allen, Alexandra. *Travelling Ladies*, Jupiter, 1980

Anderson, J. L. R. *The Ulysses Factor*, Hodder and Stoughton, 1970

Ardener, Shirley, ed. *Women and Space*, Croom Helm, 1981

Armstrong, Martin. *Lady Hester Stanhope*, Chivers, 1928

Baker, Anne, ed. *Morning Star* (biography of Florence Baker, based on her own writings), William Kimber, 1972

Ballard, G. *The Memoirs of Several Ladies*, London, 1775

Barnes Stevenson, Catherine. *Victorian Women Travel Writers in Africa*, Twayne, Boston, 1982

Barr, Pat. *A Curious Life for a Lady* (biography of Isabella Bird Bishop), John Murray, 1970

Barton, Humphrey. *Atlantic Adventurers*, Adlard Coles, 1953

Bedford, John, Duke of. *The Flying Duchess*, Macdonald, 1968

Blanch, Lesley. *The Wilder Shores of Love*, John Murray, 1954

Boase, Wendy. *The Sky's the Limit*, Osprey, 1979

Bolitho, H. and Mulgan, J. *The Emmigrants*, Selwyn and Blount, 1939

Borden, Charles A. *Sea Quest*, Robert Hale, 1968

Botting, Douglas. *The Pirates*, Time-Life Books, 1978

Boxer, C. R. *The Dutch Seaborne Empire*, Hutchinson, 1965

Braithwaite, R. *Drunken Barnaby's Four Journeys*, London, 1778

Bramson, A. and Birch, N. *The Tiger Moth Story*, Airlife Publications Ltd., 1982

Broadley, A. M. and Melville, L. *The Beautiful Lady Craven*, London, 1914

Brownlow, trans. *The Hodaeporicon* (Willibald's journey, written down by Huceburg), London, 1891

Bruce, Ian. *The Nun of Lebanon* (biography of Lady Hester Stanhope), Collins, 1951

Buchan, James. *The Expendable Mary Slessor*, Edinburgh, 1980

Burgoyne, Elizabeth. *Gertrude Bell*, Benn, 1961

Burke, John. *Winged Legend* (biography of Amelia Earhart), Arthur Barker, 1970

Burton, Isabel. *The Inner Life of Syria, Palestine and the Holy Land*, London, 1875

    The Life of Richard Burton, London, 1893

Butler Bowdon, W. *The Book of Margery Kempe*, Oxford University Press, 1954

Campbell, Olwen. *Mary Kingsley, A Victorian in the Jungle*, Methuen, 1957

Cambell, R. *The London Tradesman*, London, 1747

Cameron, J. 'Memoir of Maria Sibylla Merian' in Naturalists' Library 30 (*Entomology 4*), Edinburgh, 1841

Carey, William. *Travel and Adventure in Tibet* (contains Annie Taylor's diary), London, 1902

Carrington, C. E. *John Robert Godley of Canterbury*, Cambridge University Press, 1950

Chambers, Anne. *Granuaile*, Wolfhound Press, Dublin, 1983

Clark, Ronald. *The Victorian Mountaineers*, Batsford, 1953

Clarke, D. H. *An Evolution of Singlehanders*, Stanford Maritime, 1976

Collis, Louise. *The Apprentice Saint*, Michael Joseph, 1964 (biography of Margery Kempe)

Courtney, Janet. *The Women of my Time*, Lovat Dickson, 1934

Crow, Duncan. *The Edwardian Woman*, Allen and Unwin, 1978

Cunnington, Willett. *Feminine Attitudes in the Nineteenth Century*, Heinemann, 1935

Davidson, Lillias Campbell. *Hints to Lady Travellers*, London, 1889

Defoe, Daniel. *A Tour Through the Whole Island of Great Britain*, London, 1724

Delamont, Sara and Duffin, Lorna. *Nineteenth-Century Women*, Croom Helm, 1978

Doughty, Charles. *Travels in Arabia Deserta*, Cambridge University Press, 1888/Cape, 1921

Duffy, Maureen. *The Passionate Shepherdess* (biography of Aphra Behn), Cape, 1977

Dyhouse, Carol. *Girls Growing up in late Victorian and Edwardian England*, Routledge and Kegan Paul, 1981

Ellis, M. H. *John MacArthur*, Angus & Robertson, 1955

Emerton, Ephraim, trans. *Letters of St Boniface*, Columbia University Press, 1940

Ewing, Elizabeth. *Women in Uniform*, Batsford, 1974

Fiennes, Ranulph. *To the Ends of the Earth*, Hodder and Stoughton, 1983

Fleming, Peter *News from Tartary*, Cape, 1936/Futura, 1980

Flint, J. E. 'Mary Kingsley, a reassessment' in *Journal of African History*, 4 (1963)

Fox Schmidt, Margaret. *Passion's Child*, (biography of Lady Jane Digby) Hamish Hamilton, 1979

Fraser, Lovat. *Pirates*, Cape, 1921

Galton, Francis. *The Art of Travel*, Murray, 1893

Gibbs-Smith, C. and Warner, O. *Balloons and Ships*, Ariel, 1965

Gibbon, Monk. *Mount Ida* (contains extensive section on Ella Maillart), Wolfhound Press, Dublin, 1983

Gies, Frances and Joseph. *Women in the Middle Ages*, New York, 1978

Gladstone, Penelope. *Travels with Alexine*, John Murray, 1970

Godley, Charlotte. *Letters from New Zealand*, Christchurch, 1951

Gore, J., ed. *Mary, Duchess of Bedford*, Murray, 1938

Grey, Elizabeth. *Winged Victory* (biography of Amy Johnson), Constable, 1966

Gwynn, Stephen. *The Life of Mary Kingsley*, Macmillan, 1933

Hahn, Emily. *Aphra Behn*, Cape, 1951

Hall, Richard. *Lovers on the Nile*, Collins, 1980

Hart-Davis, Duff. *Peter Fleming*, Cape, 1974

Hartman, M., ed. *Clio's Consciousness Raised*, Harper & Row, New York, 1974

Heath, Lady Mary and Wolfe, Stella. *Woman and Flying*, Longman, 1929

Heywood, Thomas. *The Exemplary Lives of Nine Women*, London, 1640

Hill, Bridget. *Eighteenth-Century Women*, Allen and Unwin, 1984

Hopkirk, Peter. *Trespassers on the Roof of the World*, John Murray, 1982

Howard, Cecil. *Mary Kingsley*, Hutchinson, 1957

Hughes, J. *Invincible Miss* (biography of Mary Kingsley), Macmillan, 1968

Johnson, Capt Charles (Defoe). *General History of the Robberies and Murders of the most Notorious Pyrates*, London, 1724

Johnson, Henry. *Life of Kate Marsden*, London, 1895

Kingsland, Gerald. *The Islander*, New English Library, 1984, companion to Lucy Irvine's *Castaway* (Gollancz, 1983)

Latourette, Kenneth Scott. *A History of Christian Missions in China*, SPCK, 1929

Letts, M., trans. *The Pilgrimage of Arnold von Harff*, Hakluyt Society, 1946

Levison, W. *England and the Continent in the Eighth Century*, Oxford University Press, 1946

Longford, Elizabeth. *Eminent Victorian Women*, Weidenfeld and Nicolson, 1981

Lurie, Alison. *The Language of Clothes*, Heinemann, 1981

Merian, Maria. *The Wondrous Transformation of Caterpillars*, Scholar Press, 1978 (a collection of her engravings)

Meryon, Charles. *Memoirs* (contains many references to Lady Hester Stanhope), London, 1845

Middleton, Dorothy. *Victorian Lady Travellers*, Routledge & Kegan Paul, 1965

Miller, Luree. *On Top of the World*, Paddington Press, 1976

Mitchell, Juliet. *Psychoanalysis and Feminism*, Allen Lane, 1974

Mondey, D., ed. *Aviation*, Octopus, 1980

Moolman, Valerie. *Women Aloft*, Time-Life Books, 1981

Morris, Christopher, ed. *Journeys of Celia Fiennes*, Cresset Press, 1947

Oakley, Ann. *Subject Women*, Martin Robertson, 1981

Oddie, E. M. *The Odyssey of a Loving Woman*, New York, 1936

O'Faolain, Julia and Martines, Lauro. *Not in God's Image*, Virago, 1979

Parkes, Joan. *Travel in England in the Seventeenth Century*, Oxford University Press, 1925

Paston, G. *Lady Mary Wortley Montagu*, Methuen, 1907

Perham, Margery and Simmons, J. *African Discovery*, Faber, 1957

Power, Eileen. *Medieval Women*, Cambridge University Press, 1975

Primrose, Catherine, ed. *The Life and Letters of Lady Hester Stanhope*, London, 1914

Ransford, Oliver. *The Dark Interior* (biography of David Livingstone), John Murray, 1978

Rattray-Taylor, Gordon. *The Angel Makers*, Heinemann, 1958
Sex in History, Thames & Hudson, 1953

Roberts, Brian. *Ladies of the Veld*, Murray, 1965

Robson, Isabel. *Two Lady Missionaries in Tibet*, London, 1909

Ropes, A., ed. *Letters of Lady Mary Wortley Montagu*, London, 1892

Sandberg, Graham. *The Exploration of Tibet*, Cosmo Publications, 1973

Severin, Tim. *The Brendan Voyage*, Hutchinson, 1978

Sinclair, Andrew. *The Better Half*, Cape, 1966

Smith, Constance Babington. *Amy Johnson*, Collins, 1967

Stenton, Doris Mary. *The English Woman in History*, New York, 1972

Stoddart, Anna. *Life of Isabella Bird Bishop*, London, 1906

Sumption, Jonathan. *Pilgrimage*, Faber, 1975

Sykes, Sir Percy. *History of Exploration*, Routledge, 1934

Tarr, Laszlo. *History of the Carriage*, Vision Press, 1969

Taylor, E. *Pioneer Women*, Sheldon Press, 1930

Taylor, M. and Mardey, D. *Milestones in Flight*, Jane's, 1983

Thubron, Colin. *The Venetians*, Time-Life Books, 1980

Turner, J. *Famous Flights*, Weidenfeld & Nicolson, 1978

Vicinus, Martha. *Suffer and Be Still*, Methuen, 1972

Welch, Ann. *Happy to Fly*, John Murray, 1983

Wey, William. *Itineraries*, London, 1859

Woodcock, G. *The Incomparable Aphra*, London & New York, 1948

Woodward, F. J. *Portrait of Jane* (biography of Jane Franklin), Hodder & Stoughton, 1951

Essays and articles in journals:

Frank, Katherine. 'Voyages Out: nineteenth-century women travellers in Africa', a paper given at the Women's Public Lives Institute, University of Kansas, 1981

MacLulich, T. D. 'Canadian Exploration as Literature' in the *Journal of Canadian Literature*, 81, Summer 1979

Tallmadge, John. 'From Chronicle to Quest' in *Victorian Studies*, 23, spring 1980

'The Lady Errant' in the *Spectator*, 29 August 1891

Anthologia Hibernica (contains an account of the meeting between Queen Elizabeth I and Granuaile), Mercier and Co., Dublin, 1793

Some works by women travellers

Batten, Jean. *My Life*, Harrap, 1938

Bell, Gertrude. *The Desert and the Sown*, Heinemann, 1907/Virago 1985

       Amurath to Amurath, Heinemann, 1911

Bird Bishop, Isabella. *A Lady's Life in the Rocky Mountains*, Murray, 1879/Virago, 1982

       Unbeaten Tracks in Japan, Murray, 1880/Virago, 1984

       The Golden Chersonese, Murray, 1883

       Journeys in Persia and Kurdistan, Murray, 1891

       The Yangste Valley and Beyond, Murray 1899/Virago, 1985

Black, M. L. *My Seventy Years*, Canada, 1938

Blunt, Lady Anne. *Bedouin Tribes of the Euphrates*, Murray, 1879

       A Pilgrimage to Nejd, Murray, 1881

Bullock, Fanny Workman and William Hunter. *Algerian Memories*, Unwin, 1895

       In the Ice World of Himalaya, Unwin, 1900

       Through Town and Jungle, Unwin, 1904

       Ice-bound Heights of the Mustagh, Constable, 1908

       The Call of the Snowy Hispar, Constable, 1910

       Two Summers in the Ice-wilds of Eastern Karakoram, Unwin, 1917

Bulstrode, Beatrix. *A Tour in Mongolia*, Methuen, 1920

Buxton, Cindy and Price, Annie. *Survival South Atlantic*, Granada 1983

Cable, Mildred and French, Francesca. *A Desert Journal*, Constable, 1934

       The Gobi Desert, Constable, 1942/Virago, 1984

Cameron, Agnes Deans. *The New North*, London and New York, 1910

Cochrane, Jacqueline. *The Stars at Noon*, Robert Hale, 1955

Craven, Lady Elizabeth. *A Journey Through the Crimea to Constantinople*, London, 1789

Cumming, Constance Gordon. *A Lady's Cruise in a French Man-of-War*, Blackwood, 1882
    In the Hebrides, Chatto & Windus, 1883
    In the Himalayas, Chatto & Windus, 1884
    Memories, Blackwood, 1904
David-Neel, Alexandra. *My Journey to Lhasa*, Heinemann, 1927/ Virago, 1983
    With Mystics and Magicians in Tibet, John Lane, 1931
Davidson, Robyn. *Tracks*, Paladin, 1982
Davison, Ann. *Last Voyage*, Peter Davies, 1951
    Home was an Island, Peter Davies, 1952
    My Ship is so Small, Oldhams, 1958
    By Gemini, Peter Davies, 1962
Dixie, Lady Florence. *Across Patagonia*, Bentley, 1880
    Defence of Zululand, Chatto & Windus, 1882
    Towards Freedom: an appeal to thoughtful men and women, London, 1904
Dodwell, Christina. *Travels with Fortune*, W. H. Allen, 1979
    In Papua New Guinea, Oxford Illustrated Press, 1983
    An Explorer's Handbook, Hodder & Stoughton, 1984
    A Traveller in China, Hodder & Stoughton, 1985
Earhart, Amelia. *The Fun of it*, Putnam, 1932
Eberhardt, Isabelle. *Notes de Route*, Paris, 1908
Fanshawe, Lady. *Memoirs*, John Lane, 1907
Fiennes, Celia. *Through England on a Side Saddle*, London, 1888
Fountaine, Margaret. *Love Among the Butterflies*, Collins, 1980
Francis, Clare. *Come Hell or High Water*, Magna Print Books, 1979
Gordon, Lucie Duff. *Letters from Egypt*, Routledge & Kegan Paul, 1969
Hobson, Sarah. *Through Persia in Disguise*, John Murray, 1973
Hore, Annie Boyle. *To Lake Tanganyika in a Bath Chair*, London, 1886
Hubbard, Mina. *A Woman's Way through Unknown Labrador*, New York, 1808
Irvine, Lucy. *Castaway*, Gollancz, 1983
Jackson, Monica and Stark, Elizabeth. *Tents in the Clouds*, Collins, 1956
James, Naomi. *At One with the Sea*, Stanley Paul, 1979

Johnson, Amy. *Sky Roads of the World*, Chambers, 1939

Kingsley, Mary. *Travels in West Africa*, Macmillan, 1897/Virago, 1982

le Blond, Mrs Aubrey (Mrs Fred Burnaby). *The Story of an Alpine Winter*, Bell, 1907
> *Mountaineer in the Land of the Midnight Sun*, Unwin, 1908
> *Day in Day Out*, John Lane, 1928

Maillart, Ella. *Forbidden Journey*, Heinemann, 1937/Century, 1983
> *Turkestan Solo*, Heinemann, 1938/Century, 1985

Manning, Ella Wallace. *Igloo for the Night*, Hodder & Stoughton, 1943
> *Summer in Hudson Bay*, Hodder & Stoughton, 1949

Markham, Beryl. *West With the Night*, Harrap, 1943/Virago, 1984

Marsden, Kate. *On Sledge and Horseback to Outcast Siberian Lepers*, London 1892

Miller, Christian. *Daisy, Daisy*, Doubleday, 1981

Mitchison, Naomi. *You May Well Ask*, Gollancz, 1979
> *Mucking Around – Five Continents over Fifty Years*, Gollancz, 1981

Murphy, Dervla. *Full Tilt*, Murray, 1965/Century, 1983
> *Tibetan Foothold*, Murray, 1966
> *The Waiting Lanp*, Murray, 1967
> *In Ethiopia with a Mule*, Murray, 1968/Century, 1985
> *On a Shoe String to Coorg*, Murray, 1976/Century, 1985
> *Where the Indus is Young*, Murray, 1977/Century, 1983
> *A Place Apart*, Murray, 1978
> *Wheels Within Wheels* (autobiography), Murray, 1979
> *Eight Feet in the Andes*, Murray, 1983/Century, 1985
> *Muddling through in Madagasgar*, Murray, 1985

North, Marianne. *Recollections of a Happy Life*, London, 1893

Petherick, Mr and Mrs. *Travels in Central Africa*, London, 1869

Reitsch, Hanna. *The Sky my Kingdom*, Bodley Head, 1955

Scott, Sheila. *I Must Fly*, Hodder & Stoughton, 1968
> *On Top of the World*, Hodder & Stoughton, 1973

Selby, Bettina. *Riding the Mountains Down*, Gollancz, 1984
> *Riding to Jerusalem*, Sidgwick and Jackson, 1985

Shalom, Sabina. *A Marriage Sabbatical*, Frederick Muller, 1984

Sheldon, May French. *Sultan to Sultan*, Boston, 1892

Shepherd, Dolly. *When the 'Chute Went Up*, Robert Hale, 1984

Stark, Freya. *The Valleys of the Assassins*, Murray, 1936/Century, 1982

The Southern Gates of Arabia, Murray, 1936/Century, 1982

A Winter in Arabia, Murray, 1940/Century, 1983

Perseus in the Wind, Murray, 1948/Century, 1985

Beyond Euphrates, Murray, 1951/Century, 1983

The Coast of Incense, Murray, 1953/Century, 1985

Alexander's Path, Murray, 1958/Century, 1984

Dust in the Lion's Paw, Murray, 1961/Century, 1985

Swale, Rosie. *Back to Cape Horn*, Collins, 1986

Welch, Ann. *Happy to Fly*, John Murray, 1983

Index

Index

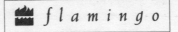

Flamingo is a quality imprint publishing both fiction and non-fiction. Below are some recent titles.

Fiction
☐ No Other Life *Brian Moore* £5.99
☐ The Kitchen God's Wife *Amy Tan* £4.99
☐ A Thousand Acres *Jane Smiley* £5.99
☐ Spidertown *Abraham Rodriguez* £5.99
☐ Tess *Emma Tennant* £5.99
☐ Pepper *Tristan Hawkins* £5.99
☐ Dreaming in Cuban *Cristina Garcia* £5.99
☐ Happenstance *Carol Shields* £5.99
☐ Blood Sugar *Suzannah Dunn* £5.99
☐ Postcards *E. Annie Proulx* £5.99

Non-fiction
☐ The Gates of Paradise *Alberto Manguel* £9.99
☐ Sentimental Journeys *Joan Didion* £5.99
☐ Epstein *Stephen Gardiner* £8.99
☐ Love, Love and Love *Sandra Bernhard* £5.99
☐ City of Djinns *William Dalrymple* £5.99
☐ Dame Edna Everage *John Lahr* £5.99
☐ Tolstoy's Diaries *R. F. Christian* £7.99
☐ Wild Swans *Jung Chang* £7.99

You can buy Flamingo paperbacks at your local bookshop or newsagent. Or you can order them from HarperCollins Mail Order, Dept. 8, HarperCollins*Publishers*, Westerhill Road, Bishopbriggs, Glasgow G64 2QT. Please enclose a cheque or postal order, to the order of the cover price plus add £1.00 for the first and 25p for additional books ordered within the UK.

NAME (Block letters)_____

ADDRESS_____

_____

_____